THE
CHRISTIAN
WORLD
OF THE
MIDDLE AGES

In memory of
Fr. W.R. Corbould

The
CHRISTIAN
WORLD
OF THE
MIDDLE AGES

BERNARD HAMILTON

BCA

This edition published 2003
by BCA
by arrangement with Sutton Publishing Limited
CN 114023

Typeset in 11/13pt Bembo.
Typesetting and origination by
Sutton Publishing Limited.
Printed and bound in England by
The Bath Press

CONTENTS

LIST OF MAPS AND ILLUSTRATIONS

Coloured Plates

PREFACE

The period covered by this book, 300–1500, represents more than half the life-span of the Christian religion. During those centuries not only did it become the dominant faith of Western Europe, but also spread north-west to the Viking settlements in Iceland and Greenland as well as north-east, from the Byzantine Empire to the peoples of Russia. In Egypt, north Africa and the Near East, the early success of Christianity was tempered from the mid-seventh century by the foundation of the Islamic Arab Empire, which stretched from the Indus Valley to Morocco. In all those lands which remained under Islamic rule throughout the Middle Ages Christianity either died out or became a minority religion, though that process took centuries to complete; but beyond the Islamic frontiers in Africa and Asia there were flourishing Christian societies in this period. These were found within the Chinese Empire, among the nomadic peoples of Mongolia and Central Asia, in the Hindu states on the Malabar coast of South India, in the Nubian kingdoms which spanned the Nile to the south of Philae, in the Empire of Ethiopia and in the Caucasian kingdoms of Armenia and Georgia.

A great deal has been written in English about the medieval Western Church, and a substantial amount about Byzantium and its cultural heirs in the Balkans and Russia, and there are also some, though rather fewer, studies of the oriental and African churches. To my knowledge there is not any single general history written in English of the Church throughout the world in the medieval centuries, and it is that gap which I have tried to fill.

I have taken as my starting point the decision made in 312 by Constantine the Great to make Christianity a lawful religion in his empire. This marked the end of the age of persecutions and allowed the Church to develop freely as part of Roman society. I conclude the study in c. 1500, by which time the Western European powers had developed the capacity to travel to most parts of the world by sea. This enabled them to found overseas dominions in which they established the Christian Church in its Western form – initially Latin Catholic, but later, in the case of the Dutch and the British, Protestant. This occurred even in areas like South India where an organized Christian community already existed. This Western religious imperialism marks a significant break with the medieval world in which a great many different types of Christianity had flourished in Asia and Africa.

A brief explanation of the nomenclature used in this book may be helpful. The term Catholic Church is reserved for the undivided Church of the fourth century from which most of the other medieval Churches traced their origins. I have sometimes referred to the medieval Western Church as the Western Catholic Church, but more frequently as the Latin Catholic Church, because of the liturgical language which it used. I have avoided the term Roman Catholic because it implies that the Church was dominated by the Papacy to a degree which only happened after the Council of Trent.

I have used the term Orthodox to describe those Churches which accept the authority of the first Seven General Councils: this applies to the Patriarchate of Constantinople and those Churches which are in full communion with it. An important group of Churches rejected the Council of Chalcedon (451) and therefore also the later Councils recognized by the Orthodox Churches. Collectively these Churches may be described as 'non-Chalcedonian', but this is a term I have seldom needed to use, and I have called the constituent Churches in this group by their customary names: the Armenian Church, the Coptic Church (of Egypt) and the Ethiopian Church. However, I have described one Church in that group, the Syrian Orthodox Church, in an old-fashioned way, as the Jacobite Church. I do not intend any disrespect by this usage; my sole reason for adopting it is to avoid the difficulty which might otherwise be experienced by readers in distinguishing between this Church and the Orthodox Church in Syria (i.e. those people in communion with the Orthodox Patriarch of Antioch). The name Jacobite comes from Bishop Jacob Baradaeus, who first gave that Church an organization independent of the Chalcedonian hierarchy.

The principal Church in Asia in the Middle Ages was headed by the Patriarch of Seleucia–Ctesiphon. Its members call it the Church of the East, and I have used this name, but this raises a technical problem, because this name has no adjectival form. I have therefore used the word Chaldean to describe members of this Church and as a general-purpose adjective for everything relating to it. Chaldean was the term used by medieval Western writers when referring to this Church. By Chaldean they meant Syriac, the liturgical language of the Church of the East, and it therefore seemed an appropriate term for me to adopt.

All the dates in this book relate to the Christian era, unless otherwise specified.

I have spent much of my adult life teaching, reading and writing about medieval Christendom, and therefore the number of scholars who have made it possible for me to write this book and to whom I should like to express my thanks is considerable. First, I owe to the late Dom David Knowles such understanding as I have of the importance of the Benedictine tradition and of twelfth-century Christian humanism in the shaping of Western Christendom. I am indebted to Professor Joan Hussey for awakening in me what has proved to be a lifelong interest in the Byzantine world and the Orthodox Church. The late Fr. Jean Leclercq, with his broad human sympathies, did much to make the monastic centuries and their thought-world come alive for me. The conversation and writings of Peter Brown have been a source of stimulation throughout my life, encouraging me to think of Christian history in the widest possible cultural, intellectual and religious context, an approach which has proved very relevant to the present study. The late Fr. Joseph Gill helped me to appreciate how remarkable was the achievement of the Council of Florence (1437–44) when, for the only time in Christian history, all the Churches were briefly united. George Every has enriched my understanding of the complexity of Byzantine Orthodoxy and the need to examine it not only from the viewpoint of Constantinople, but also from that of Alexandria,

Antioch, Calabria and Kiev. I am deeply indebted to my friend Charles Beckingham for guiding me through the labyrinth of Prester John studies and for helping me to understand the civilization of Ethiopia. I should like to express my thanks to David Morgan and Peter Jackson for elucidating the place which Christianity occupied in the Mongol Empire. I am grateful to Kevork Hintlian and to Gérard Dédéyan for important insights they have provided into the civilization of medieval Armenia. Andrew Palmer has been of great help in elucidating the early history of the Syrian Orthodox/Jacobite Church, while Jean Richard, through his wide-ranging studies has illuminated the whole field of medieval Western relations with the Churches of Africa and Asia. John Wilkinson and Denys Pringle have proved invaluable guides to the pilgrim literature and archaeological evidence concerning Jerusalem and its unique place in the medieval Christian world. Finally, I wish to express my thanks to the late Fr. W. Robert Corbould, who was my parish priest when I was in my teens and who first made me aware of the rich diversity of the Christian medieval tradition, and it is to him that I dedicate this work.

As always, I would like to thank my wife for her support on all levels while I have been working on this project. I have specially valued her good humour when confronted by the moodiness which so often, at least in my case, seems to accompany book production. My thanks are, of course, also due to Sutton Publishing who commissioned this book, but particularly to Christopher Feeney and Elizabeth Stone who have been very helpful and patient in steering it to its completion.

The material I have used in preparing it has come from a number of libraries and I would particularly like to thank the librarians and staff of the School of Oriental and African Studies and of the Warburg Institute. Without the resources of those libraries it could not have been written. I should also like to thank the staff of the London Library, of the Library of the University of Nottingham, and of the Society of Antiquaries of London for their kind assistance.

Given all the help which I have received (and which I have only listed in part), this ought to be a remarkable book. I am, however, only too aware of my own limitations, and ask my readers' indulgence for the many shortcomings which, despite the best efforts of my friends and advisers, no doubt remain in the text, and which are all my own work.

Bernard Hamilton
Nottingham 2002

ACKNOWLEDGEMENTS

My thanks to Dr Andrew Sargent for allowing me to reproduce his photographs of the keep of Chastel Blanc (p. 111), the castle of Marqab (p. 112) and the cathedral of Tortosa (p. 113).

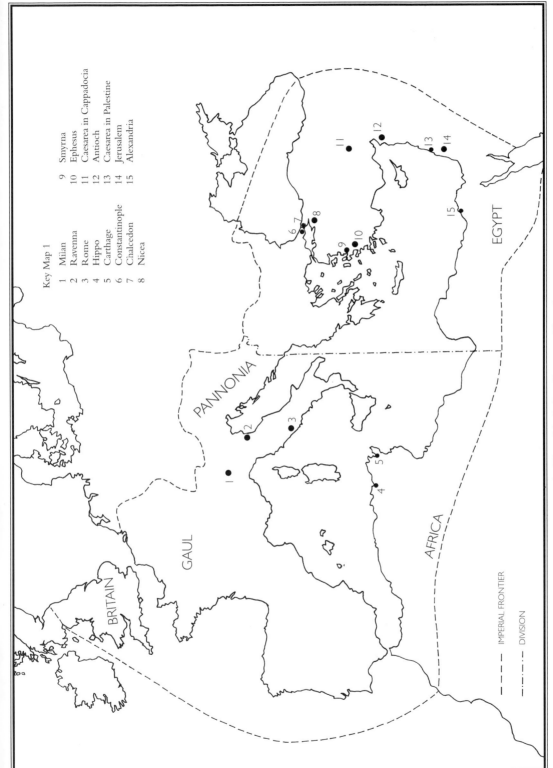

Key Map 1

1 Milan
2 Ravenna
3 Rome
4 Hippo
5 Carthage
6 Constantinople
7 Chalcedon
8 Nicea
9 Smyrna
10 Ephesus
11 Caesarea in Cappadocia
12 Antioch
13 Caesarea in Palestine
14 Jerusalem
15 Alexandria

BRITAIN
GAUL
PANNONIA
AFRICA
EGYPT

IMPERIAL FRONTIER
DIVISION

1 The Christian Roman Empire

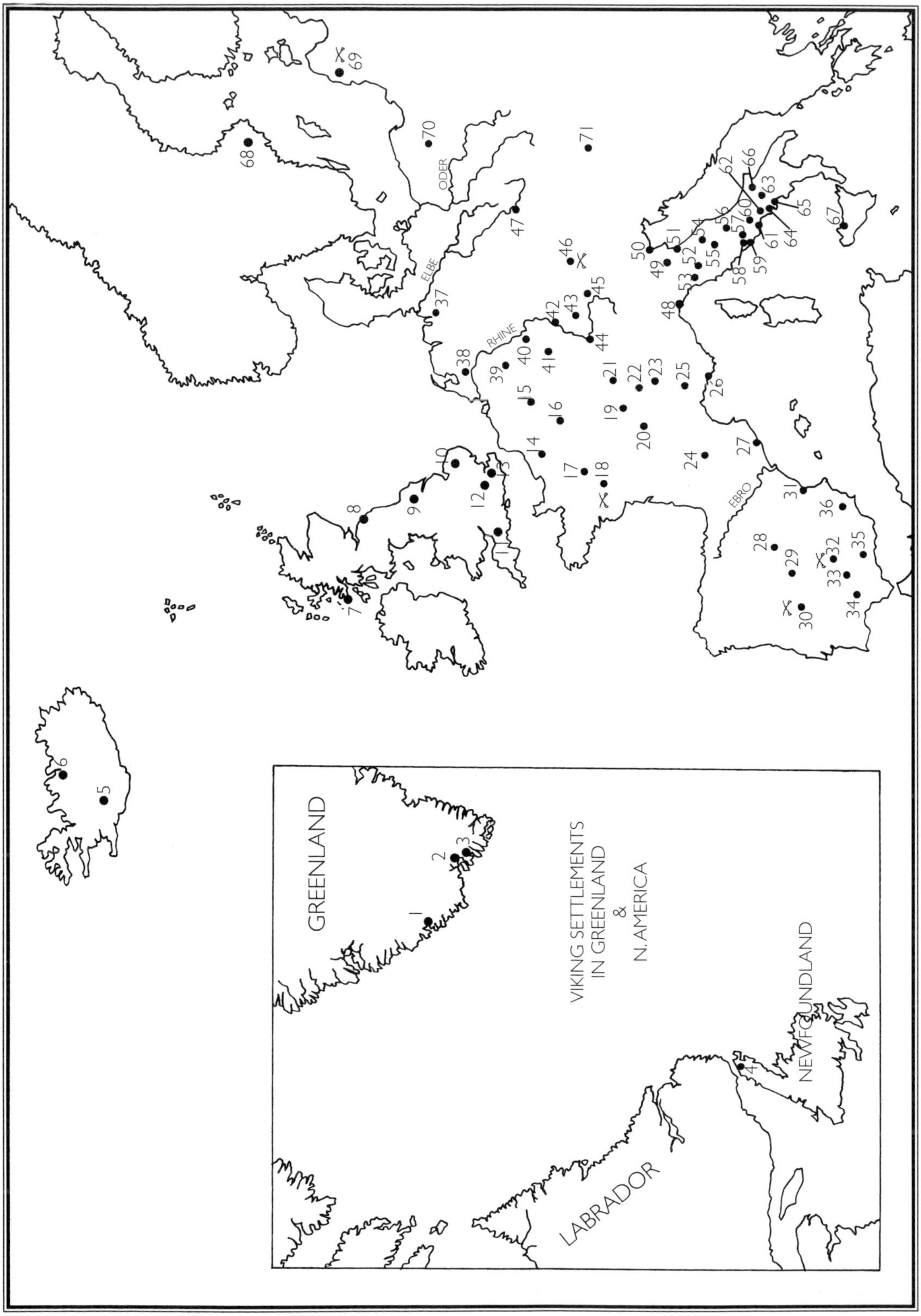

2 The Medieval Western Church

VIKING SETTLEMENTS
IN GREENLAND
&
N.AMERICA

GREENLAND

LABRADOR

NEWFOUNDLAND

ODER

ELBE

RHINE

EBRO

Key Map 2

RUSSIAN

DVINA

VOLGA

PRINCIPALITIES

ILKHANATE
OF THE
GOLDEN
HORDE

MORAVIA

DANUBE

TRANSYLVANIA

MOLDAVIA

DNEIPER

HUNGARY

CARPATHIANS

WALLACHIA

ALANIA

BOSNIA

CROATIA

SERBIA

MACEDONIA

BULGARIA

THRACE

EPIRUS

MOREA

CRETE

CYPRUS

3 The Church in Byzantine Lands

Key Map 3

1   Novgorod
2   Kazan
3   Moscow
4   Kiev
5   Suceava
6   Bolino-Polje
7   Arges
8   Cherson
9   Peč
10 Kossovo
11 Nicopolis
12 Trnovo
13 Philippopolis
14 Dragovitia
15 Adrianople
16 Dyrrachium
17 Ochrida
18 Pelagonia
19 Thessalonica
20 Heraclea
21 Constantinople
22 Nicaea
23 Gallipoli
24 Meteora monasteries
25 Athens
26 Mistra
27 Ephesus
28 Ankara
29 Iconium
30 Caesarea in Cappadocia
31 Trebizond
32 Colonea
33 Tefrike
34 Melitene
35 Antioch

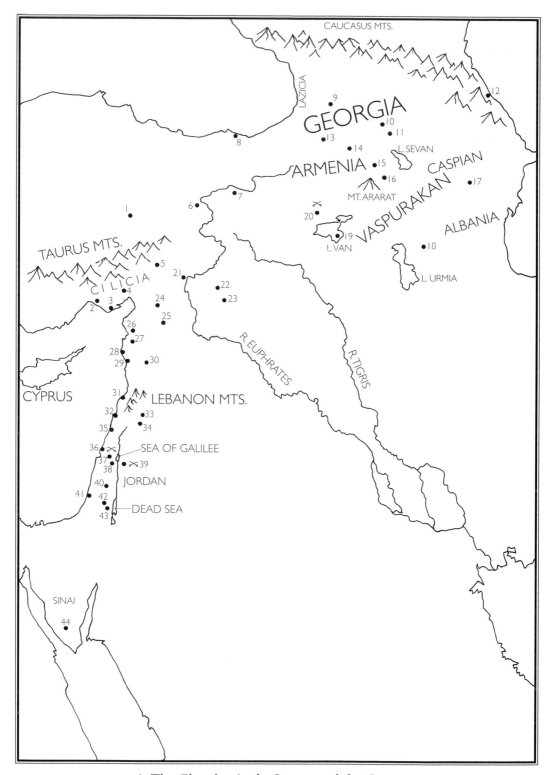

4 The Churches in the Levant and the Caucasus

Key Map 4

1	Caesarea in Cappadocia	23	Harran
2	Tarsus	24	Deir Siman
3	Ayas	25	Aleppo
4	Sis	26	Antioch
5	Marash	27	Cursat
6	Melitene	28	Latakia
7	Mananalis	29	Jabala
8	Trebizond	30	Apamea
9	Ghelati	31	Tripoli
10	Mtskheta	32	Beirut
11	Tiflis	33	Saidnai'a
12	Derbent	34	Damascus
13	Kars	35	Tyre
14	Ani	36	Acre
15	Ejmiazin	37	Hattin
16	Dvin	38	Nazareth
17	Partaw	39	Yarmuk
18	Tabriz	40	Nablus
19	Aghthamar	41	Jaffa
20	Manzikert	42	Jerusalem
21	Hromgla	43	Bethlehem
22	Edessa	44	Mount Sinai monastery

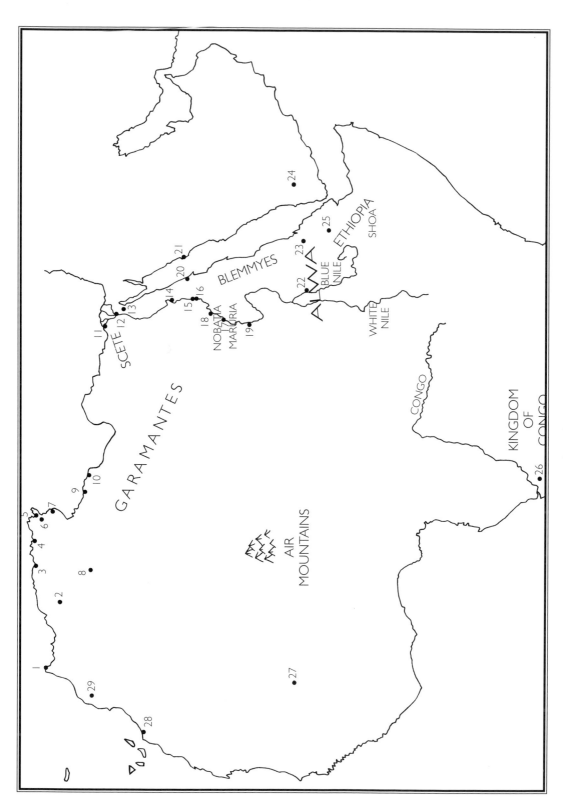

5 The Church in Africa

Key Map 5

1	Ceuta
2	Tahert
3	Bugia
4	Hippo
5	Carthage
6	Kairouan
7	Mahdia
8	Wargla
9	Tripoli
10	Leptis Magna
11	Alexandria
12	Cairo
13	St Antony's monastery
14	Thebes
15	Aswan
16	Philae
17	Faras
18	Ibrim
19	Dongola
20	Aidabh
21	Jiddah
22	Soba
23	Aksum
24	Sana
25	Lalibela
26	San Salvador
27	Ghana (now Kumbi Saleh)
28	Sta Cruz de Mar Paqueña
29	Marrakesh

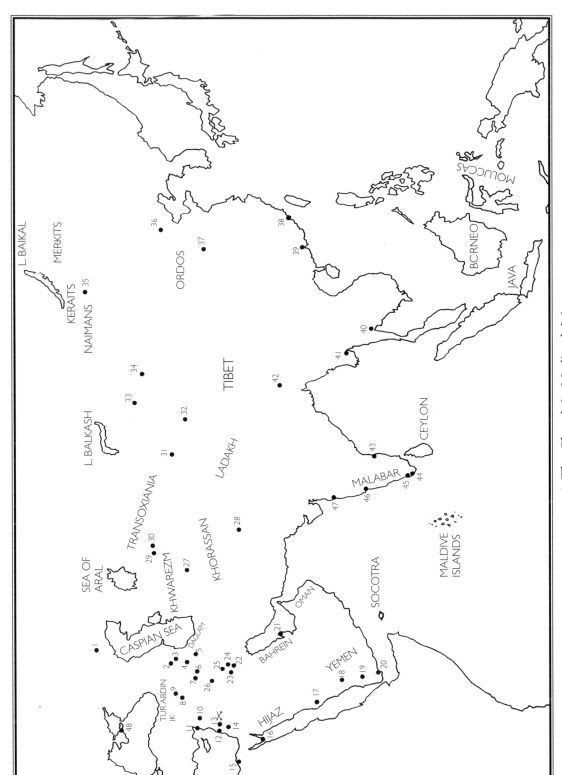

6 The Church in Medieval Asia

Key Map 6

1	Sarai	25	Baghdad
2	Nakhidjevan	26	Takrit
3	Tabriz	27	Merv
4	Maragah	28	Ghazna
5	Sultaniya	29	Bokhara
6	Irbil	30	Samarkand
7	Mosul	31	Kashgar
8	Nisibis	32	Khotan
9	Gezira	33	Almaligh
10	Aleppo	34	Turfan
11	Antioch	35	Karakorum
12	Acre	36	Khanbaliq
13	Ain Jalut	37	Sianfu (Xian)
14	Jerusalem	38	Zayton
15	Damietta	39	Canton
16	Raithu	40	Ayudya
17	Mecca	41	Pegu
18	Najran	42	Lhasa
19	Sana	43	Mylapore
20	Aden	44	Quilon
21	Qatar	45	Cochin
22	Kufa	46	Goa
23	al-Hira	47	Tama
24	Seleucia–Ctesiphon	48	Caffa

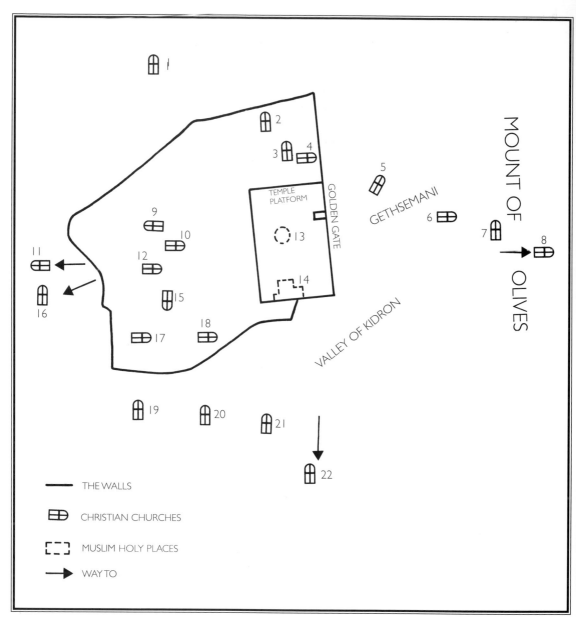

TEMPLE
PLATFORM

GOLDEN GATE

GETHSEMANI

VALLEY OF KIDRON

MOUNT OF OLIVES

THE WALLS

CHRISTIAN CHURCHES

MUSLIM HOLY PLACES

WAY TO

7 The Medieval City of Jerusalem

Key Map 7

1 Church of St Stephen
2 Jacobite cathedral of St Mary Magdalene
3 Church of Bethseda
4 Crusader church of St Anne
5 Church of Our Lady of Josaphat
6 Church of the Pater Noster
7 Church of the Ascension of the Lord
8 The convent of Bethany
9 Cathedral of the Holy Sepulchre/Anastasis
10 Church of St Mary of the Latins
11 Georgian monastery of the Holy Cross
12 Hospitaller church of St John
13 Dome of the Rock
14 al-Aqsa mosque
15 Jacobite church of St Mark
16 Church of St John the Baptist, Ain Karim
17 Armenian cathedral of St James
18 The 'new church' of St Mary built by Justinian
19 Church of Our Lady of Sion
20 Church of St Peter in Gallicantu
21 Church of the Pool of Siloam
22 Orthodox monastery of St Sabas

INTRODUCTION
THE CHURCH IN
LATE ANTIQUITY

In *c.* 298 when the Emperor Diocletian was presiding at a sacrifice to receive omens about war with Persia, Christians in his bodyguard crossed themselves to ward off the powers of evil they believed were being invoked. The augurs declared that because of this they were unable to read the livers of the sacrifices or to deliver the oracle, and this led the emperor to initiate a new persecution of the Church. He first ordered that all those in the imperial service should make sacrifice to the gods of Rome, and then in 303 ordered the confiscation of the Christian scriptures, the destruction of churches, the prohibition of assemblies for Christian worship and the arrest and imprisonment of all bishops and clergy who were not willing to offer sacrifices. In 304 he extended the requirement to sacrifice to all his subjects. The enforcement of these laws depended on the zeal of local and regional officials, which was very variable; nevertheless, in many places persecution was quite severe. There is no record of the number of Christians who died for their faith. W.H.C. Frend has estimated that there were some 3,000–3,500, but this figure may be too high: as J.H.W.G. Liebeschuetz has pointed out, from Eusebius's detailed account of what happened in his own part of Palestine it appears that only eighty-six people were killed out of a Christian population numbering some tens of thousands.[1] Even so, a great many Christians did suffer in lesser ways, ranging from imprisonment to prolonged legal and social harassment.

By this time Christianity was almost 300 years old, yet it had never been a *religio licita*, a religion recognized by Roman law. That meant that it was a punishable offence merely to be a Christian. It would be totally wrong to suppose that Christians had been subject to constant persecution and had had to practise their faith clandestinely throughout this time. Until the mid-third century persecutions were not centrally coordinated and the application of the law was entirely in the hands of provincial and local authorities. This meant that some Christian communities enjoyed long periods of peace, but it also meant that members of the Church were subject to arbitrary and at times deadly harassment, against which there was no redress. Thus St Polycarp, Bishop of Smyrna, who had grown up as a Christian, was arrested in *c.* 155 when he was eighty-six years old and burnt by the local magistrates because he would not renounce his faith.

In 249 the Emperor Decius ordered all his subjects to perform cult sacrifices and to obtain certificates from the magistrates to prove that they had done so. Although this may not have been designed as a specifically anti-Christian measure, many Christians were executed or imprisoned for refusing to conform, and this legislation was the model for the anti-Christian laws promulgated by the Emperor Valerian in 257–60. His successor Galienus issued an edict of toleration for Christians in 260 which, while not giving their religion legal recognition, granted them immunity from the enforcement of the law. The Church then enjoyed peace for almost forty years, and during that time its numbers grew considerably. It is not known how many Christians there were in the empire by 300 but all the evidence suggests that they were very numerous in Egypt, Palestine, Syria and Asia Minor, though less so in the West, particularly in the northern provinces, but that they were not in a majority anywhere.

Diocletian abdicated in 305. He had set up a complicated system of devolved government in his vast empire, and in the next few years there were frequent changes of rulers. By 311 the Empire was ruled by four men: Licinius and Maximian in the East, and Constantine and Maxentius in the West. The anti-Christian legislation of Diocletian remained in force and was implemented in the East until 311, but not very systematically imposed in the West. In 312 Constantine, who was ruling in Britain and Gaul, went to war with his colleague Maxentius who ruled Italy. Constantine later claimed that as he neared Rome, shortly before the critical battle with his rival, he had seen a vision of a cross in the sun inscribed with the words: '*In hoc signo vince*' ('In this sign conquer'). He related this story towards the end of his life to his biographer, Eusebius of Caesarea, and it may well have grown in telling over the years, but that he

The baptistery of Dura Europus on the Euphrates, c. 240, with frescoes of the miracles of Christ and the three Maries at the Sepulchre.

Christ the Good Shepherd, Rome, fourth century.

had some religious experience in 312 seems almost certain, for he ordered his troops to mark the symbol on their shields, which was the Greek abbreviation for the name Christ χριστος. In the Battle of the Milvian Bridge on 28 October 312 Maxentius was killed and Constantine became sole Emperor of the West. He made an alliance with his eastern colleague Licinius, who in April 313 defeated Maximian and became sole Emperor in the East. On 15 June Licinius issued an edict stating that when he and Constantine had met at Milan they had agreed 'to grant full toleration to Christianity as to all other religions', and to restore all property of the Church confiscated during the persecution.[2] In 320 Licinius reneged on this agreement and began to persecute Christians under his rule once again and that gave Constantine a pretext for intervening. In 324 he deposed Licinius and became sole ruler of the whole empire. The persecution had ended: Christianity had, after 300 years, become a lawful religion, and the Church experienced peace.

*Head of Constantine
the Great, Rome
c. 312.*

The edict of toleration did not specially favour Christianity, but put it on an equal footing with other religions, yet Constantine's own attitude to the Church was not one of indifference. Although he was not baptized until shortly before his death, he brought up his sons as Christians and made Christianity the religion of his court. Christian clergy were exempted from the payment of tax and bishops were given the right to hear civil cases in their courts if both parties so wished. In this way the Church began to be integrated into the imperial administration. In accordance with the terms of the edict of toleration, Constantine encouraged bishops to apply for subsidies from the provincial authorities to restore buildings damaged or destroyed in the persecutions, and consequently a large-scale programme of church building was undertaken throughout the Empire. Constantine endowed churches in the Holy Land (see Epilogue), but his greatest munificence was shown to the church of Rome. Before 312 the Christians there had not possessed any imposing buildings, only assembly rooms in the city and cemeteries outside the walls (these were the catacombs – multi-level galleries for inhumation burials carved out of the rock). Constantine endowed a cathedral and an adjacent baptistery on the site of the Lateran Palace. Because there was no tradition of church building, the cathedral was modelled on a basilica, a multi-aisled rectangular building used as an imperial assembly hall, and this became the standard form for new churches. Constantine, or more probably his mother, the Empress Helena, had a basilica built in her own Sessorian Palace nearby, which later became the Church of Sta. Croce. Nevertheless, the Christian Church did not become dominant in Rome at this time: the two large imperial foundations were remote from the main centres of public life there, and all the other churches which the emperor founded were at the shrines of the martyrs outside the walls, the greatest of which was the huge basilica built over the tomb of St Peter in the Vatican cemetery.[3] Constantine endowed the church of Rome with estates in many western provinces, which by the end of his reign produced an annual income of 25,000 gold pieces.

Statue of Mithras, now in the Louvre.

He can have derived no immediate political advantage from his patronage of the Church, since Christians were a minority in the Western provinces and, as his careful siting of his churches there shows, he was at pains not to antagonize the powerful pagan aristocracy of Rome. However, the Church may have proved more of a secular asset after he had become sole rule of the empire. Garth Fowden has argued persuasively that the imperial cult, which had been designed to unify the empire, broke down irretrievably in the third century because of the manifest weakness of the institution and traditional Roman religion could not act as a substitute because it was essentially local in character. By Constantine's day there were two universalist faiths which were spreading in the empire, Christianity and Mithraism, each of which had the potential to become a new unifying force. Recent research suggests that Mithraism had evolved in the second half of the first century AD and was responding to some of the same religious needs in the Roman world as early as Christianity did. The distribution of known *mithraea* is an indication of its popularity, specially among soldiers. Nevertheless, compared to the number of Christians in the empire in Constantine's day, Mithraism seems to have been a decidedly minority cult. In any case, the question of its establishment did not arise, because Constantine became a Christian, not a Mithraic initiate. Christianity, once it had been legalized, did prove to have the necessary qualities of universalism.[4] In other words, it is arguable that Constantine became a Christian from personal conviction, but by the end of his reign could see advantages for the empire as a whole in the religion he professed.

Constantine's reasons for delaying baptism are uncertain. The fact that he was not a member of the Church meant that he was not bound by its rules and could therefore remain *pontifex maximus* and officiate as head of state at pagan ceremonies. Yet he may have been more influenced by the Church's teaching that baptism conferred remission of sins and have seen this as a reason for delaying his reception until he could no longer sin. He was not unique among fourth-century Christians in being baptized on his death-bed.

The Church which Constantine patronized and finally joined called itself the Great Church, or the Catholic, that is universal, Church. It was the largest and best organized Christian group, but there were many others. Some consisted of enthusiasts, like the Montanists, who had originated in Asia Minor in *c*. 150, believed the end of the world was imminent, and encouraged their members, women as well as men, to prophesy. Others attracted conservatives, such as the Church of the Novatians, who had separated from the Catholic Church in the 250s as a protest against what they regarded as the too easy reconciliation of members who had apostatized during the Decian persecution. The later Novatians did not differ in faith from the Catholics but were opposed to any kind of innovation or laxity in church practice. Others sects differed from the Great Church over doctrinal issues; for example, the Adoptionists, followers of Paul of Samosata, Bishop of Antioch in the 260s, believed that Jesus was an ordinary man who became the Son of God by adoption when the Word of God had descended on him. The most heterodox group were the followers of Marcion (d. *c*. 160), who taught that the creator God of the Old Testament was different from the God of Love who had taken pity on the human race which he had not made, and sent his son, Jesus Christ, to redeem them from their creator.

Marcion had much in common with the Christian Gnostics who looked to Jesus as their founder, but claimed to have received from him knowledge (*gnosis*) of the esoteric meaning of the Christian faith. Gnosticism was not tied down to any defined set of texts, like the New Testament, and its adherents encouraged speculation about the nature of the universe and man's place in it, often expressed in very fanciful terms. The most powerful Christian Gnostic school was that of Valentinus, an Egyptian who taught in Rome from *c.* 135–160 and was concerned, like all Gnostics, to make Christianity a truly spiritual religion. Some sense of this is found in his hymn, 'Summer', recorded by St Hippolytus:

> I see that all is suspended on spirit,
> I perceive that all is wafted upon spirit.
> Flesh is suspended on soul,
> And soul depends on the air,
> Air is suspended from ether,
> From the depths come forth fruits,
> From the womb comes forth a child.[5]

In Constantine's day Valentinian Gnosis was still very powerful in both the eastern and western provinces, although many new schools of Gnosticism had developed.

A new religion, Manichaeism, which also claimed to be a valid form of Christianity, had entered the Roman world in the late third century. Its founder, Mani (d. 276), was a Persian nobleman who had been brought up as a Christian Gnostic, but had been much influenced by Zoroastrianism, the traditional religion of Iran. The religion which Mani founded shared with Gnosticism a contempt for the material world, and drew from Zoroastrianism a belief in a dualist cosmogony: that is, that the powers of Light and Good and those of Darkness and Evil were autonomous and in contention for control of the cosmos. Mani formulated his theology in terms of a myth of struggle between the forces of Light and Darkness, and taught that this had led to the formation of our universe, which is composed of evil matter in which particles of the good light are imprisoned, among them the souls of living creatures, and he taught that the souls of men and of all living creatures were either liberated at death or were reincarnated. The God of Light sought to restore all the imprisoned light particles to his realm, and his agent was a spiritual being, Jesus the Brilliant Light, who manifested himself in this world in a succession of prophets, including the historical Jesus of Nazareth and Mani. Their function was to tell men about their true condition and to provide them with the knowledge of how to escape from the evil, material creation. Mani founded a church with an elaborate hierarchy, designed to symbolize the time mechanism which operated the universe. At its head was the Archegos, an office held by Mani. His followers were divided into Hearers, who were in sympathy with the aims of the faith, and Elect who were fully initiated members of the Church and were cared for by the Hearers. The Elect were dedicated to a spiritual way of life in so far as that was compatible with staying alive: they were ascetic, celibate and vegan. They viewed even such food as they did eat as a necessary evil, as their form of grace makes plain:

I did not mow thee, did not grind thee, nor knead thee, nor lay thee in the oven, but another did do this and bring thee to me. I eat thee without sin.[6]

The pale Manichaean Elect, who met together to sing hymns to the Light and regarded a loaf of bread as a possible occasion of sin, were some of the most high-minded people who have ever lived.

Whenever possible, Manichaean missionaries used the religious vocabulary of the people among whom they worked in their preaching. In Persia they claimed to be part of the Zoroastrian tradition; in India they taught within a Buddhist framework; and when they entered the Roman Empire at some time after 275, they used Christian terminology, claiming that Mani was the Paraclete whom Jesus had said he would send to perfect his ministry. Probably because of their Persian connections, Diocletian proscribed the Manichaeans in 297, ordering their leaders to be burned together with their books. This persecution proved ineffective, and Manichaeism continued to spread in the Roman Empire for some 300 years. Its best known adherent was St Augustine of Hippo who became a Manichaean Hearer while a student and remained one for many years.

The Catholic Church which Constantine patronized had developed a strong and uniform organization which is well documented from the second century: the Christian community in each city was headed by a bishop supported by a group of priests and deacons. These clergy were responsible for the conduct of public worship and the pastoral care of the Christian community in their area. Bishops claimed to be the successors of the Apostles whom Jesus had appointed and considered themselves the true guardians of the apostolic teaching. Those who wished to join the Church had to receive instruction for at least three years. They were then baptized, normally at a ceremony held on the night before Easter. St Hippolytus of Rome (c. 170–c. 236) relates how, when the candidates were standing in the baptismal pool, the officiating priest asked each of them:

Dost thou believe in God the Father Almighty? Dost thou believe in Jesus Christ, the Son of God, who was born of the Holy Spirit and the Virgin Mary, who was crucified in the days of Pontius Pilate, and died, and rose the third day living from the dead, and ascended into Heaven, and sat down at the right hand of the Father and will come to judge the living and the dead? Dost thou believe in the Holy Spirit in the Holy Church, and the resurrection of the flesh?[7]

When the baptism was completed the candidates dressed again and knelt before the bishop who laid his hands on their heads to confer the Holy Spirit. Then he and all those present joined in the celebration of the eucharist of Easter Day.

The profession of belief made by the baptismal candidates is the oldest known version of the creed. This was a summary of the faith, but during their long preparation the candidates would have received detailed instruction. They would have learnt that God is the sole creative principle, that his nature is love and that the universe which he created had been perfect. Evil had entered it because God had given men and women free will and they had made wrong choices, motivated by selfishness and malice. Such acts were

The baptism of Christ, mosaic in the Arian baptistery, Ravenna, late fifth century. The figure on the left is a personification of the river Jordan.

sinful because they separated man from his creator. Once the first human beings had sinned, their descendants became naturally inclined to sin. Theologians described this inclination as original (that is, inherited) sin. Thereafter, although human beings might wish to lead perfect lives in accordance with God's will, they were no longer capable of doing so.

Although the power of evil is made very evident in the New Testament, little is said about its origin. Jesus taught his followers to pray 'deliver us from evil', and spoke of the evil power which opposed his work and which he called by a variety of names – Satan, the Devil, the Prince of this World. St Paul taught that the story in the Book of Genesis about how Adam and Eve had been driven from Paradise for disobeying God's command exemplified the way in which human self-will had allowed sin and death and the forces of evil to enter God's creation. He also explained how the whole of creation, and not just man, needed and would benefit from the redeeming work of Christ. From a very early date Christian writers sought to give a coherent account of the origin and nature of evil, using these and other biblical passages and also drawing on the Jewish apocryphal tradition (e.g. Jude, v. 9). They inferred that angels, like men, had been created with free will and that some of them, led by Lucifer, had misused it and rebelled against God. Lucifer had become the Devil, and with the fallen angels ruled over Hell. The Devil and his angels carried on a perpetual war against God and were responsible for marring the perfect universe which God had made, so that it had become hostile to man. Until the coming of Christ the Devil had claimed dominion over the souls of dead men and women because they had all been sinful, but Christ freed the souls of those who repented when, after the Crucifixion, he descended into Hell. This image of a cosmic conflict between the rebel angels led by Lucifer and the angels loyal to God, commanded by St Michael, in which humanity had a central role, was accepted by most Catholic Christians in the Middle Ages as an explanation of the origin and nature of evil. Yet although the Church never condemned this view, it was never defined as true belief by any medieval Church Council.[8]

Christian tradition affirmed that the defeat of evil and the restoration of perfection had been achieved by the Son of God, Jesus, who became man and was born of a virgin mother, Mary. In him a new creation began. By suffering and dying on the cross he exemplified God's love for men, and he then descended into Hell to fight the mystery of evil on its own supernatural ground and won. Having defeated death and sin he rose from the dead and became the firstborn of the new creation. Leaving on earth the Church which he had founded, God the Son returned to Heaven and the Third Person of the Trinity, the Holy Spirit, descended on Christ's followers at Pentecost to fortify them to continue his ministry. Although individual theologians attempted to explain how the incarnation, and more particularly the death and resurrection of Jesus, had effected the reconciliation of men to God, none of their opinions ever received the official endorsement of the medieval Catholic Church, which was content to express its faith in the words of the Nicene Creed: 'for us men and for our salvation he [Jesus] came down from Heaven'.

It was part of the apostolic tradition that at some future time Christ would return to judge the living and the dead. He himself had said that he did not know when this would happen (Matt. 24:36) but despite this, speculation about dates was rife throughout the Middle Ages and beyond. In the meantime it was the task of the Church to complete the work which Jesus had begun. St Paul had expressed that work in this way in one of the very earliest documents of the Church: 'if any man be in Christ he is a new creature: old things are passed away; behold all things are become new.' (II Cor. 5:17) The Christian life was dedicated to living in harmony with God, and it was conceived of as a battle, fought on two levels: first against the selfish instincts of the individual Christian, and secondly against the spiritual powers of evil who, although defeated by Christ, were still fighting a spirited rearguard action and, with the help of wayward humanity, were seeking to frustrate the divine plan.

St Peter the Apostle, a mosaic from the Arian baptistery, Ravenna.

Procession of virgin saints, wearing court dress, Sant' Apollinare Nuovo, Ravenna.

Unlike Gnostics, Catholic Christians had a high regard for the material world. Christ's work had only been possible because he had become fully human. Because God was the creator of everything, the whole creation had to be restored to its original perfection, not just the souls of men. This was symbolized by the Church's belief in the resurrection of the body: just as Christ had risen bodily from the dead, so all his followers would enjoy not merely immortality of the soul, but also the transformation of their bodies. But this was only part of a process which would culminate in the creation of a new heaven and a new earth in which evil would have no part.

There was uncertainty among Christian theologians about whether at the end of time only part of the creation would be redeemed and whether those who rejected Christ, both men and angels, would suffer eternal damnation. This was certainly the majority opinion, but some thinkers, notably St Clement of Alexandria and Origen in the third century and St Gregory of Nyssa in the fourth, held that the entire creation would, in the end, attain salvation, a doctrine known as *apocatastasis*, which was later condemned in the form in which it was expressed by Origen because it appeared to deny God's creatures the freedom to choose their own destinies.

Church members were expected to pray regularly each day. In the age of persecution such prayers had been said privately, but when cathedrals were built in the fourth century it became common to hold daily services in the morning and at the time the lamps were lit in the evening. These consisted of the recitation of psalms and prayers and lay people were encouraged to attend. At the centre of the Christian life was the celebration of the eucharist. The earliest account of this sacrament is that given by St Paul:

> The Lord Jesus the same night in which he was betrayed took bread; and when he had given thanks, he brake it, and said: 'Take, eat; this is my body which is broken for you: this do in remembrance of me.' After the same manner also he took the cup, when he had supped, saying: 'This cup is the new testament in my blood; this do ye, as oft as ye drink it, in remembrance of me.' For as often as ye eat this bread, and drink this cup, ye do shew the Lord's death till he come. Wherefore whosoever shall eat this bread and drink this cup of the Lord unworthily, shall be guilty of the body and blood of the Lord. But let a man examine himself, and so let him eat of that bread and drink of that cup. For he that eateth and drinketh unworthily, eateth and drinketh damnation to himself, not discerning the Lord's body. (1 Cor. 11: 23–9).

The Church in the fourth century believed that the eucharist was not only a commemoration of Christ's death, but also a showing forth in time of an act which had eternal validity: that is to say it enabled the congregation to be spiritually present at Calvary, and to petition Christ crucified for their needs and for the needs of all the world. This sacrament emphasized the importance of hallowing the physical creation: bread and wine, the everyday food and drink of people in Mediterranean lands, became the body and blood of Christ, the means by which the faithful entered into communion with God.

The eucharist, which in the Western Church came to be called the Mass, was celebrated every Sunday, the day of Christ's resurrection, and the normal minister was the bishop. A great variety of liturgical rites was used in local churches, but they all conformed to the same general pattern: an introductory service, consisting of prayers and readings, which anybody might attend, followed by the part of the liturgy at which only the baptized might be present, when the bread and wine were consecrated and the faithful received Holy Communion.

Jesus had given his followers an impossible rule of life: 'Be ye therefore perfect, even as your Father which is in Heaven is perfect.' (Matt. 5:48.) The means to achieve this, he had told them, was love, love of God, and love of all other human beings as though they were oneself. This course of action was hindered by the strong drives to selfishness which all people experience and theologians identified the seven sins, each of which could destroy the new life and indeed the desire for it in a Christian. The poet Prudentius (348–c. 410) wrote a mock epic, the *Psychomachia*, or Spiritual Battle, about the war between the seven deadly sins and the virtues which are opposed to them. The sin of lechery was combated by chastity, that of gluttony by abstinence, that of sloth by diligence, that of avarice by generosity, that of anger by patience, that of envy by loving-kindness, and that of pride by humility. Christian morality consisted in promoting in oneself these and other virtues.[9]

It was universally recognized that nobody could live a perfect life and that minor sins such as irritability or pomposity were part of being human. Nevertheless, the Church considered that three sins were so serious that those who committed them incurred excommunication: these were apostasy, denial of one's faith; committing murder; and committing adultery, that is breaking one's own or somebody else's marriage vows, normally in a public and persistent way. Those guilty of these offences had to make confession to the bishop, and do public penance for as long as he determined. During that time the offender had to sit on the penitents' bench in church during the first part of the liturgy, but was not allowed to stay for the consecration or to receive Holy Communion. The penance always lasted for several years and sometimes the penitent was only reconciled when he was dying. In the early fourth century a Christian might only be absolved once from serious post-baptismal sin; a second offence would lead to his permanent exclusion from the Church.

The Church recognized that there were different ways of living the Christian life. Most people would pursue normal careers and many of them would marry. The Church laid down rules about marriage, but the ceremony at this time and for long afterwards was an entirely secular one arranged by the families concerned. Other Christians had a vocation to the contemplative life of prayer. This might take a number of forms, but from the late third century it became increasingly common for such people to become monks and nuns, a development which originated in Christian Egypt (see p. 139). The contemplative life entailed vows of celibacy (the renunciation of sex) and poverty (the renunciation of personal property), though beyond that there was a great deal of variation in the rules of life followed by solitaries and in communities.

The Church accepted the Jewish scriptures of the Old Testament as authoritative and divinely inspired. They were read in the Greek translation made for the Jews of

The three Magi bearing gifts for the infant Christ, Sant' Apollinare Nuovo, Ravenna.

Alexandria and known as the Septuagint, because that was the version in which the writers of the New Testament cited them. The Septuagint contains a group of books not found in the Hebrew scriptures, which are generally called the Apocrypha, and throughout the Middle Ages they formed part of the text of the Old Testament.

Christians took longer to decide what books should be included in the New Testament. From *c.* 130 there seems to have been general agreement about the inspiration of the Four Gospels and the thirteen letters attributed to St Paul. The remaining books gained acceptance more slowly, while some Christian groups wanted to include other writings, such as *The Shepherd of Hermas*. The earliest complete list of the books of the New Testament in the form which is now standard dates from 367 and is found in the Festal Letter of St Athanasius of Alexandria; a similar list was drawn up in Rome for Pope Damasus in 382.[10]

Authority in the Church was vested in bishops, who held the place of the Apostles, and when disputes arose they were settled by council at which normally only the bishops voted, though other church members might attend and speak. The author of the Book of Acts certainly supposed that conciliar government was part of the apostolic tradition (Acts 15:6–31), but in the age of persecution only local councils had been able to meet. In Constantine's day, although all bishops were equal in dignity, three were recognized as pre-eminent in the Roman world, those of Rome, Alexandria and Antioch in Syria. The Bishop of Rome, like his colleague at Alexandria, was known as pope, or father, and in Constantine's day he enjoyed undoubted primacy of honour, taking precedence over all other bishops as successor of St Peter and bishop of the ancient imperial capital. The popes claimed to have inherited the powers which Christ gave to Peter:

> Thou art Peter and upon this rock I will build my church; and the gates of hell shall not prevail against it. And I will give thee the keys of the kingdom of heaven: and whatsoever thou shalt bind on earth shall be bound in Heaven: and whatsoever thou shalt loose on earth shall be loosed in Heaven. (Matt. 16:18–19).[11]

This text is first known to have been invoked by Pope St Stephen I (254–7) during a dispute with St Cyprian of Carthage about baptism, but it was only gradually, during the Middle Ages, that the popes became aware of how widely their powers as vicars of St Peter might be interpreted.

Once Christianity had become a *religio licita* it was possible to hold a General Council representing the entire Church.[12] In 325 Constantine summoned the first assembly of this kind to Nicaea in order to resolve the Arian controversy. Arius, a priest of Alexandria, was represented by his opponents as teaching that there had been a time when God the Father existed and God the Son did not; in other words, that the Son was not equal to God but a creature made by God. Henri Marrou was probably correct in suggesting that in fact Arius 'was trying to express an ontological superiority [of God the Father] rather than a chronological priority'.[13] Seen in those terms, the dispute was concerned with defining what was meant by 'Son of God', and that could only be resolved by trained theologians. However, the dispute could also be presented in a simplified way which every Christian could understand: was Jesus Christ God, or was he simply a part of God's creation? In our very different society this is still a matter which can arouse strong feelings in religious discussions. In the fourth century Arius's views as popularly understood proved very divisive.

The Council was attended by 318 bishops from all over the Christian world, some from beyond the imperial frontiers. Constantine, though not yet a member of the Church, convened the assembly and presided at it, though only the bishops voted. This anomaly showed that there was a potential in Christian society for a conflict between Church and State, and although that did not happen at Nicaea, it was to become one of the dominant themes of Christian history during the Middle Ages. The Council of Nicaea was important because for the first time since the apostolic age an assembly could meet which was representative of the whole Church and able to reach decisions binding on all its members. At Nicaea Arius's teaching was unanimously condemned and the belief affirmed that Jesus Christ shared one being with God the Father and the Holy Spirit, that he was, indeed, fully God and fully man. The council also legislated about lesser matters such as the date on which Easter should be kept.

In practice the decisions of Nicaea proved difficult to implement. Many churchmen continued to hold modified forms of Arius's teaching: the opinion that Christ was like his Father in all things, though not of one being with him, proved particularly attractive. Bishops who held such views were allowed to remain in office, and one of them, Eusebius of Nicomedia, received Constantine into the Church when he was dying in 337. His son and successor, the Emperor Constantius (337–61), was a convinced moderate Arian and exiled some of the bishops who upheld the rulings of Nicaea, replacing them by men with Arian sympathies.

Constantius was succeeded in 361 by his cousin Julian, known as the Apostate, because although brought up a Christian, he rejected that faith when he became emperor and restored traditional Roman paganism as the official religion of the state. He did not persecute Christians, but placed all forms of Christianity on an equal legal footing, hoping that through their quarrels his opponents would undermine their own credibility. It is impossible to know whether his religious policies could have succeeded, because his death in 363 at the end of a disastrous campaign against Persia, and his lack of an heir, brought his changes to a sudden end. All his successors were Christians, and the favoured position of the Church in the empire was never subsequently called in question.

Julian's policy of tolerating all forms of Christianity had allowed pro-Nicene bishops, exiled under Constantius, to return to their sees. Although some of Julian's immediate successors were moderate Arians they did not attempt to persecute Catholics, and for the next twenty years Catholics and Arians co-existed in a single church. In 379 power passed to two emperors who supported the Council of Nicaea, Theodosius I (379–95) and Gratian (375–83), and under their auspices the second General Council of the Church met at Constantinople in 381. All forms of Arianism were condemned, the decisions of the Council of Nicaea were upheld, and there is evidence to suggest that the Council endorsed the Nicene Creed in its present form.[14] Thereafter, Arians living in the empire became a very small minority and the bishops of the Catholic Church were united in accepting the faith as defined by the first two general councils.

The Church had not been damaged by the Arian controversy, which was symptomatic of its intellectual vitality. Large numbers of people joined the Church during the fourth century and it was fast becoming the religion of the majority. The privileges of the clergy were increased under Theodosius: in 384 they were made answerable to the bishops' courts alone for all offences, criminal as well as civil, while bishops were declared to be subject only to the judgment of their peers. The Church had also become better organized during the fourth century. It began to model its hierarchy on that of the imperial administration: the bishops were like provincial governors; metropolitan archbishops, who supervised whole groups of dioceses, were like imperial vicars; while the incumbents of the great sees of Rome, Alexandria and Antioch, which were later to be called patriarchates, corresponded to imperial prefects. Because of court patronage Christians had begun to be appointed to the highest offices in the state: the first Christian consul, for example, was nominated in 323. By the end of the fourth century a large number of men of great ability not merely wanted to be

Christians, but wanted to be ordained. Men like Ambrose and Augustine in the West, and John Chrysostom, Gregory of Nazianzus and Basil of Caesarea in the East, are evidence of this trend. The Catholic Church was being run by some of the most gifted and able men in their generation, and so when on 8 November 392 Theodosius I made Catholic Christianity the official religion of the Roman Empire, this seemed almost a natural development.

No pagan was compelled to join the Church, but the public and private performance of pagan religious ceremonies was forbidden by law. Eighty years after the Edict of Milan there had been a complete reversal of roles: paganism had now become a *religio non licita*. Although this legislation proved very difficult to enforce and most pagans continued to worship in the traditional ways, they were now subject to random harassment, such as the destruction of temples. Most Christians, despite their long experience of persecution, did not regard the toleration of other religions as a virtue.

In 395 Arcadius, Theodosius's son and successor in the eastern provinces, made all forms of Christianity illegal except that of the established Catholic Church. This law also proved almost impossible to enforce and other Christian sects survived in some places as late as the mid-eighth century, but they had all died out by *c.* 800 and it was from the Catholic Church of the fourth century that virtually all the churches of medieval Christendom described in this book were descended, which explains why, despite many superficial differences, they had so much in common.

CHAPTER ONE

THE MEDIEVAL WESTERN CHURCH

THE FORMATION OF WESTERN CHRISTENDOM

Changes in Western Society

When Theodosius the Great died in 395 the empire was divided between his two sons: Arcadius ruled the eastern provinces and Honorius the western (see Map p. xviii). It is customary to refer to the eastern provinces after this time as the Byzantine Empire. Honorius and his successors ruled in Ravenna, protected from sudden attack by marshes and linked by sea to the eastern provinces. Considerable social and political changes took place in the Western Empire during the fifth century. They were in part caused by the Huns, a warlike, nomadic people who in the fourth century began to build an empire in southern Russia and eastern Europe, which led Germanic tribes to seek refuge across the Roman frontier. When the waters of the upper Rhine froze over on 31 December 406, a large body of Suevi and Vandals crossed into imperial territory. The Suevi finally settled in north-western Spain, while the Vandals occupied the rest of the peninsula. The Visigoths, who had settled in Roman territory in the Balkans in 376, led by King Alaric moved into Italy, where they sacked Rome in 410. In 412 they settled in Aquitaine and, after the Vandals established a kingdom at Carthage in 429 (see p. 171), took over their lands in Spain as well. Meanwhile the Burgundians had gained control of south-eastern Gaul. The parts of the West which remained under direct Roman rule were gradually eroded. In 476 the German general Odoacer deposed his master, the Western Emperor Romulus (contemptuously called Augustulus, the Little Emperor), and transferred his allegiance to the Emperor Zeno in Constantinople. Then in 486, the Franks, who had formerly lived along the north-eastern frontier of Gaul, led by their young King Clovis (481–511), conquered most of Gaul north of the Loire. Thus within a century of the death of Theodosius the Western Empire had become a group of Germanic kingdoms.

The immigrant peoples did not consider that they were conquering Roman territory, but merely settling inside it. With the exception of the Vandals in north Africa, they were prepared to accept imperial overlordship and in return to defend the empire. Their help was indeed valuable, as the Visigoths proved when they fought alongside the Romans and defeated Attila, King of the Huns, when he invaded Gaul in 451. The Germanic kings wanted to preserve Roman institutions, which most of them admired, and some of them were extremely successful in doing so. It is possible to gain some idea of what the changes seemed like to contemporaries from the letters of Sidonius Apollinaris (*c.* 430–86), a member of the senatorial aristocracy of southern Gaul.

Sidonius was educated in the classical tradition, possessed huge estates and was trained for a conventional career in the imperial administration. When his father-in-law, Avitus, briefly became Western Emperor (455–6), Sidonius wrote a panegyric in his honour and a statue was erected to him in the Roman forum. The Emperor Anthemius (467–72) appointed Sidonius prefect of Rome in 468–9. Then, in 471, he was elected Bishop of Clermont by the local people and tried unsuccessfully to defend the city, which was still directly under Roman rule, against the Visigothic King Euric. After a brief imprisonment by the Visigoths, Sidonius returned to his see, where he used his great wealth to benefit his flock. As his career shows, although there was much continuity, radical changes were taking place in the Roman Empire of the West by the 470s.

With the exception of the Franks, most of the Germans who settled in the empire were Arians. They owed their faith to Ulfilas, a Christian living under Gothic rule, who in *c.* 341 had been sent as an ambassador to the Emperor Constantius, who arranged for him to be consecrated Bishop of the Goths at a time when the court was moderate Arian.[1] Ulfilas translated the liturgy and the Bible into Gothic, omitting the four books of Kings which he considered too bloodthirsty for his converts. Missionaries trained by him worked among the other Germanic peoples of central and eastern Europe, so that by the time they entered Roman territory many of them had been converted to Arianism. It is probable that they remained Arian because they were attached to the vernacular Gothic liturgy rather than for theological reasons. Except in the Vandal kingdom of Africa the Arian rulers did not persecute Catholics, but the difference in religion was important, because it kept the German settlers separate from the Roman population. Indeed, the latter came to identify the Catholic Church and its Latin liturgy with the traditional civilization of Rome. Latin at that time was the everyday speech of much of Italy, while in other parts of the West it was known by a quite wide cross-section of the urban population. The Roman aristocracy, many of whom had previously been hostile to Christianity, joined the Catholic Church, and some of them, like Sidonius, became bishops.

The Franks were pagans, but King Clovis received Catholic baptism in *c.* 496 together with many of his followers. He was already familiar with Christianity as his wife, Clothilde, was a Catholic Burgundian princess, but he attributed his conversion to the victory granted him by the Christian God over the Alemanni. His Catholicism ensured him the support of the Church hierarchy and of the Roman aristocracy of Gaul, and in 507 he was able to defeat the Visigoths at Vouillé and annex all their lands in Gaul. Because he was the only Catholic king in the West he was honoured by the Emperor Anastasius at Constantinople who conferred on him the dignity of a consul.

The conversion of the Franks to Catholicism and their dominance in Gaul may have been one reason which inclined the Emperor Justinian (527–65) to attempt to restore imperial power in the West. The rapid success of his forces against the Vandal kingdom of Carthage in 533–4 (see p. 172–2) encouraged him to attack the Ostrogothic kingdom in Italy. The Arian Ostrogoths, who had settled in the province of Pannonia in the 450s,

Noah's Ark. An allegory of the Church in which the faithful are saved from spiritual destruction. Spanish manuscript, 1150–1200.

had been used by the Emperor Zeno to overthrow Odoacer in 489 and had established a kingdom in Italy. In the reign of Theodoric (d. 526) late Roman civilization in Italy had enjoyed a final flowering. It took Justinian almost twenty years (535–54) to bring the whole of Italy under direct imperial rule and to destroy Ostrogothic power, and the cost was high. The entire peninsula had been impoverished and Rome had suffered two long sieges during which the aqueducts had been cut, so that its population declined drastically.

Soon after Justinian's death in 565, the Lombards, a Germanic people whose rulers were Arians, invaded Italy and by 590 had conquered Lombardy, Tuscany and the Duchy of Benevento in southern Italy. Venice, the Exarchate – a band of territory extending across central Italy from Ravenna to Rome – Apulia, Calabria, the maritime cities of Naples, Amalfi and Gaeta, together with Sicily remained under Byzantine rule. Consequently, the Papacy was subject to the Eastern Emperor even though most of Western Christendom was governed by German kings.

Arianism gradually died out. The Arian churches in north Africa and Italy did not survive the destruction of the Vandal and Ostrogothic kingdoms by Justinian. The Burgundians had accepted Catholicism in the time of King Sigismund (516–23), while in Spain the Suevi became Catholics in the 560s and the Visigoths in 589. Finally, the Lombards became Catholic after the death of King Rothari in 652.

The Response of the Western Church

The Western provinces of the Roman Empire were in the main coterminus with the Western Church, which worshipped in Latin and looked towards Rome as the senior bishopric. That Church proved itself to be very resilient during the troubled years which followed the death of Theodosius. Despite the edict of 392 paganism remained strong, specially among the senatorial aristocracy. The members of this articulate and powerful group were shocked by the Gothic sack of Rome in 410, which, they argued, was a direct consequence of the abandonment of the worship of the traditional gods of Rome. St Augustine of Hippo responded to this criticism by writing what was in effect a Christian philosophy of history, *The City of God*. He argued that human history was an ongoing conflict between two cities, the City of God, consisting of those who tried to act in conformity with God's will, and the City of the World, which was made up of those who through self-regard or wilful defiance opposed God's will, a conflict which was part of a wider cosmic battle between the forces of Good and Evil which would only end with the Last Judgement. Augustine refused to make a crude equation between the City of God and the Church, since not all Christians did the will of God and not all pagans were opposed to it. Divine approval could not be assessed in terms of worldly success, as Augustine's opponents urged it should be, for as he pointed out, Rome had suffered comparable vicissitudes to the Gothic sack while it was a pagan city.

Although by *c*. 500 the Roman aristocracy had for the most part been received into the Catholic Church, paganism still remained strong among the peasantry. The evidence for this in the enactments of church councils and in anecdotes in the lives of saints is convincing because of its unanimity. In part this reflects the lack of resident clergy in rural areas. By 400 bishoprics had been established in all the main cities of the West and the whole area was divided into dioceses, some of which were very large. There were churches in most of the old Roman cities, and landowners built some in the countryside, but there was as yet no system of rural parishes. Although a high proportion of the rural population had probably been baptized by itinerant priests, few of them had received any serious instruction in the faith, or had much opportunity to practise it regularly. Monasteries came to have a very important role in the work of evangelization.

Early western monasticism was strongly influenced by eastern Mediterranean models. John Cassian (*c*. 360–430), founder of St Victor at Marseilles, was particularly influential, for he had spent ten years in Egypt and brought a deep understanding of the spirituality of the Desert Fathers to the Western Church (see Chapter Four). He wrote the *Institutes*, an account of the way of life of the monks of Egypt, and the *Conferences*, reports of his discussions of the monastic life with some of the most distinguished Egyptian abbots, and these works became spiritual guides for western monks.

In the early sixth century a specifically western form of monastic observance developed which was attributed to St Benedict of Nursia. In his *Dialogues* Pope Gregory I

(590–604) relates that Benedict (*c.* 480–*c.* 550) when a young man had become a recluse at Subiaco near Rome, where he later founded a monastery. In *c.* 529 he founded another monastery at Monte Cassino near Capua, of which he became abbot and for which he wrote his Rule. There seems no longer any doubt that Benedict did write the Rule which bears his name; what is in dispute is the degree of originality in his work. There is now general, though not total, consensus that he made extensive use of an anonymous work written in *c.* 500–530, known as the *Regula Magistri*, or Rule of the Master. This is a much longer Rule and it never became influential, but Benedict was indebted to it just as he was to the works of John Cassian and of St Basil.[2]

St Benedict describes his work as 'a little Rule for beginners'. It marks a complete break with the Egyptian monastic tradition because it makes no provision for extreme asceticism but is characterized by moderation and common sense. Members of the community have to be trained to live and work and pray together, and that means that they must be considerate of others and obey the abbot, but Benedict accepted that individual monks have different strengths and weaknesses. All the brethren are required to recite the long night office in chapel, but Benedict accepts that some people find it more difficult to get up than others and no penalty is attached to those who come late to chapel provided they arrive before the end of the first psalm. The Rule, in fact, sets out to train a community which is a well-run household. Benedict required a monk to take a fourth vow at his profession, that of stability – the promise to stay for the rest of his life in the community in which he was professed. This did not preclude the possibility that some monks might feel a vocation to become hermits, because they would still remain attached to the community. Benedict was concerned to discourage *gyrovagi*, gadabout monks, of whom there were many, who, while keeping their vows, spent their lives wandering from one monastery to another. Although the Rule of St Benedict was later to become immensely influential, this was a slow process. In the early Middle Ages it was only one rule among many observed in western monasteries.

The primary function of monastic communities was to worship God in liturgical prayer, but they soon acquired social commitments as well. They were given landed endowments and therefore had to assume responsibility for the spiritual wellbeing of their tenants, while lay people who were not necessarily their tenants also came to them for help and advice and attended their chapels on great feast days. Yet arguably the greatest contribution which the monasteries made to the formation of a Christian Europe was the witness which they bore to the Catholic faith, for in their chapels the Divine Office was sung eight times every twenty-four hours, without a single day's intermission, for centuries on end.

Monasteries were not uniformly distributed, and in many rural areas the peasantry's knowledge of Christianity and their opportunities to practise it remained slight. Even so, the spiritual landscape of the West was changing in ways that affected everybody. One example of this was the popular cult of relics. The early Christians had revered the martyrs who, in accordance with Roman customs, had been buried outside the city walls. In the early Middle Ages urban churches were built in honour of those saints and their relics were brought into the cities and placed beneath the altars, while relics from Rome and elsewhere were translated with great solemnity to new churches in other

The Benedictine abbey of Saint-Guilhem-le-Desert in southern France, founded in 804.

parts of Europe, and it later became obligatory for every altar in Catholic Christendom to contain a relic. Peter Brown has rightly pointed out how revolutionary this was, because in the pre-Christian, Graeco-Roman world the bodies of the dead had been considered polluting and might not be buried inside the city walls, whereas in the medieval world relics were considered important as a point of physical contact with the saints who stood in the presence of God and could pray for the needs of Christians on earth. This sensibility persisted throughout the medieval centuries. When in 1458 the skull of St Andrew was brought to Rome from Patras by a refugee Byzantine prince, Pope Pius II, a distinguished humanist scholar, held it aloft and admonished the crowd outside St Peters:

Here, here the Spirit of God alighted [at Pentecost] . . . here were the eyes that often beheld God in the flesh, the mouth that often spoke to Christ. Behold a mighty shrine.[3]

The saints were not at all like the pagan gods, who could grant or withhold benefits from their votaries without reference to any other power. The saints were the servants of God. They could only ask him to help their devotees, but they could not forgive sins or guarantee salvation. Real power belonged to God alone.

Living holy men and women who led lives of extreme asceticism were also held in great esteem, since it was believed that God would answer their prayers and sometimes enable them to perform healing miracles or to prophesy accurately about the future. Many of them were recluses who lived in remote places, but local people sought them out and asked them to right injustices. The holy man had no counterpart in the ancient world, and he was powerful. Because they believed that God listened to him, landlords and princes would take notice of what he said. Again, regard for this kind of spiritual authority lasted throughout the Middle Ages. When Louis XI of France was dying in 1483, he had the Calabrian hermit, St Francesco of Paola, brought to his bedchamber to pray for his soul, considering his intercession superior to that of other people.

The cosmic conflict in which Christians were involved came to be reflected in human experience. The Devil sometimes appeared in person to tempt man, and lesser demons frequently did so, but the angelic powers also manifested themselves to men, including St Michael, captain of the heavenly host, who attracted many votaries, particularly among warriors.

The Conversion of Ireland and Scotland

A further sign of the vitality of the fifth-century Western Church was the successful evangelization of the independent Celtic peoples of the British Isles. The chronicler Prosper

The cosmic conflict. St Michael fights the Dragon above his shrine church, the Mont St Michel, from the Très Riches Heures of Jean, Duc de Berry.

of Aquitaine records that in 431 Pope Celestine I sent Palladius to be bishop 'to the Irish believing in Christ'. The relation between this mission and the more famous work of St Patrick is not at all clear. Kathleen Hughes suggested that Palladius was sent to southern Ireland, which had contacts with continental Europe and where there would certainly have been some Christian merchants living, while Patrick worked in the north, west and centre of the island, areas which were less cosmopolitan and still entirely pagan, and this view is persuasive though unprovable.[4] In his *Confession*, or spiritual autobiography, St Patrick relates how he had grown up in a Christian family in Roman Britain, but, aged sixteen, had been captured by pirates and sold into slavery in the west of Ireland. Although he later escaped, he felt a vocation to return to Ireland and, having been consecrated a bishop, he began to preach the faith of Christ there. All the evidence suggests that Patrick's mission took place in the second half of the fifth century. No doubt other clergy were involved in the evangelization of Ireland of whom no historical record survives. Although Ireland had not formed part of the Roman Empire a Latin liturgy was introduced there, because the Catholic authorities associated vernacular liturgies with the heretical Arians, who were ruling much of the West.

Irish monasticism, like that of early Gaul, was strongly influenced by the Egyptian and Syrian traditions which involved extreme forms of asceticism. The Irish monastic legislator St Columbanus (d. 615) had a very different view of community life from St Benedict, as his description of a perfect monk shows:

> Let him not do as he wishes . . . Let him come weary to his bed and sleep walking, and let him be forced to rise while his sleep is not yet finished.[5]

The earliest enactments of Irish canon law, embedded in later codes, suggest that at first the Irish shared the same ecclesiastical organization as the rest of Western Europe: bishops were appointed with jurisdiction over defined territories and monasteries were founded within those dioceses. Yet as the monastic movement grew in strength in the later sixth century abbots and their monasteries came to appear more important than bishops and their cathedrals. This was partly because most cathedrals came to be served by monastic communities and all bishops were monks. In fact a good deal of variety existed. Some bishops combined their office with that of abbot, while some abbots appointed bishops who were members of their communities. This kind of organization looked very different from that of the rest of the Western Church, and the Church in Celtic lands also had distinctive forms of piety and of liturgical usage. Nevertheless, it was not a separate church, but an integral part of Catholic Christendom with which it shared a common faith and order.

Irish monks were responsible for completing the conversion of Scotland. In the sixth century much of the country was ruled by the Picts,[6] but although, as archaeological evidence shows, the southern Picts were already Christian by the late fifth century, the northern Picts were still pagans in 563 when the Irish St Columba, or Columcille, founded a monastery at Iona. He and his brethren took the Christian faith to the rest of the western isles and to the northern Picts. In the course of that mission Columcille met the Loch Ness monster and so far as I am aware is the only person ever to have had speech with it.[7]

The Conversion of England

The history of the former Roman province of Britain in the fifth and sixth centuries is very poorly documented and it is difficult to determine what happened to the Catholic Church, which had certainly existed there in the fourth century. In the fifth century Britain was invaded by pagan Angles and Saxons from Frisia, north-western Germany and Denmark, who established a group of independent kingdoms in the east of the island. The Britons fought back and the Anglo-Saxon advance to the west was slow. In this period the independent British became entirely Christian, but adopted a Celtic type of church organization. The British Church made no attempt to evangelize the Anglo-Saxons.

In 597 Pope Gregory I sent a mission to King Ethelbert of Kent led by Augustine, a monk from Gregory's own foundation, St Andrew's monastery in Rome. Ethelbert was already familiar with Catholicism because he was married to a Frankish Christian princess, and within a few years he and many of his subjects were baptized. Augustine

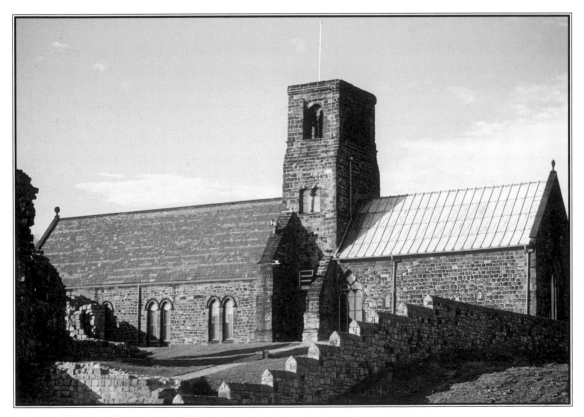

St Paul's Church at Jarrow, dating from 681. The historian Bede lived in the adjacent monastery.

became the first Archbishop of Canterbury, but it was not until 686 that all the Anglo-Saxon kingdoms had come to accept the Catholic faith. They had received it from a variety of sources: St Birinus who converted the West Saxons worked independently of Canterbury; St Felix who converted East Anglia came from Burgundy; while King Oswald of Northumbria, who had spent his youth in exile at Iona, invited the Celtic St Aidan to be first Bishop of Lindisfarne when he came to the throne in 634. St Aidan endeared himself to the Northumbrians by his combination of asceticism, affability and liberality. He walked all over his huge diocese because he wanted to get to know his flock, and talked freely to everybody he met, irrespective of their rank; and when the king's son presented him with a fine horse to make his journeys easier, Aidan offended the prince by giving it away to the first beggar he met.

The Christian Anglo-Saxons continued to fight the British, but henceforth respected the churches in the lands which they conquered. For example, when the West Saxons advanced into Somerset in 658 they found a Celtic monastery at Glastonbury, which had a wooden chapel, said by the brethren to be the first church built in Britain. The Saxons endowed the monastery lavishly and reverenced the wooden church, which survived unaltered until the great fire of 1184. Anglo-Saxon and Celtic Christians were thus working together without too many problems by the middle of the seventh century, but the English at that time had many independent churches, just as they had many independent kings.[8] In 667 Pope Vitalian nominated a Greek monk, Theodore of Tarsus, as Archbishop of Canterbury. Theodore had been educated in the schools of Athens and was said to be sixty-seven years old when he reached England in 669. When he died twenty-one years later he had, through tact, firmness and hard work, brought the English Church into being, with fourteen bishops all acknowledging the primacy of Canterbury and able to meet in councils to legislate for the whole province. It was a remarkable achievement because England at that time did not exist: there were still seven independent English kingdoms, but henceforth there was only one English Church.

The Vision of a United Europe

In 711 Spain was invaded from north Africa by Muslim forces composed chiefly of recruits from Mauretania and therefore known as Moors. They easily defeated the Visigoths and by 718 had gained control of the whole peninsula. In the early eighth century Muslim fleets captured the Balearics, Sardinia and Corsica, and in the ninth century the Muslims conquered Sicily. They did not persecute their Christian subjects, but they did cut off the churches of Spain and the islands from regular contact with the rest of the Western Christendom.

The Moors of Spain conducted savage raids into France but met with strong resistance. The Frankish kingdom in the mid-eighth century was powerful and included not only the whole of France but also much of western Germany. Although Clovis's descendant, Childeric III, was king, real authority rested with his Mayor of the Palace, Pepin. In 751 Pope Zacharias sanctioned Pepin's seizure of power: Childeric was deposed, and Pepin was anointed king by a French bishop. This was a revival of a ritual used in ancient Israel, which was later adopted throughout western Christendom and formed the basis for the theory of the divine right of kings.[2]

Zacharias's predecessor, Gregory III (731–41), had excommunicated Emperor Leo III of Constantinople because of his religious policies (see p. 67). This quarrel, which lasted for fifty years, weakened Byzantine control over central Italy and in 751 the Lombards conquered the Exarchate of Ravenna, but when they sought to incorporate Rome into their kingdom Pope Stephen III (752–7) appealed for help to King Pepin of France, who in 755 forced the Lombards to hand over the Exarchate to the pope. When they reneged on this settlement, Pepin's son Charlemagne (768–814) annexed the Lombard kingdom in 774.

While his generals conquered the march of Barcelona from the Moors, Charlemagne extended Frankish territory in the Danube valley as far as Austria. He also conquered the pagan Saxons in 795, thereby extending his eastern frontier to the Elbe. He fixed his capital at Aachen and the palace school there acted as a magnet for learned churchmen from all over the West, including Alcuin of York. Charlemagne ruled a considerable part of the Christian West, and his clerical advisers were concerned to give institutional permanence to this conglomeration of territories acquired by inheritance and conquest, for they believed that this would ensure peace among Christians. Charlemagne seemingly agreed with this policy and on Christmas Day 800 was crowned Emperor of the West by Pope Leo III in St Peter's basilica. He had not expected a hostile reaction from Byzantium (see p. 90), and later tried to distance himself from the proceedings by claiming that his coronation had been planned without his knowledge by Leo III, which is inherently unbelievable. The long-term consequences of Charlemagne's coronation were more important than the immediate ones. The Christian Empire of the West was to last for a thousand years and a precedent had been created whereby only a pope could crown a western emperor. Moreover, later popes were able to claim that emperors derived their power from God through them. After this time the Papacy became free from Byzantine control. The former lands of the Exarchate became the States of the Church, which made the popes sovereign rulers. Nevertheless, the western emperors, as protectors of the Holy See, often attempted to dominate the Papacy and the Papal States.

Charlemagne's predecessors had worked closely with the Church in promoting Christianity among their subjects and had been greatly aided by Celtic and Anglo-Saxon missionaries such as St Boniface of Exeter (d. 753). Until Charlemagne's day coercion had had no place in Christian evangelization, but when he conquered Saxony he ordered that the entire population should be baptized on pain of death, ignoring the protests of his priestly advisers.

In other ways he was prepared to take the advice of Alcuin and his colleagues about Church policies. They were particularly concerned about the standard of clerical education. Although some lay schools, which trained notaries, survived in Italian cities, the Church had become the chief repository of learning in the West since the late Roman educational system had collapsed in the sixth century. The Church preserved literacy: the clergy needed to read Latin in order to conduct public worship and service books and Bibles had to be produced in multiple copies. Monasteries needed schools to train novices, and schools were also attached to some cathedrals to train priests, and in such schools small libraries were built up. Nevertheless, the standard of education among the clergy by Charlemagne's day was very uneven, and on the advice of Alcuin and his circle the emperor enacted that schools should be attached to every cathedral and monastery to train priests and monks.

Alcuin wanted to impose a uniform liturgy throughout the empire, based on service books which he obtained from the papal court. He also sought to introduce the Vulgate as the standard text of the Bible. Latin translations of the Bible had been made in north Africa and southern Gaul by *c.* 200 and continued in use in the early Middle Ages. These and other early versions contained many variant readings and St Jerome (d. 420) had sought to establish a new standard Latin text based on the Hebrew and Greek

An ivory diptych with scenes from the resurrection appearances of Christ.

originals. His translation was known as the Vulgate, the Scriptures in the common speech. Although Alcuin's liturgical reforms met with only a limited response, his attempt to promote the Vulgate was more successful and it did in the long term come to be regarded as the authoritative version of the Latin Bible.

The reform movement continued after Charlemagne's death. At the Synod of Aachen in 817, St Benedict, Abbot of Aniane (d. 821), tried to standardize monastic observance in the empire by persuading all communities to adopt the Rule of St Benedict. This measure met with only partial success, but it did ensure that that Rule became more widely known.

Since the sixth century the Church had attempted to preserve the secular learning of the classical world. Cassiodorus (c. 490–c. 580) had taken an important initiative in this regard, by founding a monastery at Vivarium near Naples, where he set the brethren to copy what he considered the most important Latin texts, and to make Latin translations of key Greek texts, because few people in Western Europe any longer read Greek. Cassiodorus's concern to preserve the classical heritage was shared in some degree by other clergy, and consequently some classical texts found a place in monastic and cathedral libraries.

The scholars at Charlemagne's court collected and copied these texts. Many of the exemplars they used dated from late antiquity, and the copyists modelled their own script, the Carolingian minuscule, on the half-uncial script of the late Roman world. They also imitated the late classical illuminations they found in those manuscripts. Carolingian codices produced for the court are a visual delight, for they are often beautifully illuminated and always easy to read. The work of these scholars was important, for almost all the Latin classics now available derive from Carolingian exemplars. Charlemagne's grandson, Charles the Bald, King of the West Franks (843–77), placed an Irishman, John Eriugena (d. c. 877), in charge of his palace school at Laon. John was unusual among his western contemporaries in knowing Greek and was influenced by Neoplatonism (see p. 75).

The reform initiated by Alcuin and his circle had had a limited success. By the 870s there were some monasteries and cathedrals with well-regarded schools and well-stocked libraries run by clergy trained in both the classical and Christian traditions of scholarship. Nevertheless, the majority of bishops and abbots remained largely unaffected by these educational reforms.

New Challenges

The Carolingian Empire, which Alcuin and his friends had called into being to preserve the peace of Europe, proved an inadequate instrument for that task. The imperial family had no concept of a state, but thought in terms of partible inheritance and quarrelled over the division of lands, while their empire faced new enemies. In Italy Muslim raiders from Sicily made settlements on the mainland as far north as the Papal States, where they sacked the basilica of St Peter's in 844; while northern Europe began to suffer from Viking raids towards the end of the eighth century. Contemporary western chronicles were written by churchmen who portrayed the Vikings as barbarous because they were pagans. Modern historians have pointed out that Viking armies did not behave any worse than Christian armies did at that time, and that the Vikings made valuable contributions to the development of the West by opening up new trade routes and were a civilized people, skilled as poets and artists and unparalleled as shipbuilders. All this is true, but so were the complaints of churchmen, for the Vikings were in search of plunder and because they were pagans were not deterred from attacking cathedrals and monasteries, which were often poorly defended and whose communities had not been trained to fight, but which contained treasures. The Vikings came from Norway and Denmark in ships with shallow draughts, which could sail far up the main rivers of Germany, France, Britain and Ireland. They often established inland bases for a season, rounded up local horses, and fanned out in raiding parties. A relatively small group of mounted warriors could cause havoc over a wide area, and haphazard raiding of this kind continued for the best part of a hundred years. This was a threat which western governments proved quite inadequate to meet. By the late ninth century Viking raids began to give way to permanent settlement. In England, East Anglia, the east Midlands and the kingdom of York came under direct Viking rule, while in 911 the Vikings settled in Normandy, where their leader, Rollo, was recognized as duke by Charles the Simple, King of France.

A new threat appeared in 895 when the Magyars settled in the plains of Hungary. They too were a pagan and warlike people, trained to ride long distances. They raided southern Germany and south-eastern France, which had hitherto been largely immune from invasion, and Italy, where in 936 they reached the outskirts of Rome. Like the Vikings, the Magyars also sacked churches and monasteries in their search for plunder. As in the fifth century, the Western Church proved very resilient when faced by these new challenges.

The Conversion of the North

When Alfred of Wessex made peace with the Danish King Guthrum in 878 and ceded much of eastern England to him, he made this settlement conditional on Guthrum's being baptized, and a similar condition was imposed on Rollo by Charles the Simple in 911 when he invested him with the Duchy of Normandy. Many other Vikings were baptized with their leaders and in all the Christian lands where they settled – England, Ireland and northern France – all the Vikings fairly soon came to adopt the religion of the local people. This suggests that they were not numerous and that they intermarried with their Christian subjects. The evangelization of the Vikings in Scandinavia was arguably speeded up through their contacts with the Christian Vikings of the West.

King Harald Bluetooth of Denmark (936–86) was converted in *c.* 960 by a mission from Bremen led by the priest Poppo, and Harald's son Swegn (d. 1014) attempted to suppress all pagan cults in the kingdom. The first Christian king of Sweden was Olof Sköttkonung (1000–24), but paganism proved more resilient there than in Denmark. In 1092 Adam of Bremen reported that sacrifices were still being made in the temple of Odin at Uppsala, but gradually the new faith became dominant and in 1164 Uppsala became the metropolitan see of the Swedish Church.

King Olaf Tryggvason of Norway had become a Christian in England, while he was raiding there. During his brief reign, 995–1000, Christianity was certainly established in Norway, although it is now generally agreed that the degree of his success in evangelizing the Viking world was exaggerated by later writers such as the author of the Orkneyinga Saga, written soon after 1200, who records how Olaf Tryggvason:

Sailed east with five ships . . . until he reached Orkney. At Osmundwall he ran into Earl Sigurd, who . . . was setting out on a viking expedition. Olaf asked . . . Sigurd to come over to his ship . . . 'I want you and all your subjects to be baptized', he said when they met. 'If you refuse, I'll have you killed on the spot, and I swear that I'll ravage the island with fire and steel.' The Earl . . . surrendered himself into Olaf's hands. He was baptized and . . . after that, all Orkney embraced the faith.[10]

In Norway Olaf Tryggvason's work was consolidated by St Olaf (1016–30), who had been baptized at Rouen in 1013, and who was responsible for breaking the hold of paganism and establishing the Catholic faith.

Olaf Tryggvason was certainly responsible for the formal conversion of Iceland, which had been settled by the Vikings in *c.* 870. There were already some Christians there in his reign and in 999/1000 he sent back as his envoys two Christian Icelandic chiefs, who were visiting his court, with a formal request that the island should adopt the Christian faith. His message was considered by the Althing, the assembly of the free men, which had legislative powers. It was decided that the Icelanders could not live under two different laws, which would prove divisive in their small community, and that they should therefore all adopt the law of the Christians. Three provisos were made, that it should remain lawful to sacrifice in private to the Norse gods, to eat horseflesh, and to expose unwanted children, all practices contrary to Christian law. Yet although there is sound evidence that the Althing did reach this decision, as Orri Vésteinsson has pointed out, Christianity made quite slow progress in Iceland. The first Bishop, Isleifr Gizurarson, was not

A fortified medieval church on the Baltic island of Bornholme.

consecrated until 1056. This took place at Bremen and his visit to Germany was remembered because he presented the Emperor Henry III with a polar bear from Greenland.[11] In the early twelfth century a second see was set up for northern Iceland at Holar, and by the early thirteenth century paganism had become sufficiently remote that the Icelandic scholar, Snorri Sturlason, felt the need to write *The Prose Edda* partly to explain to his fellow islanders the mythological references in early Icelandic poetry.

Colonists from Iceland led by Eric the Red reached Greenland in 986 and their primary settlement, known as the eastern settlement, was in the south-west of the island. According to a much later tradition, Eric's son Leif visited the court of Olaf Tryggvason and brought Christianity to Greenland where, although Eric rejected it, his wife Thjodhild was converted and built a church near her home at Brattahlid. This story has received some measure of confirmation from the discovery in 1961 of the remains of a very small early-eleventh century church at Brattahlid. Later the Vikings established a second settlement to the north-west (known as the western settlement) and in 1125 Arnald, the first Bishop of Greenland, was appointed, with his see at Gardar. A parish network was developed in Greenland, with at least four churches in the western settlement and twelve in the eastern, while a house of Austin canons and a Benedictine convent were also founded there.

The *Saga of Eric the Red* and the *Greenland Saga* both report the exploration of the north American coast and the discovery of Vinland by members of the Greenland colony. The remains of a Viking settlement have been found at L'Anse aux Meadows in northern Newfoundland, but no Viking church has yet been discovered in north America, though a Bishop Eric, called a papal legate in one source, is reported to have visited Vinland in the early twelfth century.[12]

The most northerly evidence so far discovered of a Christian Viking presence is the Kingiqtorsoaq stone found on an island off the west coast of Greenland at 72° 58' N, which reads:

> Erling Sighvatsson and Bjorni Thordarson and Endridi Oddson on the Saturday before Rogation Day raised these cairns. . .[13]

The western settlement in Greenland was abandoned by the 1360s, but the eastern settlement was still active, and clergy were present there, in 1410. In 1448, however, Pope Nicholas V appealed to the bishops of Iceland to supply a bishop and priests for Greenland because the people there 'have been without a bishop for thirty years after the attack by the heathen, on which occasion most of the churches were destroyed and the inhabitants were taken prisoner'.[14] The heathen were the Inuit, who moved into southern Greenland in the later Middle Ages. So far as is known this appeal met with no response and the eastern settlement died out or was abandoned in *c.* 1500.

The Conversion of Central Europe

During the tenth century the Latin Church also expanded into central Europe. In Bohemia the ducal family were Christian although paganism remained strong in the country at large. When Duke Wenceslas (*c.* 922–9), a devout Christian, was assassinated by his brother Boleslas I, this was not part of a pagan reaction, for Boleslas was also a Christian, but was probably a protest against the amount of time which Wenceslas devoted to his religious duties at the expense of his military responsibilities.[15] A bishop of Prague was first appointed in 972 and Bohemia became fully Catholic in the eleventh century.

King Henry I of Germany (918–36) began to contain the Magyar raids and that menace was ended by his son Otto I (936–73), who decisively defeated the Magyars at the Lechfeld in 955. He was then free to consolidate German rule over the pagan Wends between the Elbe and the Oder and to found bishoprics there. Because Christianity was associated by the Wends with German domination, when they successfully revolted against Otto II in 982 they not only expelled the German garrisons, but also burnt down the new cathedrals and reverted to paganism. Otto's death in 983, followed by the long minority of his son Otto III, assured Wendish independence.

Beyond the Oder lay Poland, ruled by Duke Meiszko I (*c.* 960–992). Born a pagan, he married a Christian Bohemian princess and was baptized in 966. His son, Boleslas I, was staunchly Catholic, and when Otto III's friend, St Adalbert of Prague, undertook a mission to Prussia in 997 and was martyred there, Boleslas ransomed his body and interred it with great solemnity in his capital, Gneisno. In 1000 Otto III went to Adalbert's shrine as a pilgrim, accompanied by the saint's brother, Radim, who had been consecrated Archbishop of Gneisno in Rome in 999 by Pope Sylvester II. Otto's visit therefore marked the creation of an autonomous Polish Church directly subject to the pope.

After their defeat at the Lechfeld, the Maygars settled in Hungary and became open to Christian influences. These were numerous as some of the indigenous population had been Christian, as were almost all the prisoners the Maygars had seized in their raids. In 995 Duke Geisa I (972–97) and his son Waik were baptized. Waik took the name of Stephen, and in 1001 Otto III conferred the title of king on him, while Sylvester II licensed the creation of an autonomous Church in Hungary under the Archbishop of Gran. In his very long reign (997–1038) St Stephen the first-crowned placed the Catholic Church in Hungary on very secure foundations.

Reconquest in the Western Mediterranean

Unlike the Vikings and Magyars, the Muslims in the Western Mediterranean could not be converted and assimilated to the culture of the West by Christian missions because Muslim law prescribed the death penalty for those who spoke against the Islamic faith and for those who apostatized from it. In Moorish Spain Eulogius, priest of Cordoba, together with twenty-seven followers, was executed in 859 for criticizing Islam and trying to make converts. Most Spanish Christians were content to observe the law and to enjoy the quite wide toleration which it offered them, although there was a high rate of conversion to Islam, which seems to have accelerated in the mid-ninth century. As Hugh Kennedy has commented:

Alfonso IX of Leon (1188–1230) receives the surrender of Badajoz from the Moors.

> We can be sure that before 711 there were no Muslims in the area and that by the twelfth century the Christians of al-Andalus [Moorish Spain] were a small minority, but there is no direct evidence for the change.[16]

Those who remained Christian began to speak Arabic and became known as Mozarabs, a term meaning 'would-be Arabs'. They continued to worship in Latin and, in the case of the clergy, to write in it.

It was clear that in the Western Mediterranean Christian expansion could only be achieved by force of arms. The wars of reconquest began in Italy, where in 915, with the help of the Byzantine navy, a Christian coalition organized by Pope John X cleared the Roman Campagna of the Muslim raiders who had settled there. Then the combined Pisan and Genoese fleets drove Muslim pirates from Sardinia in 1015–16. Soon after this, fighting men from Normandy began to serve as mercenaries in the armies of the south Italian princes and in due course to carve out principalities for themselves there. In 1059, by the Treaty of Melfi, Pope Nicholas II invested Count Richard of Capua and Robert Guiscard Duke of Apulia with the lands they had conquered, and granted to Robert the lordship of Sicily as well if it might be recovered from the Muslims. The Sicilian campaign, initiated by Guiscard's brother Roger in

1 *Apse mosaic of Sant' Apollinare in Classe, Ravenna, c. 549, showing the saint as shepherd of his flock.*

2 *St John Chrysostom, an eleventh-century mosaic in the monastery church of Hosios Loukas, Greece.*

3 *Abraham and Sarah entertain three angels under the oak at Mamre, sixth-century mosaic, San Vitale, Ravenna.*

6 *The Derynaflan Chalice, Irish, Co. Tipperary, ninth century.*

7 *The crown of the Holy Roman Empire, second half of tenth century, now in the Kunsthistorisches Museum, Vienna.*

1061, was a long and difficult war of sieges which only ended in 1091 with the fall of Noto and the capture of Malta.

In Spain, Galicia and Navarre which had become independent in the eighth century, together with the March of Barcelona captured by Charlemagne, formed bases for the Christian wars of reconquest. The offensive began after 1009 when the Caliphate of Cordova broke up into a number of independent and mutually hostile kingdoms. The first phase culminated in 1085 in the capture of Toledo by Alfonso VI of Castile, an event which drove the Moorish kings to seek help from the Almoravid Sultan of Morocco, the zealous and militant Yusuf Ibn Tashufin. Yet although in 1086 his army inflicted a crushing defeat on the Christians at Sagrajas and halted their advance, the Muslims did not regain much territory.

In 1095 Pope Urban II summoned the First Crusade. Its purpose was to 'liberate the Church of God in Jerusalem', but it inevitably had consequences for the wars in Spain which were also being fought against Muslims. Alfonso I, the Battler, of Aragon (1104–34) saw the latter as an integral part of the crusade movement and spoke of reaching Jerusalem by way of Morocco. The Spanish wars of reconquest did not automatically rank as crusades, although popes gave crusade status to some specific campaigns.[17] The Spanish kings tried to persuade the Military Orders of the Templars and Hospitallers, founded to defend the Holy Land (see pp. 112–13), to work in Spain, but, meeting with only a limited response, established Military Orders of their own, such as those of Calatrava, Alcantara and Santiago, which played a significant part in garrisoning frontier castles.

Yusuf Ibn Tashufin and his successors alienated their Mozarabic subjects by enforcing the discriminatory laws against non-Muslims too harshly. Many Mozarabs sought refuge in the north with the Christian Kings and in 1125 Alfonso I of Aragon brought thousands of them back from the province of Granada, where he had campaigned, and settled them in the Ebro Valley. The Mozarabs had a liturgy which was very different from the forms used elsewhere in the Western Church and the Papacy attempted to make them conform to the Roman liturgy, but the Mozarabic rite persisted in the churches of Toledo throughout the Middle Ages and was given protected status there by Cardinal Ximenes (1495–1517).

Although the power of the Almoravid Sultans collapsed in the mid-twelfth century, the Almohad Caliphs of Morocco who replaced them had even greater resources and the Christian frontier in Spain only moved forward slowly. Then in 1212 a confederate army under Peter II of Aragon defeated the Moors at Las Navas de Tolosa, thereby precipitating the break-up of the Almohad Empire, which enabled the Christians to complete the reconquest. James I of Aragon conquered the Balearic Islands between 1229 and 35, and in 1238 annexed the Moorish kingdom of Valencia. His contemporary, Ferdinand III of Castile and Léon, better known as San Fernando, captured the old Moorish capital of Cordoba in 1236, annexed the kingdom of Murcia in 1243, made Granada tributary in 1246, and in 1248 captured the great city of Seville. The Portuguese meanwhile had pushed southwards into the Algarve. Thus by the time San Fernando died in 1252 the whole peninsula was under Christian control apart from the client kingdom of Granada.

In both Sicily and Spain the conquerors made Catholicism the established religion, but they also had many Muslim subjects, and in the case of Spain many Jewish subjects as well. Although some Muslims had been massacred during the Spanish wars of reconquest such incidents were exceptional, the product of war rather than of ideological hatred, and the kings of Christian Spain were anxious to keep the Muslims contented because they formed an essential part of the labour force. In both Sicily and Spain non-Christians were required to pay a religious poll tax to the crown, and in return were guaranteed freedom of worship and security of property.

At Palermo in the twelfth century the finance office of the Norman kings was staffed by officials known as sheikhs, who kept the records in Arabic. In the Muslim villages of western Sicily the mosques remained open and muezzins called the faithful to prayer, while the kings welcomed Muslim scholars to their cosmopolitan court. But just as Christian numbers dwindled in lands under Muslim rule, so the reverse was true. In the early thirteenth century there were revolts among the surviving Muslims in Sicily, and Frederick II (1198–1250) transferred most of them to Lucera in Apulia, where they remained until they lost their privileged status and were forced to become Christians in the reign of Charles I of Anjou (1266–85).

Alfonso X of Castile (1252–84) described himself as King of the Three Religions, because Christians, Jews and Muslims all lived under his rule. Muslim religious teachers discouraged this, holding that no Muslim should live under infidel rule if he had the means to move away, and consequently the Muslim landowners and townsfolk tended to go to Granada and Morocco. But large numbers of Muslim peasants still remained in the Christian kingdoms at the end of the fifteenth century. Although the Catholic hierarchy was never entirely happy about the toleration of infidels, it made little attempt to evangelize them, chiefly, it would seem, because most priests were unwilling to learn Arabic.[18] The kings did not wish the Moors to be converted either, because the religious taxes they paid formed an important part of royal income.

This policy of toleration only changed at the very end of the Middle Ages. There was a wave of anti-semitic riots in some towns in the 1390s, which led to the forcible conversion of some Jews. Then in 1483 Ferdinand V of Aragon and his wife Isabella I of Castile instituted the Spanish Inquisition which, unlike the medieval papal inquisition, was under royal control. This tribunal prosecuted converted Jews who had continued clandestinely to practise their former faith. In 1492 the remaining orthodox Jews of both kingdoms were offered the choice of conversion or explusion, a measure perhaps in part designed to pay for the war of Granada which ended in that year, since the property of some 50,000 Jews who went into exile escheated to the crown.

The annexation of Granada by Ferdinand and Isabella brought an additional quarter of a million Muslims under Castilian rule. At first they were granted toleration, but Cardinal Ximenes, head of the Spanish Church, disregarding the terms of the capitulation of Granada, encouraged the clergy to convert the Moors there by force. This led them to rebel, and in 1502 Isabella, considering that they now constituted a security risk, offered to all Moors throughout Castile (including those of Granada) the choice of conversion or exile. Most of them were poor people who lacked the means to leave. They therefore accepted mass baptism, but could only be nominal Christians

The thirteenth-century church of Vera Cruz, Segovia, built during the Spanish wars of reconquest.

because they had received no instruction. They were known as *Moriscos*, or Christian Moors. Ferdinand V did not implement this policy in Aragon, where Moorish communities continued to practise their faith until the reign of his successor, Charles V (1518–56).

The Conversion of the Baltic Lands

Although some attempt had been made to reintroduce Christianity among the Wends who lived between the Elbe and Oder, the majority of them were still pagans in 1146 when Pope Eugenius III allowed the Second Crusade to be diverted to attack them on the grounds that their lands had once been Christian and were being reclaimed for the

Church. The Northern Crusade of 1147 achieved very little, but the Wends were subdued between 1161 and 1172 by Henry the Lion, Duke of Saxony, and Waldemar the Great, King of Denmark. Paganism was suppressed, the Ottonian bishoprics were restored, and the Wends were evangelized with the help of the newly founded Cistercian Order.

In the eastern Baltic, Finland, Prussia, Estonia, Livonia and Lithuania were still pagan. Finland was gradually conquered and converted to Catholicism by the Swedes, and Estonia was evangelized by the Danes, who had conquered it in 1219. In c. 1180 Meinhard, a German priest from the province of Bremen, began to work among the Livonians and was later consecrated as their bishop by Archbishop Hartwig of Bremen (1185–1207). The third bishop, Albert, appointed in 1199, was Hartwig's nephew. He was extremely ambitious, and with virtually no resources succeeded in creating a prince-bishopric in Livonia. In 1204 Pope Innocent III allowed him to wage a perpetual crusade, that is, to raise troops as he considered necessary without a fresh papal mandate. He recruited crusaders every year in Germany, while his assistant, the priest Theoderic, founded a small Military Order, the Sword Brethren, to hold down conquered territory.

The Livonian crusade had no conventional justification; the territory had never been Christian and the crusade there was simply a war of aggression. Despite papal disapproval, the crusaders adopted a policy of forcible conversion, offering pagans whom they defeated the choice of baptism or death. Bishop Albert built churches in the conquered territories and appointed priests to instruct and minister to the new converts, and in 1225 Pope Honorius III sent a legate, William of Modena, to supervise the Livonian church settlement. William insisted that the new converts should be well-treated, that they should not be required to pay taxes apart from the tithe and should not be subject to harsh labour services. When Albert died in 1229 the whole of Livonia had been conquered, but in 1236 the Lithuanians inflicted a crushing defeat on the Sword Brethren who were its principal defenders. They had a reputation for treating the native population brutally, and this may have influenced Gregory IX's decision to hand over the Order and its lands to the Teutonic Knights in 1237.

The Teutonic Order, whose members were all German knights, had been founded in 1198 to defend the Holy Land, but it could not find enough scope there for its activities because so few territories remained in Frankish control (see p. 113). Thus, when the Polish Duke, Conrad of Masowia, offered the Order the march of Culmerland so that they might defend his duchy against the pagan Prussians, the Knights welcomed this invitation to diversify their activities. By the Golden Bull of Rimini the Emperor Frederick II in 1226 conferred on the Order all the pagan lands which they might conquer as a fief of the Holy Roman Empire.

The Order began to campaign against the Prussians in 1230 with the help of crusaders recruited in Gemany, and enlisted the aid of the newly founded Dominican Order to evangelize their Prussian subjects. By 1249 they had completed their conquest and papal representatives mediated the Peace of Christburg between the Order and the Prussian princes. The terms were quite generous: Prussians who became Christians should enjoy free status and keep their property; they might become priests and, if noble, might join the Teutonic Order – that is, they were offered a theoretical share in future government.

In return the Prussians undertook to pay tithes, to fight for the Order against its enemies and to abandon all pagan cults. It was stipulated that if these terms were broken the Prussians would be severely punished.

After they acquired Livonia in 1237, the Teutonic Knights became involved in war against the Lithuanians who controlled the land routes between Livonia and Prussia. When the Mongols destroyed the cities of western Russia in 1240 the Lithuanians moved into those territories and became more powerful (see p. 84). In 1260 they defeated the Teutonic Knights at Durben and this sparked off serious revolts against the Order in both Livonia and Prussia. Peace was not fully restored in Livonia until 1290. In Prussia the Order had regained control by 1283 but imposed harsh new terms; those who had rebelled, and that included most Prussians, had their lands confiscated and lost their free status, becoming serfs on the estates of the Order and its German lay vassals. As serfs they were not eligible to become either priests or knights. Prussia thus became a German principality.

The Lithuanians remained pagan in the fourteenth century and the Order was therefore still able to organize crusades against them. Every year men came from Western Europe to take part in such *reysen*. Jonathan Riley-Smith has aptly commented:

> Were it not for the brutality and the real hardships that were part of them, one is tempted to write of the *reysen* as packaged crusading for the European nobility, and their popularity demonstrated how attractive this package could be when wrapped in the trappings of chivalry.[19]

The Lithuanians were good fighters and proved remarkably resilient in the face of these attacks, but in 1386 the *raison d'être* of the Baltic crusades disappeared when Jogailo, King of Lithuania, was baptized and married Jadwiga, Queen Regnant of Poland, thus uniting the two kingdoms and ensuring the establishment of the Catholic Church throughout Lithuania.

This completed the expansion of medieval Western Christendom. It now shared common frontiers with the Orthodox Christian states of eastern and south-eastern Europe, and only the Lapps, living beyond the arctic circle in Scandinavia, remained virtually untouched by Christianity.

THE FLOWERING OF CATHOLIC EUROPE

Church Reform in Western Europe

In 897 Pope Stephen VI convened a synod in the Lateran basilica to examine charges against his predecessor, Formosus (891–6). The corpse of the dead pope was exhumed, dressed in full pontificals and placed on a throne in the choir. At the end of the proceedings Formosus was condemned and his body was solemnly unfrocked and flung into a common grave. This macabre episode occurred because the Papacy had been caught up in the political intrigues for control of the Western Empire after the collapse of Carolingian power, a struggle in which Stephen and Formosus had supported different candidates. The synod of the corpse was symptomatic of the way in which the Western Church was being manipulated by powerful laymen.

The state of chronic warfare produced by the Viking, Magyar and Muslim raiders throughout much of the West led to the abandonment of monastic life in some areas, not only because monasteries were sacked, but also because rulers in need of resources to raise troops seized monastic lands or granted them to their vassals. Even in communities that did survive, monastic observance was often adversely affected by the violence of society. Thus when the great abbey of Farfa to the north of Rome, which had been sacked by Muslim raiders in 898, was rebuilt some twenty years later, the brethren refused to live in community, but married and divided up the estates of the house between them and only met to discuss estate management.

As royal power grew weaker in many parts of Europe in the late ninth century, so senior church appointments passed into the hands of local lords, who tended to treat them as secular posts, nominating members of their own families to office, or putting the offices up for sale, a practice known as simony and forbidden in canon law.[20] Many of the men appointed in this way were unsuited by training or temperament to be churchmen, while it became quite common for young children to be nominated to benefices which they would hold when they came of age, but for which their fathers drew the revenues during their minority. Corruption of this kind was not universal, but it was sufficiently widespread to trouble the consciences of devout laymen.

Such practices led to the foundation of reformed monasteries of strict observance, because the monastic profession was seen as the ideal form of the Christian life. Cluny in Burgundy was founded in 909/10 by Duke William III of Aquitaine, who sought to keep his foundation free from the evils of lay control by placing it directly under the protection of the pope. In England St Dunstan refounded the abbey of Glastonbury in 940 with the support of his kinsman King Edmund, while at Gorze in Lorraine the reform was initiated in 933 by Bishop Adalbert of Metz. The brethren of these houses were often called in to reform other communities; for example, Prince Alberic of Rome gave St Odo of Cluny oversight of all the monasteries in and around the city in 936. By the eleventh century families of reformed monasteries, with administrative and jurisdictional links, began to develop. Cluny, under the rule of three exceptionally long-lived abbots, St Maiolus (954–94), St Odilo (994–1049) and St Hugh (1049–1109), evolved into a religious Order in which the Abbot of Cluny had authority over the priors of daughter houses, of which there were some 2,000 by 1100 situated all over Latin Christendom. The reformed monasteries acquired extensive endowments from pious laymen, their brethren were recruited from local noble families, and consequently men such as St Hugh of Cluny became extremely influential. Most of the reformed congregations followed the Benedictine Rule and in many houses the plainsong setting of the liturgy became increasingly elaborate, and since it was customary to celebrate a solemn Mass each day in addition to the Divine Office, a large part of the brethren's time was spent in chapel.

The solitary life of a hermit, devoted to contemplative prayer, continued to be regarded as the most perfect form of the Christian life. St Romuald of Ravenna

A twelfth-century fresco of Christ in majesty from the Cluniac priory of Berze-la-Ville in Burgundy.

(d. 1027) founded the Camaldolese Order to train hermits. St Peter Damian joined it in *c.* 1035 and even after he became Cardinal Bishop of Ostia in 1057, a position second only to that of the pope in the Catholic hierarchy, he continued to spend as much time in his hermitage at Fonte Avellana as his other duties allowed.

In the years 950–1050 some reform-minded bishops were also appointed, and they attempted to reform the lower clergy. This led to a renewed study of canon law, exemplified by the *Decretum*, the collection made by Bishop Burchard of Worms (d. 1025).

Although popes gave encouragement and support to individual reformers, they made no attempt to direct the movement until after 1046, when the Emperor Henry III intervened to settle a disputed papal election. He secured the deposition of the rival claimants and appointed a series of popes from Germany and Lorraine, trained in the north European reform tradition. They had two principal aims, to suppress simony and to eliminate concubinage. Where possible, simoniac bishops and abbots were deposed and replaced by men of good character appointed in accordance with canon law. The papal reformers failed to enforce clerical celibacy, but succeeded in outlawing clerical marriage. This meant that priests' children were illegitimate and could not themselves become priests without special dispensation. That prevented the growth of a clerical caste, which had been a distinct possibility in the early Middle Ages.

In 1059 Nicholas II reformed papal electoral procedure by setting up the College of Cardinals to replace the older system whereby the pope was chosen in open forum by 'the clergy and people of Rome'. This reform excluded lay intervention either by the Roman nobility or by the Western Emperor. Inevitably the popes' attempt to reform the higher clergy brought them into conflict with rulers who relied on their bishops to assist them in civil administration, for a good administrator might be a very worldly churchman. Pope Gregory VII (1073–85) clashed with the Emperor Henry IV (1056–1105) about the choice of an archbishop of Milan, and this escalated into a quarrel about church appointments in general which lasted long after Gregory's death and came to involve many other western rulers. The dispute was resolved in the early twelfth century by a series of concordats, typified by the Concordat of Worms of 1122 which governed relations between the pope and the emperor. This enacted that bishops and abbots should be freely elected by their cathedral or monastic chapters in the presence of the emperor or his representative. Superficially it seemed that the secular authorities had won, for how could a cathedral chapter refuse to elect the emperor's candidate if the emperor were present? Yet any chapter had the right to appeal to the pope against an election result on the grounds that canonical procedures had not been observed. Kings were reluctant to antagonize the Papacy unless some really important issue was at stake, because the popes had proved to be dangerous enemies, who could excommunicate a ruler, thereby encouraging his fractious vassals to renounce their allegiance to him. So although the Papacy failed in its attempt to free church appointments from lay control, it did successfully assert its right to scrutinize them.

Between 1150 amd 1250 there were further disputes between the Papacy and the empire, in which the popes succeeded in keeping the Papal States independent of imperial control. The popes wished to avoid becoming imperial civil servants, because that would inhibit them from carrying out their wider duties in the Western Church

The Romanesque church of Notre-Dame-la-Grande, Poitiers, France, eleventh–twelfth centuries.

impartially. Papal control over the Western Church grew considerably in this period. The routine use of legates enabled the popes to make their presence felt throughout the West; the codification of canon law and the huge growth in new papal legislation increased the amount of judicial business which came before the papal courts, and the curia grew in size. Papal power was exemplified in the successful launching of the First Crusade by Pope Urban II in 1095 and also in the business transacted by the Fourth Lateran Council. This met in Rome in 1215 and legislated about the succession to the Holy Roman Empire, transferred the lands of the Count of Toulouse to Simon de Montfort without reference to the King of France, and launched a new crusade to recover Jerusalem.

The Growth of Lay Piety

In the early Middle Ages, except for some members of the high nobility who employed domestic chaplains and the populations of some Italian cities well provided with churches, most lay people were not able to go to church very often. This changed when, as part of the reform movement, parish churches began to be built in considerable numbers. The reformed monasteries took a lead in this, building churches in the villages on their estates and appointing priests to serve them. A resident priest was able to give children basic religious instruction and although at this time the parish clergy were not trained to preach, the high visual content of the eucharistic liturgy as it was re-enacted year by year would have reinforced among lay people their understanding of the central tenets of the Christian faith. There is evidence that some monastic landlords attempted to ensure that their tenants performed ritual penance at the beginning of each Lent, received absolution on Holy Thursday and were thus able to make their communion on Easter Day. There is also widespread evidence from the eleventh century of spontaneous lay piety, which took the form of pilgrimages to local or distant shrines.

The First Crusade appealed to fighting men who took the Christian faith seriously. The Church considered acts of violence of all kinds as sinful and worthy of penance, but traditional penances involved various forms of public humiliation, like fasting on bread and water, or standing at a church door on feast days dressed in a shift and holding a lighted taper. In the crusade indulgence of 1095 Urban II declared that anybody who was willing to take part in a war to liberate Jerusalem from the Muslims might, after making confession of his sins to a priest, substitute his participation in the crusade for all penance. The crusade was certainly not an easy option, for it was lengthy and dangerous in a way that other kinds of penance were not, but it was congenial to warriors because it was congruent with their sense of honour, and so they took the cross in large numbers.

Most of the population of Western Europe were peasants. Some of them wanted more involvement in the practice of the Christian life and this desire was met when, in the late eleventh century, some monasteries, notably the Benedictine congregation of Hirschau in Bavaria, began to admit lay brethren. These were peasants who took monastic vows, but who, because they did not know Latin, did not take part in the long choir offices but met together in chapel at set hours to recite simple prayers and spent most of their time in manual labour. This system was adopted by other religious foundations in the twelfth century, particularly by the Cistercian Order.

Some late eleventh-century reformers, like Robert of Arbrissel, recruited postulants from all classes and both sexes, including both married and single people, but their followers had to take monastic vows, and husbands and wives lived in separate communities within the same institution. These reformers met with a quite wide response, but after their deaths the Orders they had founded soon lost their distinctive characters.[21]

In the early thirteenth century new forms of lay piety came into being through the work of the Orders of Friars, the Dominicans and Franciscans. Their members were known as mendicants, or beggars, because at first both Orders refused to accept endowments and their brethren had to take it in turns to beg for necessities. The Dominican Order, or Order of Preachers, was founded to combat heresy, specifically Catharism (see pp. 49–50). Its founder, Dominic Guzman (1170–1221), became convinced that the success of heretical preachers was in large measure due to the ignorance of the Catholic laity about fundamental Christian teaching. Pope Honorius III licensed the Order in 1217. Dominicans were normally trained as priests and were given a good education by the Order. The most able members were sent to complete their studies in university theology faculties.

Unlike monks, who devoted themselves to a life of prayer, the Dominicans were engaged in the work of public ministry. Their convents were built in towns, and they preached regularly, both in their chapels and in the open air, and sought to give their congregations a proper doctrinal understanding of the Christian faith. The Order attracted men of considerable intellectual ability, whose learning was made available to all classes of society during preaching tours.

The other new Order, that of the Friars Minor, or Little Brothers, was founded by St Francis of Assisi (1182–1226). He saw voluntary poverty as a virtue which enabled those who embraced it to dedicate their lives to Christ unencumbered by material concerns. Unlike Dominic, Francis did not want his brethren to be priests or even well educated.

The hallmark of the early Franciscans was simplicity: they preached about the life and teaching of Jesus as set out in the four Gospels, and sought to carry out his injunction to love one's neighbour by giving help to those in need. St Francis was unusual among reformers in being patient. He was so convinced that he was acting in accordance with God's will that he believed his work was unstoppable. He therefore refused to accept any privileges for his Order and if a bishop or even a priest refused permission to him and his followers to work in his diocese or parish, Francis did not contest this decision, but moved on elsewhere. This attitude kept the movement entirely orthodox in its early days.

In 1209 Francis and his few supporters, for the most part idealistic young drop-outs, dressed like tramps, arrived at the papal court and asked Innocent III to recognize them as a religious Order on a par with the Cistercians and Carthusians. Surprisingly, he did so. He may well have been influenced by the example of the Waldensians,

St Francis of Assisi receives the stigmata (the five wounds of Christ); painting by Giotto (c. 1266–1337)

whose great idealism and dedication had been lost to the Church because Alexander III had delegated final responsibility for them to local bishops (see p. 49). Innocent appointed Cardinal Ugolino, the future Pope Gregory IX, as protector of the Order. This was sensible, for although Francis had a great charisma – within a few years his friars were numbered in thousands – he had no organizing capacity, and the Papacy had to introduce some necessary safeguards, like a year's novitiate before a postulant could take life vows. Franciscan poverty was almost total: the brethren owned nothing but their patched habits and some service books and lived in wooden huts built on waste land.

Dominican and Franciscan convents of nuns were founded, but these were conventional communities devoted to contemplative prayer. Because of prevalent social attitudes women were not allowed to undertake the work of active ministry, even though many of them, like St Clare, very much wanted to do so.

In 1214 St Francis addressed an encyclical letter 'To all Christians, religious, clerics and layfolk, men and women; to everyone in the whole world,' inviting them to join him in his work in so far as they were able.[22] It was unprecedented for a letter of this kind to be written by a man who was not the pope, or even a bishop, but it led to the foundation in 1221 of the Third Order of St Francis made up of lay people, many of them married, who bound themselves to observe as much of the Rule as was compatible with living an ordinary life. They formed religious associations with Franciscan chaplains, whose members met together regularly for worship and undertook voluntary work as enjoined by the Rule. The Dominicans also developed a Third Order in the course of the thirteenth century. Such Orders marked a recognition by the Western Church that lay life was fully compatible with the devout practice of the Christian faith.

After St Francis's death his Order lost much of its distinctive character. The rule of poverty was relaxed, many Franciscans became priests, and some received a university education. Both Orders were given special privileges, including the right to run parishes, and by 1300 there were few towns of any size in Western Europe which did not have at least one house of mendicant friars. By their preaching both Orders considerably raised the standard of knowledge of the Christian faith among the laity.

The new Orders of friars played a central part in implementing the decree of the Fourth Lateran Council of 1215, which ruled that all Catholic men over the age of fifteen and women over the age of twelve should make their confession and receive Holy Communion once a year at Eastertide.[23] In the case of penitents who had committed only minor sins the penances which were enjoined were usually private ones, such as the recitation of certain prayers, though public penances continued to be imposed for very serious sins. At its best this penitential system gave lay people the opportunity of discussing with their priests the problems which they experienced in trying to lead the Christian life. Before 1215 many parish priests were not used to hearing routine confessions and offering advice to their penitents, so the members of newly founded Mendicant Orders were valued as confessors and helped to popularize the regular use of this sacrament. The work of the friars helped to produce a devout urban laity, and that was one of the most important developments in the later medieval Western Church.

A Tradition of Dissent

Some devout lay people who could find no means of expressing their piety within the Catholic Church responded to dissenting preachers. Small movements of this kind are first reported in various parts of the West in the early eleventh century, but they did not take root.[24] In the early twelfth century charismatic preachers like Tanchelm of Utrecht and Henry of Le Mans attracted large followings, but their movements lacked organization and did not survive their founders' deaths for long.

The Waldensians proved more resilient. Their founder, Peter Valdès, was a rich merchant of Lyons who in *c.* 1160 formed a band of lay helpers who took vows of poverty and devoted their lives to preaching and working among the urban poor. He received the limited support of Pope Alexander III (1159–81) who did not object to lay preachers provided that they obtained a bishop's licence. When refused a licence some Waldensians broke away from the Church. Initially they were entirely Catholic in faith, but because they had no priests, services of preaching and prayer came to take the place of the eucharist as their central act of worship, and they caused some scandal by allowing women to preach. After a time they began to diverge from the Catholic Church on some doctrinal issues also.

The largest dissenting group were the Cathars whose name comes from the Greek word καθαροι, meaning 'the pure', for they claimed to hold the Christian faith in its

The ruined Cathar stronghold of Montségur in southern France.

pure form. They were a western branch of the Byzantine Bogomils (see pp. 87–90). They were certainly present in the West by 1143 and may have been there for much longer. They had a strong organization, consisting of bishops who ruled territorial dioceses and deacons who had charge of local congregations. They based their teaching entirely on the New Testament, which they interpreted in a different way from most other Christians.[25]

The Cathars were divided into various sects, but they were all dualists: they believed that the Good God was entirely spiritual, and that the material world had been created either by an evil principle or by a malign demiurge. The human dilemma was that men had divine souls created by the Good God which were imprisoned in material bodies and which would remain imprisoned through a process of reincarnation. The Cathar creed was stated very simply by Pierre Garsias of Toulouse:

> God is very good. But nothing in this world is good. It must therefore be the case that He has not made anything which exists in this world.[26]

The Cathars believed that Christ, the Son of the Good God, had founded the Cathar Church and given it the unique sacrament of deliverance, baptism in the Holy Spirit by the laying-on of hands, performed by a professed Cathar (normally a bishop). This involved the recipients in a total conversion of life: the men or women who received it had to abandon all family ties and all property, adopt a celibate and vegan lifestyle, and live in community with other Cathars of the same sex. If they persevered in this way of life, when they died their souls would escape from the round of reincarnation and be restored to the realm of the Good God. Less dedicated Cathars led ordinary lives and were baptized on their death-beds. The baptized Cathars were known as the perfect, the others as believers.

The movement attracted many followers in southern France, Catalonia, north and central Italy and Flanders in the twelfth and thirteenth centuries. The role of women in the Cathar Church was very restricted, since all offices were held by men, who usually carried out all public duties, such as preaching. Cathar believers were not members of the church and were not allowed to pray because their church taught that the Good God could not hear the prayers of the unbaptized, though they might attend Cathar meetings.

It is ironic that St Dominic, who founded his Order with the specific intention of combating Catharism through sound argument and persuasion, should be associated with the Inquisition. In the late twelfth century, partly as a result of the revived study of canon law, which made churchmen aware of the arguments for the coercion of obdurate heretics used centuries before by St Augustine of Hippo and others, the Church had begun to legislate about the prosecution of heretics. These laws had been codified by the Fourth Lateran Council in 1215, but no effective means of enforcing them had been found. As an experiment, Pope Gregory IX in 1233 ordered the Dominicans in southern France to undertake the work of inquisition for heresy and they later co-opted other clergy, including Franciscans, to help them. The inquisitors had powers to summon and question suspects about heresy and in their courts the normal rights of the accused were suspended; they were not told the charges against them or allowed the services of defence lawyers. After 1252 inquisitors were allowed by the pope to license the torture of obdurate suspects, but it is impossible to discover how frequently this power was used in Cathar trials.[27] Convicted heretics were most commonly required to perform some public penance, such as wearing distinctive yellow crosses on their clothes at the Inquisition's pleasure, or making pilgrimages to designated shrines; some were condemned to incarceration in the Inquisition's prisons; while a small number were handed over to the secular authorities to be burnt at the stake.

The power of the Inquisition should not be exaggerated. It was entirely dependent on the co-operation of the secular authorities to enforce its rulings, and if they withdrew their support it was paralyzed. At any given time there were only about two dozen inquisitors at work in the whole of Western Europe, and no central authority existed to coordinate the activities of provincial tribunals. Although it is true that Catharism had almost totally disappeared from Western Europe within seventy years of the Inquisition's foundation, it is difficult to believe that such a poorly organized institution could have been chiefly responsible for this. It seems far more likely that it was the pastoral work of the Mendicant Orders which eroded support for Catharism, although persecution may have accelerated its decline, but not all scholars would agree with that view.[28]

The work of the Inquisition was not restricted to the investigation of Catharism, but included all forms of heresy. In 1307 Philip IV of France used the Inquisition to extort, by means of torture, confessions of idolatry, sodomy and apostasy from the Knights Templar, who were an international religious Order subject to the pope alone. Armed with this evidence and despite the pope's reluctance, Philip forced Clement V to dissolve the Order at the Council of Vienne in 1312, and the French crown derived considerable profit from the disposal of the Templars' wealth.[29]

The Waldensians proved resilient in the face of persecution and have survived until the present day. New dissident movements developed in the later Middle Ages. Among them were the Fraticelli, members of the Franciscan Order who claimed to remain true to their founder's ideal of poverty. When they refused to accept papal adjudication about this they were declared heretical and were subject to persecution.

The Lollards, who emerged in England in the late fourteenth century, were inspired by the teachings of John Wycliffe (d. 1384), an academic theologian who denounced abuses in the church such as non-residence and pluralism, as well as established Catholic devotions such as pilgrimages, and criticized the terms in which eucharistic doctrine had been formulated (see pp. 56–7). Although the Inquisition did not operate in England, parliament in 1401 enacted the statute *De heretico comburendo*, threatening Lollards who would not recant with burning at the stake. Despite some persecution, the Lollards survived into the sixteenth century. They rejected papal supremacy and believed that the only valid religious authority was the Bible as interpreted by themselves.

The Bible had not previously been a contentious issue between Catholics and dissenters. The Latin Bible had been translated into the vernacular in a literal, word-for-word way, as a teaching aid for novices in monastery schools, and Bible stories had been paraphrased in vernacular poems for lay audiences since the early Middle Ages.[30] Literary translations of the Bible began to be made in the vernacular from the tenth century, and by 1300 complete texts of the Bible existed in most western European languages except English, perhaps because the English nobility, who might have commissioned such a translation, still spoke Norman French. It seems likely that the English translation which the Lollards used, the so-called Wycliffe Bible, was mostly made after his death. The Council of Oxford in 1407 enacted that no layman should possess a text of the Bible in a translation made since Wycliffe's day without a bishop's licence. Such licenses were sometimes granted, though not to Lollard preachers who nevertheless read these scriptures to their followers. Similar restrictions did not obtain in other parts of the Western Church, where vernacular Bibles were freely read.[31]

Wycliffe's writings influenced John Hus, the Rector of the University of Prague. He was far more orthodox than Wycliffe, but by encouraging a pietist movement among the Slav-speaking population of Bohemia he antagonized the German bishops who dominated the hierarchy. Hus appealed against their censures to the Council of Constance in 1415, but refused to accept the Council's criticisms about some points of his teaching, claiming that his views were not contrary to the Bible. This assertion of the paramountcy of private judgement against the authority of a reforming General Council of the Church led to Hus's being burnt by the Council as a heretic. His followers regarded him as a martyr and that ensured the persistence of the Hussite movement in Bohemia. However, the movement did not spread further: its radical wing, the Taborites, took up arms and were defeated in battle in 1434; and after 1457 the pietist wing became known as the Bohemian Brethren and later evolved into the Moravian Church.

By the fifteenth century the Inquisition had become moribund throughout most of Europe. Yet the principle of the religious coercion of dissenters had been accepted as normative by the Western Church, an attitude which lamentably was taken over by the Protestant Churches as well as by Tridentine Catholics in the sixteenth century.

Intellectual Challenges to the Western Church

In the second half of the eleventh century the need for an increased number of literate administrators in church and state led, all over the West, to the growth of centres of study, the more successful of which evolved into universities. In these institutions all teaching was in Latin and students were trained to debate using syllogistic logic, which they studied in the Latin translation of the logical works of Aristotle. It was natural that, having been taught to argue logically, university masters should have applied logic also to the study of theology.

This did not produce any great problems in the field of biblical study. Since at least the third century it had been accepted that the sacred text had four levels of meaning, literal, moral, allegorical (that is, the way in which it related to Christ and his Church), and mystical (that is, the way in which it related to God and to eternal truths). The literal and moral meanings are straightforward. The allegorical meaning may be illustrated by the gifts which the Wise Men brought to the infant Jesus, gold, to show that he was a king, frankincense, to show that he was a priest, and myrrh, which was used to preserve the bodies of the dead, to show that he was a sacrificial victim. The mystical meaning of scripture may be exemplified by the city of Jerusalem, which in some contexts was interpreted as a symbol of Heaven. An axiom of medieval commentators was, *Si absurdum allegorice* ('If [a passage] fails to make sense, it must be understood allegorically'). Thus commentators argued that when St Matthew's Gospel relates that the Devil took Jesus to the top of a high mountain and showed him all the kingdoms of the world (Matt.: 4, 8), this passage cannot be understood literally because such a mountain cannot exist in a spherical world, so it must be the intention of God, who inspired the writer, that this account should be understood allegorically.

Problems arose when theologians differed about the interpretation of the Christian faith. Peter Abelard (d. 1142), who taught logic in the schools of Paris, wrote a treatise called *Sic et Non (Yes and No)*, listing 158 sets of contrary opinions of this kind about biblical exegesis and Christian belief. This kind of critical approach to the faith led to the whole of Christian doctrine being reformulated in terms of Aristotelian logic, a system known as scholastic theology, which resolved the inconsistencies which Abelard and others had revealed.

The reconquest of Moorish Spain and Muslim Sicily and the conquest of the Crusader States in the twelfth century brought a flood of new learning into the West. Latin translations were made of Greek and Arabic works, among which the metaphysical and scientific works of Aristotle were of particular importance. Many of these reached the West in Latin translations made from Arabic translations of the original Greek. Because Aristotle's logical works formed the chief instrument of the new approach to western learning, all his works enjoyed great prestige, but his philosophical works raised problems. For whereas Christian thinkers assumed that the only secure basis of knowledge was divine revelation, Aristotle assumed that the only secure basis of knowledge was empirical observation. Moreover, the Muslim philosopher Averroes (d. 1178), who had written the fullest modern commentary on Aristotle, which was also translated into Latin, assumed that if there was a conflict between human reason and divine revelation, the explanation based on human reason should be accepted. In the schools of Paris in the 1260s Siger of Brabant led a group of radicals who were influenced by Averroes and held that matter was eternal and that one could not therefore meaningfully speak of the beginning and end of the world.

The Mendicant Orders, which were prepared to support gifted brethren to study indefinitely in the university theology faculties, attracted the vocations of some intellectual heavyweights. These friars met the challenges posed by the new sources of learning. The Dominican, St Thomas Aquinas (d. 1274), responded to the Aristotelian challenge first by establishing, with the help of Greek exemplars, what the true text of Aristotle was, and secondly by using Aristotle's methods to examine the Christian faith. In his two chief works, the *Summa contra Gentiles (The Defence of the faith against the pagans)* and the unfinished *Summa Theologica (The Compendium of Theology)*, he argued that by extrapolating concepts from empirical observations of the physical world an observer would be led to a knowledge of God consonant with the Christian revelation. Unlike Averroes, Thomas believed that revelation and reason were complementary: reason could lead to a belief in the existence of God, but revelation alone could inform man about the nature of God. Similarly, although Thomas agreed with Averroes that reason suggests that matter has existed eternally in dependence on God, whereas revelation explains that it has been created by God, a Christian should accept this revelation as true because it is not contrary to reason, but complementary to it.

St Thomas's fellow Dominican, Vincent of Beauvais (d. 1264), compiled a huge encyclopaedia in which he incorporated the new learning in a Christian framework. He called it the *Speculum Maius,* or *Great Mirror,* because he conceived of the creation in all its aspects, including human speech, as a huge mirror, which if rightly focused revealed part of the mind of its Creator.

Later Western thinkers instinctively drew back from this seemingly harmonious synthesis of faith and reason. The Franciscan theologian William of Ockham (d. 1349) held that it was impossible to provide convincing proofs for the existence of God, and that human reason had limitations which should be recognized. In the late Middle Ages western theologians on the whole accepted that whereas the empirical world was measurable by reason the supernatural world might be known only through revelation.

THE END OF THE MIDDLE AGES

Pope Boniface VIII (1294–1303) quarrelled acrimoniously with Philip IV of France about the superiority of the Church to the state, and the pope was preparing to excommunicate Philip when the king sent an armed escort to bring him to stand trial before a general council of the Church. Boniface, who was an old man, died from shock at this insult and the confrontation was averted. The France of Philip IV was beginning to resemble a modern state, run by professional administrators appointed by the crown, in which royal power was based on tax revenues rather than on the loyalty of secular and ecclesiastical vassals who could be absolved from their religious oaths of allegiance by the pope, and that made it impervious to the ecclesiastical sanctions which popes had used so effectively in the previous 200 years.

Pope Clement V (1305–14) spent his entire reign in France, attempting to restore good relations with Philip IV. He settled in Avignon in 1309 and his successors remained there for almost seventy years.[32] The city was a more practical headquarters for the Papacy than Rome, because it was situated in the centre of Western Christendom not on the southern periphery. Nevertheless, there was a strong feeling throughout the Western Church that the pope, who was St Peter's vicar, should live in Rome which was St Peter's see. In 1377 Gregory XI did return there, but died almost immediately. The conclave then elected Urban VI, an Italian, whose paranoid behaviour soon alienated many of the cardinals, a group of whom withdrew from his obedience and, claiming that Urban's election had been uncanonical, chose the cardinal of Geneva as Pope Clement VII. He returned with his supporters to Avignon, thus causing the Great Schism when the Western Church was divided in allegiance between two popes, individual rulers deciding which pope their subjects would acknowledge. When a General Council of the Church finally met at Pisa in 1409 and elected Pope Alexander V, although he had the support of much of Europe, this merely complicated matters, since neither of his rivals would stand down.

A solution was finally imposed by the Council of Constance (1414–18). Gregory XII, the Roman claimant, resigned his powers to the council, which declared his two rivals deposed. In April 1415 the Council issued a decree, *Sacrosancta*, claiming that all Christians, including the pope, were subject to the decisions of a general council. The Fathers of Constance also attempted to make general councils a regular part of church government, stipulating that they should be convened at stated intervals in future. Finally, on 11 November 1417, Pope Martin V was elected by a special college set up by the council.

In accordance with the decree of Constance, Martin V summoned the Council of Basle in 1431, but died before it opened. Its members quarrelled with his successor, Eugenius IV (1431–47), who sought to move the council to Italy in order to negotiate union with representatives of the Byzantine Church. Some of the delegates obeyed the pope's summons and attended his Council of Ferrara/Florence/Rome (1438–44), but most of them remained at Basle. They had very radical ideas about Church reform and in particular wished to restrict the fiscal powers of the popes. Their opinions were viewed with sympathy by many heads of state at first, but they forfeited support in 1439 when they declared Eugenius IV deposed for challenging the authority of a general council and elected Felix V as antipope, thereby recreating the situation that the Council of Constance had been summoned to solve.

Eugenius's successor, Nicholas V (1447–55), was the first humanist to become pope. He found an elegant solution to the problem of the new schism. He negotiated with the Fathers at Basle, who agreed to elect him as pope, while in return he offered a cardinal's hat to their pope, Felix V. The attempt to make councils a normal part of Church government had failed, and in 1460 Pius II issued the bull *Execrabilis* in which he condemned as heretical the view that a general council was superior to the pope. The sympathy which some rulers had shown for the conciliar desire to limit papal power had been neutralized by the popes who, in a series of concordats, had agreed to restrict their own rights to appoint and tax the clergy.

Late Medieval Piety

Western piety in the later Middle Ages was centred on the mystery of the Incarnation. The learned and the simple shared a deep devotion to the Blessed Virgin Mary. This reflected the wonder which they felt that Christ, the Second Person of the Trinity, had before his birth and in his childhood placed himself entirely in the power of a human mother. No other created being was so closely associated with the Godhead and so according to scholarly opinion, this made Mary worthy of *hyperdoulia*, a reverence greater than that due to any other created being, though different from the worship owed to God alone. In the tenth century the Little Office of Our Lady was composed in her honour, and in some monasteries came to be recited each day in addition to the Divine Office. Lady chapels in honour of Mary were to be found in almost every parish church by the late Middle Ages; the Hail Mary, in its short biblical form, was a prayer known to everybody[33]; and Mary was believed to be the most powerful human intercessor in the court of Heaven.

The tympanum over the royal doors of Chartres Cathedral, showing Christ in majesty surrounded by symbols of the four evangelists (c. 1150).

Devotion to Christ centred on the Mass. The Church's traditional teaching that Christ was truly present in the consecrated bread and wine (see p. 13) became a matter of lively debate in the twelfth century when all Christian doctrine was redefined in terms of scholastic terminology. The eucharistic debate was an extension of the Christological debates of the fourth and fifth centuries; it was concerned with the question of how the Divine nature can be present in the material creation. The same technical terms were used to resolve it: the Fourth Lateran Council in 1215 defined the presence of Christ in the consecrated elements as transubstantiation, a definition based on the distinction made by Aristotle between the appearance of an object and its real character. The consecrated elements retained the appearance of bread and wine, but their real character was that of the body and blood of Christ.

The mere fact of definition did not, of course, preclude doubt, since the consecrated elements appeared to be unchanged; nevertheless, the definition did lead to a great growth in eucharistic piety. This found liturgical expression in the feast of Corpus Christi, which originated as a pious devotion in the Netherlands but came to be observed throughout the Western Church during the fourteenth century. It was held on the Thursday after Trinity Sunday. When Mass had ended, the consecrated Host was carried in procession through the streets by the clergy. It became customary in large cities for the guilds to stage scenes from the cycle of Mystery Plays and enact them on pageant carts in honour of Corpus Christi.

The devout centred their lives upon the eucharist, sometimes hearing three or four Masses each day. From *c.* 1400 the devotion known as Exposition developed, during which the consecrated Host was placed in a monstrance on the altar as a focus for private worship and prayer.[34] The late Middle Ages also witnessed the multiplication of requiem masses, one evidence of which was the endowment of chantry chapels in which Mass was offered daily for the repose of the founder's soul.

Personal piety also found expression in a wide range of good works. Hospitals were founded to care for the sick and indigent, almshouses to provide shelter for the old and homeless, orphanages to care for fatherless children, and confraternities to minister to the poor or to bury dead paupers and to pray for their souls.

One intensely personal aspect of medieval religion was mystical experience. Some of the mystics who were held in great esteem in the medieval church were women and they came from a wide variety of social backgrounds. St Hildegard of Bingen (1098–1180) was an aristocratic Benedictine abbess, who was credited by her contemporaries with oracular powers. In addition to her mystical writings she produced works of scholarship and was a musical composer of distinction whose work is still performed. The English anchoress, Julian of Norwich (d. after 1416), seems to have been an ordinary housewife before she renounced the world. She described her visions in everyday terms, comparing the blood dripping from the head of Christ crowned with thorns to 'round herring scales as it spread out'. One of her most striking visions, in which she expressed her sense of the greatness of God in comparison to the created universe, used an equally homely symbol:

And [God] showed me . . . a little thing, the size of a hazel-nut, on the palm of my hand, round like a ball. I looked at it thoughtfully and wondered 'What is this?' And the answer came: 'It is all that is made.'[35]

The Papacy and Christian Humanism

From 1347–9 Europe was ravaged by the Black Death, which in some places carried off almost 60 per cent of the population in a few months; yet the next generation witnessed the genesis of the Florentine Renaissance, which is a remarkable testimony to the resilience of the human spirit. There was no conflict between the renewed interest in

Graeco-Roman civilization and the Catholic religion; indeed, the Church was an important patron of artists and scholars working in the new tradition, and this gave rise to Christian humanism.

The invention of printing by John Gutenberg (d. 1468) made it possible to standardize texts. Since the time of Alcuin Western churchmen had been concerned to establish as accurate a text of the Bible as possible, and this was finally achieved with the publication in 1517 of the Complutensian polyglot under the patronage of Cardinal Ximenes, Inquisitor-General of Spain.[36] In this six-volume work the Vulgate text of the Old Testament is printed in parallel with the Hebrew and the Greek Septuagint, and the Vulgate New Testament is printed along with the original Greek text and its Syriac paraphrase. This was an invaluable tool for biblical scholarship.

In 1447 Nicholas V became the first humanist pope, and for the next hundred years men who shared those values held the Roman see.[37] At the beginning of his reign Nicholas set out his programme for the regeneration of Rome, once the capital of the ancient civilization he so much admired but now a city of ruins:

> The immense, supreme authority of the Church of Rome . . . can in the first place be understood only by those who have studied its origins and developments through the medium of the written word. But the mass of the population have no knowledge of literary matters . . . However, the grandeur of buildings, of monuments which are in a sense enduring and appear to testify to the handiwork of Our Lord, serves to reinforce it and confirm the faith of the common people, which is based on the assertions of the learned, so that it is then passed on to all those who will be enabled to admire these wonderful constructions.[38]

Under Nicholas's cultivated successors this plan was implemented. Churches were restored, Renaissance palaces were built and processional roads were driven through the city to connect the chief basilicas. Martin V had moved the papal residence from the Lateran Palace to the Vatican, where Nicholas V began to build a new palace. Sixtus IV (1471–84) built the Sistine Chapel there which became a centre of musical excellence and founded the Vatican Library which came to house the finest collection of classical manuscripts in the world. The popes also built up a fine collection of classical sculpture which they displayed in the Vatican belvedere. When Julius II became pope in 1503, Rome had replaced Florence as the cultural capital of Italy and artists and architects from all over the peninsula came there to vie for papal patronage. It was a mark of Pope Julius's supreme confidence in the creative capacities of his contemporaries that he commissioned the architect Bramante to demolish the Constantinian basilica of St Peter's and to replace it by a new church in contemporary style. The foundation stone of the new cathedral was laid on 18 April 1506: once again, the Western Church had shown itself to be very resilient when confronted by change.

CHAPTER TWO

THE CHURCH IN BYZANTINE LANDS

The City of Constantine

Once he became sole ruler of the Roman Empire in 324, Constantine the Great made the old Greek city of Byzantium his capital and it was renamed Constantinople in his honour. The emperors who ruled there until the Turkish conquest in 1453 regarded themselves with justice as successors of the caesars and styled themselves emperors of the Romans, but modern historians refer to their empire as the Byzantine Empire, from the old Greek name of the capital, because in language and civilization it was a Greek society. Constantinople had an excellent natural harbour, known as the Golden Horn, and occupied a strategic position at the crossroads between Europe and Asia, and the Black Sea and the Aegean. Before the invention of cannon its great land walls, built in the fifth century, were virtually impregnable, and the city was further protected by a circuit of sea walls.

Constantinople was a simple bishopric subordinate to the Metropolitan of Heraclea, until, in 381, the second General Council, meeting at Constantinople, declared that the see should rank immediately after Rome, 'because Constantinople is the new Rome'. In 451 Canon 28 of the Council of Chalcedon made the Bishop of Constantinople a patriarch and gave him equal privileges with those of the Roman pontiff, who retained only a primacy of honour. The papal legates refused to endorse this canon.

The Emperor Justinian I (527–65) endowed a cathedral worthy of new Rome. It was dedicated to the Holy Wisdom (in Greek, *Hagia Sophia*), was designed by Anthemius of Tralles assisted by Isidore of Miletus, and was consecrated in 537. Charles Diehl described the interior as:

> in truth incomparable. A vast rectangle, 77 metres by 71.7 in area, forms a broad nave flanked by aisles with galleries above them which pass over the narthex and extend all round the church. At a height of 55 metres from the ground this central nave is crowned by an enormous dome, 31 metres across, which rests upon four great arches supported by four massive piers . . . [This dome] has truly been described by a sixth-century writer as 'a work at once marvellous and terrifying', seeming so light and airy it was, 'rather to hang by a golden chain from heaven than to be supported on solid masonry.'[1]

An interior view of the dome in the cathedral of the Holy Wisdom, Constantinople (now the museum of Hagia Sophia, Istanbul).

The walls of the cathedral were clad in different kinds of marble, the screen and furnishings of the sanctuary were plated with silver, and the upper registers of the church were covered with mosaics. In the apse was a mosaic of the Virgin and Child enthroned; the Pantocrator, Christ the ruler of all things, looked down from the dome against a background of gold, and the four squinches of the dome were decorated by the Emperor Basil II (976–1025) with monumental six-winged cherubs. Mosaics also adorned the galleries and the narthex – the great entrance hall of the cathedral, pierced by nine doors. No church in Christendom was served by as many clergy as the Holy Wisdom. In 612 the Emperor Heraclius limited their number to eighty priests, 150 deacons, forty deaconesses, seventy subdeacons, 160 readers, twenty-five cantors and 100 doorkeepers.[2] The splendour of the liturgy performed there was unsurpassed in the medieval Christian world. Yet the Holy Wisdom was only the greatest of the several hundred churches, monasteries and oratories which existed in Constantinople during the central Middle Ages.

The Byzantines believed that their church had been founded by St Andrew the Apostle (appropriately the brother of St Peter), who had consecrated St Stachys as its first bishop, but the true patron of the city was the Blessed Virgin Mary. Her cloak had been brought to Constantinople in the reign of the Emperor Marcian (450–7) and was placed in the church of Blachernae. Whenever the city was besieged the cloak was

The cathedral of the Holy Wisdom, Constantinople, with minarets added by the Ottoman Sultans.

paraded round the walls and Constantinople was placed under the Virgin's protection. Probably after the city had successfully resisted the Avar siege in 626 the hymn 'Akathistos' was ordered to be sung in honour of Our Lady in all Orthodox churches on the first Saturday of Lent. It is still sung on that day, and it begins with this invocation by the city to the Virgin:

> Unto you, O Theotokos, invincible champion,
> Your city in thanksgiving ascribes the victory for the
> deliverance from sufferings,
> And having your might unassailable, free me from all
> dangers, so that I may cry unto you: 'Hail, O bride
> ever-virgin'.[3]

This sense of divine protection became deeply rooted in Byzantine religious sensibility. In the early tenth century, St Andrew the Fool, while attending the night office in the church of Blachernae, had a vision of the Mother of God holding her veil over the city of Constantine, and that became a favourite subject for Byzantine icon painters.

The earthly ruler of Byzantium lived in the Great Palace, a walled inner city enclosing some 100,000 square metres of land in the south-west corner of Constantinople. It was a conglomeration of palaces, churches, pavilions and gardens. In the audience chamber, in which foreign visitors were received, the throne stood at the top of a flight of steps, flanked by mechanical lions which could be made to roar and bang their tails on the ground. Beside the throne stood a tree of gilt bronze in whose leaves small mechanical birds twittered. The emperor wore heavily embroidered silk vestments, remained silent during audiences and ambassadors were required to perform *proskynesis*, that is to kneel and touch the ground with their foreheads three times as they approached the throne. While they were doing this the throne was mechanically elevated so that the emperor appeared high and remote above his court.[4]

Constantinople was the largest city in the medieval Christian world, with perhaps half a million inhabitants. Its main streets were paved and its many churches and public buildings well maintained. Next to the Great Palace was the Hippodrome, which had forty tiers of seats on each side, surmounted by a promenade, and was said to be able to seat 40,000. Chariot races continued to be held there until the twelfth century. Constantinople, the city guarded by God and by His Mother, was unique in that until 1204 it was the only surviving city of the ancient world which had never been sacked.

Church and Empire

The patriarchate at first comprised only Thrace and the eastern Balkans, together with Asia Minor to the west of the Taurus mountains. To the east and south it was bounded by the patriarchate of Antioch, and to the West by that of Rome. In 731–2 the Emperor Leo III transferred Illyricum, which comprised the western Balkans, mainland Greece and Crete, from the jurisdiction of Rome to that of Constantinople.[5] The patriarchate and the empire were seldom geographically coextensive. As a result of missionary activity the powers of the patriarch spread to areas north of the Danube and the Black Sea which had never formed part of the empire. The patriarch's relations with the emperor were not always harmonious, at first because their respective spheres of authority were not clearly defined.

The Byzantine Church considered that authority in the universal Church was vested in a pentarchy of patriarchs – those of the five ancient sees of Rome, Constantinople, Antioch, Alexandria and Jerusalem – and was exercised in general councils of the Church. After the seventh century the Orthodox patriarchs of Jerusalem, Alexandria and Antioch lived under Arab rule and, although they continued to send representatives to general councils, could take little active part in the affairs of the universal Church. Constantinople therefore became the pre-eminent eastern patriarchate and, except in the easternmost provinces, most Christians living within the imperial frontiers professed the Orthodox faith of Chalcedon.

Until 751 the fifth patriarch, the pope of Rome, was a political subject of the Byzantine emperor and a number of Greek-speaking popes were appointed in the seventh and early eighth centuries. Although the patriarchs of Constantinople had been granted equal privileges to the popes of Rome by the Council of Chalcedon the Byzantines recognized that the popes were the successors of St Peter and therefore held the unique powers of binding and loosing which Christ had conferred on that apostle (see p. 16), but this did not lead to any major conflict in the early centuries, chiefly because the popes had not fully explored the implications of their Petrine powers at that time.

In Christian thought the authority of the Roman Empire had been divinely sanctioned because Christ had been born in the reign of the first Emperor, Augustus, and had declared that the Roman governor of Judaea had the right to sit in judgment on him (Jn. 19:11). Moreover, it was believed that the Roman Empire would retain a central place in the world order throughout much of human history. St Paul, writing about the end of the world, had said that: 'The mystery of lawlessness is already at work, but there is at present someone who holds it in check until he is taken out of the midst, and then the Lawless One will be revealed, whom the Lord will destroy . . . by the appearance of His coming.'[6] From the time of St Hippolytus of Rome (d. c. 235), this cryptic passage was interpreted as meaning that Antichrist was already at work in the world but was held in check by the forces of law and order represented by the Roman Empire. When that empire should cease to exist, then Antichrist would appear openly, anarchy would prevail, and that would be the prelude to the Second Coming of Christ and the end of the world.

Eusebius of Caesarea, one of the religious advisers of Constantine the Great, described the relation of a Christian emperor to God in this way: '[he] will frame his earthly government according to the pattern of the divine original, finding strength in conformity with the monarchy of God'.[7] The Byzantine world found this ideology congenial and regarded the emperor as the representative of God in the work of secular government. In theory the imperial office was elective and was open to any citizen of Orthodox faith and free birth, and from the eighth century that included women. The electors were the senate, the people of Constantinople and the army, but elections did not always prove necessary, for an emperor could associate a colleague, often a son, with him in power, with rights of succession. Because the emperor was representative of the one God, the senior emperor was known as the *autocrator*, or sole ruler, and the co-emperor as *basileus*, or king.

In theory the emperor in Constantinople was the only divinely constituted secular authority in the world, and all other rulers should acknowledge him as their overlord. That many of them failed to do so was considered the result of human sin. As a diplomatic strategy emperors sometimes conferred the title of *basileus* on other Christian rulers. This did not imply parity, though it was sometimes misconstrued as doing so, for there could be only one *autocrator*, but he could designate as many *basilei* as he wished, both inside and outside the empire, to assist him in ruling the world.

The Church had no part in the appointment of an emperor, but from the early seventh century the emperor was crowned by the patriarch in the church of the Holy Wisdom. As a member of the Church the emperor was bound by its rules about religious observances and subject to its penitential discipline for breaches of morality. That had been established in 390 when St Ambrose had required Theodosius I to do penance for ordering the massacre of unarmed civilians at Thessalonica. Nevertheless, the emperor had considerable powers in Church affairs. He appointed the Patriarch of Constantinople from a list of three names submitted by the Holy Synod and in practice he could normally secure the deposition of a patriarch whom he found unsatisfactory.[8] The emperor convened general councils of the Church and was present at them. Because his authority rested on religious sanctions, it was a matter of political importance to him that all his subjects should hold the same faith as he did. Between 451 and 680 the emperors periodically tried to force the Church to accept a religious settlement which would satisfy the Monophysites (see Chapters Three and Four), but this usually led to conflict with some church leaders. After the Arab conquests, when it became clear that the empire had little prospect of rapidly recovering its territories in Syria and Egypt, Monophysitism ceased to be a major concern of imperial policy. In 680 Constantine IV convened the third General Council of Constantinople which reaffirmed the Christology of the Council of Chalcedon and this marked the restoration of harmony between Church and state.

This peace was disturbed again in the early eighth century by the Emperor Leo III. The Arab victories of the seventh century had posed a religious problem to the Byzantine world: if their Christian empire was divinely ordained, how could it suffer defeat at the hands of the Muslims? One answer, given by some bishops in the eastern provinces of Asia Minor from which Leo III's family came, was that God was punishing the Christians for the sin of idolatry. The second of the Ten Commandments forbade the making and worship of graven images. Traditionally there had been no prohibition in Christian art on the use of the human image, and Christ, the angels and the saints were widely represented in sculpture, mosaics and frescoes. In the late sixth and early seventh centuries in Byzantium there is evidence of a growth of religious devotion to certain of those images as focuses of prayer. The new religion of Islam placed great emphasis on the absolute distinction between God and His creation, and although the Koran does not prohibit religious representational art, it is forbidden in an *hadith*, one of

The Virgin and Child with the Empress Irene, wife of John II Comnenus (1118–43). Mosaic panel in the south tribune of the cathedral of the Holy Wisdom.

the sayings of the prophet, which began to be collected and recorded in *c.* 695. It was therefore logical for some Christians to see the victory of Islam as a punishment sent by God for the idolatry into which some of their fellow believers had fallen.

Leo III was converted to this view and in 730 made iconoclasm official imperial policy. Iconoclasm, the destruction of likenesses, meant that all religious representational art should be destroyed or covered over with whitewash. Consequently, a huge amount of early Byzantine religious art of all kinds was destroyed at this time. The policy had the support of much of the

A fifteenth-century icon of St Demetrius, patron saint of warriors.

army and of the Asian provinces, but was unpopular in the European provinces. Germanus I, Patriarch of Constantinople, resigned rather than implement it, while Pope Gregory III excommunicated the emperor. Leo's opponents were known as Iconodules, those who worshipped images. Many of them were monks, who were particularly attached to the cult of the saints and to the use of religious representational art. Leo's son Constantine V (741–75), who was equally committed to Iconoclasm, suppressed some of the monasteries which opposed his policy and executed some of his more vocal critics. Although the Iconoclast decrees were strictly enforced in Constantinople, they were more fitfully observed in the provinces. Constantine V's daughter-in-law, the Athenian-born Empress Irene, who in 780 became regent for her infant son Constantine VI, was an Iconodule and, having in 784 appointed a new Patriarch, Tarasius, who shared her views, she convoked the seventh General Council of the Church which met at Nicaea in 787 and was attended by representatives of the pope and of the three eastern patriarchs. The Council restored the icons and in formulating its decrees was influenced by St John of Damascus (d. 750), a monk in the Orthodox monastery of St Sabas near Jerusalem and a strong supporter of the devotional use of religious images. He argued that the representation of Christ in art was a legitimate expression of belief in the Incarnation; that the material world (in this case represented by wooden panels, mosaic tesserae and stone carvings) could be used as a vehicle of God's grace, and that the production of religious art was part of redeeming the whole creation which Christ had initiated when he became man. It followed, therefore, that if Christ might be represented in works of art there could be no objection to representing His creatures – his Mother, the angels and the saints. Moreover, St John argued, it was not idolatrous to honour a likeness, because all reverence paid to an image or likeness was in fact given to its prototype, the person whom it represented. The Council made an important distinction between worship (*latreia*) which might be paid only to the Three Persons of the Godhead, Father, Son and Holy Spirit, and veneration (*syndoche*) which might justly be paid to the angels and saints in recognition of the way in which God had used them as instruments of his grace. The second Council of Nicaea was the last to be recognized as a general council by the Byzantine Church.

Support for Iconoclasm remained strong, particularly in the army, and the Emperor Leo V (813–20) rescinded the acts of the Council of Nicaea and restored Iconoclasm as the religion of the empire. Some Orthodox opponents were persecuted for refusing to accept this, but the law does not seem to have been strongly enforced outside Constantinople, though it remained official policy until the death of the Emperor Theophilus in 842. His widow Theodora, regent for the child-emperor Michael III, summoned a council to Constantinople in 843 at which all Iconoclast legislation was revoked and the canons of the second Council of Nicaea declared a true statement of the faith of the Orthodox Church.

The very long Iconoclast controversy helped to define the relations between the emperor and the Church and these were set out in the new law code, the Basilics, issued under Leo VI (886–912). It was a relationship of interdependence, and although the emperor retained most of his powers in matters relating to Church administration, he was no longer allowed to determine points of doctrine, but was required at his accession to sign a profession of Orthodox faith drawn up by the patriarch. It was impossible to avoid all conflict between Church and state. Leo VI himself was excommunicated by the Patriarch Nicholas Mysticus in 906 for contracting a fourth marriage, contrary to Byzantine canon law. As his fourth wife had given the emperor the male heir he desired, he was not willing to have this marriage annulled and the matter was resolved in his favour by an appeal to Pope Sergius III. Yet on the whole such disagreements were exceptional and relations between Church and state in Byzantium were for the most part harmonious after 843.

The emperor's powers were understood in religious terms. Although he was a layman, he took his place with the clergy in the sanctuary during the divine liturgy and led his people in worship. He was not merely required to appear as God's representative in a ceremonial context, but was also expected to rule in a spirit of *philanthropia*, or benevolence, because he was the representative of Christ. The scholar emperor Constantine VII (913–59) wrote: 'It is the duty of the emperor to spread blessings everywhere and if he fails to do so he subverts the imperial power.' Constantine, who succeeded to the throne as a child, was beset by ambitious regents and co-emperors throughout much of his life and witnessed a good deal of political violence, and in order to counter these trends drew up *The Book of the Ceremonies*, setting out the ancient rituals which should be observed by the emperor and his court. The ideal which he sought to inculcate in his heirs was that the emperor should mirror on earth the divine order of Heaven, manifest in the movement of the stars in the firmament:

[Through court ceremonial] may the imperial power, being exercised in an orderly and measured way, reproduce the harmonious movement which the Creator has given to the entire universe; and may [the empire] appear to our subjects both more majestic and also more pleasing to them and more worthy of their admiration.[9]

Religion in the Byzantine World

Although the Byzantine Church shared, broadly speaking, a common faith, organization and pattern of worship with the Western Church, it occupied a different place in society. In the eastern provinces of the Roman Empire the structures of secular government and public education had remained in place in the early medieval centuries and the Church had not had to take over any of those tasks. Byzantine bishoprics were more numerous and far smaller than those of the Western Church, and although the patriarch and some of the metropolitans were socially important, there was no equivalent in Byzantium to the prince bishops of Western Europe. In each diocese there were parish churches established by the bishop, but there were comparatively few of them, whereas there were many private chapels and oratories, founded by landowners, local monasteries and lay benefactors. Although in theory rites of passage – baptisms, marriages and burial services – might only be performed by parish priests, in many rural areas where parishes were very large these were carried out by the priests of private chapels. In 692 the Byzantine Church enacted that priests had either to take monastic vows or to marry before ordination. In either case they would have the support of a community in their vocation – that of a monastery or of a family. Since bishops were not allowed to marry, this meant that the church hierarchy was recruited chiefly from monks, although unmarried laymen were also eligible to become bishops. In the Byzantine Church the primitive form of initiation, which combined baptism, confirmation and first Holy Communion in one rite, was retained even after infant baptism had become normal, but bishops delegated the right to perform confirmation to priests.

The Byzantines read the New Testament in the original Greek and the Old Testament in the Septuagint translation (see p. 15). The normal eucharistic liturgy was attributed to St John Chrysostom (d. 407), though in its final form it dates from no earlier than the eighth century. Of course, as the centuries passed, liturgical Greek became increasingly remote from the common speech, demotic Greek, but in a general sense the Byzantine liturgy remained accessible to the laity until the fall of the empire. One consequence of this was that some lay people attended mattins and vespers, which were sung daily in all cathedrals and some parish churches.

The focus of worship in the Byzantine Church was the eucharist. It was always celebrated on Sundays and great feast days, though daily celebrations seem to have been uncommon. The Byzantine liturgy was always sung unaccompanied, and an elaborate repertoire of liturgical chant was developed.[10] By the mid-ninth century the Orthodox Church was normally furnished with an iconostasis, a solid screen which divided the sanctuary from the nave, covered with icons and pierced by doors which were opened at certain points during the liturgy to enable the clergy to process from the sanctuary into the nave. In its most elaborate form, the cathedral service led by a professional choir using elaborate chants, the Byzantine liturgy could last for several hours, though in ordinary churches it was briefer. The aim of the liturgy was to bring Paradise down to earth and the elaborate chanting, the rich vestments of the clergy, the profusion of candles and incense and the liturgical rituals all combined to produce that effect.

The liturgy was enhanced by the programme of decoration used in Orthodox churches. Whereas western religious artists always enjoyed considerable freedom of expression, Byzantine artists, at least after the end of the Iconoclast controversy, had to work within a strict iconographic tradition. The composition of particular scenes was strictly regulated. In a Nativity, for example, the centre was occupied by the Virgin Mother, lying on a couch draped in imperial scarlet, and at her side the crib containing the Christ child was respectfully watched by a white ass and a brown ox; at the top of the painting was the star of Bethlehem, towards which, on the left side, the three kings were shown riding up a steep hill; on the right side a group of angels was portrayed, announcing the birth of Christ to the shepherds, and in the bottom register St Joseph was shown seated, talking to a shepherd, while a midwife bathed the new-born child. A good deal of variation was possible within these limits. The figures could be shown in hieratic poses or be treated naturalistically; the positioning of some of the minor characters could be varied; the landscape detail of the background could be changed; and additional figures could be introduced, for example, the prophet Isaiah could be shown kneeling beside the crib holding a scroll inscribed, 'The ox knoweth his owner, and the ass his master's crib' (Is. 1:3), which was the scriptural justification for their

The Virgin and Child enthroned among saints and angels. Fresco in the apse of the Dionysiou monastery, Mount Athos.

inclusion. The high religious art of Byzantium was not static, but it was subordinate to the mind of the Church, not simply to the vision of the artist.

The cycle of decorations used for church interiors evolved in the post-Iconoclastic period was designed for cross-in-square churches with central domes, which were then the most common type of church building, although it could be adapted to other architectural designs. Christ the Pantocrator was portrayed in the dome, and below him the angels in heaven; the Blessed Virgin was shown enthroned in the sanctuary apse; in the highest register of the walls were scenes from the life of Christ arranged in order of the festival calendar (these could vary in number according to the size of the church); on the lower registers of the walls and on the arches over the pillars were portrayed the patriarchs and prophets of the Old Testament and the saints and martyrs honoured by the Church.

After the restoration of the icons in 843 God the Father was never portrayed in Byzantine art. Moreover, sculptures and bas-reliefs ceased to be used in Byzantine churches, which were now only embellished with frescoes and mosaics. The positioning of mosaic tesserae involved considerable knowledge of optics and required advanced mathematical skills. Gervase Mathew observed of the mosaic of the Virgin and Child in the vestibule of the church of the Holy Wisdom that 'the intricate measuring and angling of the mosaic are best explained if it was intended to be seen at thirteen metres from its centre at man's height from the floor'.[11] The most characteristic form of Byzantine religious art after *c.* 850 was the icon, a painting (or sometimes a mosaic) on a wooden panel. These works had originated in the fifth century, but assumed a central place in Byzantine devotional life at the end of the Iconoclast period, both in church and in the home, for they symbolized the victory of Orthodoxy

In Byzantium, as in the West, the liturgy was the normal means of religious instruction. Priests instructed children in the essentials of the faith, but were not trained to preach, though bishops regularly did so. Knowledge of theology was not a clerical monopoly in Byzantium, because there was a large class of literate lay people of both sexes. The Empress Irene Ducas, wife of Alexius I (1081–1118), for example, was said by her daughter to have read a good deal of mystical theology.

Outwardly Byzantine society was completely Christianized by the central Middle Ages, but quite widespread magical practices co-existed with Orthodox belief. The most common of these were attempts to predict the future, to cast horoscopes by reading the clouds, or by studying the movement of the stars. People employed learned wizards to make amulets, or carried around with them pieces of dyed fur cut from the coats of thaumaturgic bears, which were believed to protect the wearer against misfortune. Black magic also flourished: recourse was had to sorcerers to enlist the help of demons in order to subvert the chastity of virgins or bring about the downfall of rivals and enemies.

The Byzantines accepted that lay people could lead devout Christian lives, but they considered that withdrawal from the world was the highest vocation. They held solitaries in special reverence, particularly the stylites who spent their lives praying on the tops of pillars, and the less austere, but equally single-minded, dendrites who lived in the branches of trees. The majority of monks and nuns lived in communities. The Byzantine Church never developed religious orders; instead, each new foundation was given its own rule, but those rules had much in common because almost all of them drew extensively on the ascetic works of the monastic legislator, St Basil the Great (d. 379). There were two main types of Byzantine monastery, the coenobitic house in which the emphasis was on community life, and monasteries in which the brethren lived as solitaries but met together on Sundays and feast days for communal worship. Some coenobitic communities had priories attached to them known as *skete*, for brethren who wished to live as hermits. From time to time monastic reformers sought to promote a more austere way of life. This took various forms. Abbot Alexander (d. *c*. 430) founded a community in Constantinople known as the *akoimetoi*, the unsleeping brethren, because they were divided into multiple choirs so that the psalms might be sung without intermission in their chapel; while in the ninth century St Theodore of Studium stressed the importance of monastic poverty and of manual labour.

Monasticism was an omnipresent feature of Byzantine religious life. Some of the city monasteries administered the charitable institutions – hospitals, orphanages and almshouses – whose endowment formed such a conspicuous feature of Byzantine lay piety.[12] Monasteries were also a regular feature of rural life, though many of them were poorly endowed and attracted the vocations chiefly of the local peasantry. Such houses tended to be ephemeral. There were also concentrations of monasteries in certain areas.

Part of the Georgian monastery of Iviron on Mount Athos, founded in the late tenth century.

Between the seventh and eleventh centuries the strange tufa rock formations near Caesarea in Cappadocia, which look like an enchanted landscape from a fantasy story, were adapted to house monks and hermits and were equipped with churches and chapels, many of them decorated with vivid and elaborate frescoes. A new monastic centre developed in the tenth century on Mount Athos, a peninsula near Thessalonica some thirty-five miles long, which terminates in a 6,000 foot high mountain. In 963 St Athanasius, a friend of Emperor Nicephorus I Phocas (963–9), founded the Grand Lavra there, which received considerable privileges and endowments, and the mountain soon attracted other vocations. When the Emperor John I Tzimisces issued a *typikon* regulating monastic life on the Holy Mountain in 970–2, forty-seven abbots signed it. Under the supervision of the patriarch and the emperor the monks of Athos became self-governing and their affairs were regulated by a council elected by the abbots of Athos. The Mountain was dedicated to the Blessed Virgin and it became the convention that no other woman, not even a Byzantine empress, might set foot on the domain of the Queen of Heaven. The Mountain rapidly acquired prestige and monasteries were founded there by benefactors drawn from all parts of the Orthodox world.

In *c.* 1340 Athanasius, a monk trained on Mount Athos, founded the Great Meteora monastery in Epirus. The Meteora is a strange rock formation which rises out of the plain near Kalambaka and by 1500 there were some fifteen communities there. In most cases no roads led to the summit of the rocks on which these monasteries had been built and visitors, until the nineteenth century, had to be hauled up the cliff-faces in nets lowered by the brethren. This assured the safety of the monks during the long periods of border warfare which preceded the final Ottoman conquest of the region. Despite the difficulties of bringing material to these sites, the brethren built elaborate churches and had them decorated with fine frescoes.

There was also considerable spiritual vitality in late Byzantine monasticism, which is exemplified by the development of Hesychasm. This word means 'quietness' and refers to a form of contemplative prayer by means of which, its advocates claim, it is possible to experience mystically the uncreated Light of God. The Hesychasts identified this Light with that which SS. Peter, James and John had seen when Christ was transfigured in their presence on Mount Tabor (Matt. 17:1–9). This form of prayer had its roots in the writings of classical Byzantine theologians like St Maximus the Confessor (d. 662) and St Symeon the New Theologian (d. 1022), a monk who was a mystic and a poet. The Hesychasts placed great emphasis on the personal union of the soul with God through private, contemplative prayer, and were viewed with misgiving by some churchmen because they appeared to set little value on the corporate life of the Church expressed in its public worship and its sacraments. There was a strong Hesychast movement in some of the monasteries of Mount Athos in the early fourteenth century and one of its most learned and articulate supporters was St Gregory Palamas (*c.* 1296–1359), who defended the Hesychast position against the attacks of Barlaam, a monk from Calabria, who considered some Hesychast claims to be heretical. The Orthodox Church vindicated Palamas and a synod held in the Blachernae palace at Constantinople in 1351 declared Hesychasm to be doctrinally orthodox. It had a considerable influence on later Orthodox spirituality, and Palamas was canonized in 1368.

The eleventh-century church of Daphne, near Athens.

The sheer number of monasteries meant that monks and nuns were a normal part of the social as well as the religious life of most Byzantine people. Orthodox monasteries seem to have interpreted their rules in ways which gave the individual brethren more personal space than western practice allowed: the physical arrangement of many Orthodox monasteries, in which monks had what were in effect small private houses within the compound, encouraged this. It was a system not without dangers: it could lead to spiritual laxity and it also enabled heterodoxy to develop unobserved. But the system had benefits, for it enabled monks to spend more time than their western colleagues in personal and reflective prayer. It was this quality which made them valued as spiritual advisers and gave them so much influence in the Church as a whole.

Tradition and Perfection

Kurt Weitzmann described Byzantine civilization as 'the connection between tradition and perfection', the learned tradition of classical Greece and the perfection of the Orthodox faith.[13] Those links had been formed in the early third century by Alexandrian Christians like St Clement and Origen (see p. 138), who had found the work of Plato particularly congenial. In the *Timaeus* he speculated about the nature of the world, suggesting that the Divine Craftsman (the demiurge) had brought this changing world into being in conformity with an archetype which did not change; and therefore that the world we can see is an *eikon*, or likeness, of the unchanging world we cannot see. The concept of the visible world as a transient and imperfect copy of the divine exemplar which existed in the thought of God synchronized well with Christian teaching.

Origen's younger contemporary, the pagan thinker Plotinus (d. 270), was the founder of Neoplatonism, a movement which transformed the philosophical concepts of Plato into a metaphysical system. He taught that the material world was the most distant of an hierarchical series of emanations from the First Principle, which he called the One, but that the human soul, by a process of moral and mental purification, could attain union with the One by means of contemplation. Neoplatonic philosophy was interpreted in Christian terms by an anonymous Greek writer living in Syria in *c.* 500. His treatises – *The Celestial Hierarchy*, *The Ecclesiastical Hierarchy*, *The Divine Names* and *Mystical Theology* – were mistakenly attributed to Dionysius the Areopagite, one of the few converts whom St Paul had made at Athens (Acts 17:34). Pseudo-Dionysius shared with the Neoplatonists a belief that the universe is hierarchically ordered, but substituted the nine choirs of angels – the Celestial Hierarchy, who mediated the One God to His creation – for the divine emanations of Plotinus. He taught that on earth the ecclesiastical hierarchy reflected this divine order: bishops, priests and deacons mediated divine grace to the Church which consisted of the three orders of monks, laymen and catechumens (those under instruction). With the help of divine grace, mediated partly by the angelic and ecclesiastical hierarchies, the soul might learn to use ascetic techniques of contemplation in order to enjoy the beatific vision of God. Because the works of the pseudo-Dionysius were believed to date from the very earliest age of the church they were extremely influential.

Byzantine theologians were also influenced by the argument of St Gregory Nazianzes (d. 390) that God was unknowable by human reason because any human concept was inadequate as a means of describing the Divine Being. As a result, apophatic theology, which accepts that the only valid statements which may be made about God are negative ones (e.g. that He has no limitations), came to occupy a central place in Byzantine religious thought. The Byzantines, of course, accepted that God had revealed Himself in the Incarnation of Christ and continued to do so through the work of the Holy Spirit, but held that man could respond to such revelations because he had a spiritual faculty which was non-intellectual. One consequence of this was that Byzantine thinkers made a distinction between the Inner and the Outer Learning. The Inner Learning was theology, which was concerned with divine revelation and mystical

God rests on the seventh day of creation. Byzantine mosaic in the Latin cathedral of Monreale, Sicily, built by William II (1172–89).

experience. The Outer Learning was secular scholarship, the domain of human reason. It did not prove possible to keep these two kinds of study completely separate.

Monastic schools were concerned with providing a training in theology based on a study of the Bible, the liturgy and the Church Fathers. This emphasis was reflected in monastic libraries: when St John's Patmos was founded in the late eleventh century only seventeen of the 330 books in its library were secular works. But it would be wrong to suppose that all monasteries were insulated from secular learning and hostile to it, although this was true of some monks. Many monks were professed as adults and had already received a secular education; moreover, the writings of many of the Church Fathers were so heavily influenced by the classical heritage that its impress may be seen even in the works of monks like St Symeon the New Theologian (d. 1022), who professed himself hostile to it. Books of all kinds found their way into monastic libraries and no censorship existed to exclude classical texts.

Byzantine religious writings consisted of works of biblical exegesis, very heavily dependent on the Greek Fathers; and lives of the saints, which ranged from creative fiction to scholarly biography. There was also a large corpus of dogmatic theology, the systematic study of divine revelation, which culminated in the work of St John of Damascus (d. 749) whose treatise *Concerning the Orthodox Faith* was a compendium of Orthodox doctrine. Later dogmatic theology was largely, though not exclusively, concerned either with polemic – disputes with other churches, notably the Western Church, about the different ways in which they understood their common faith – or with dualist heresy. Both these issues will be considered later in this chapter.

The finest Byzantine poetry was inspired by religious themes. Liturgical poems, known as canons, were set to music and incorporated in the liturgy, while St Symeon the New Theologian described some of his mystical experiences very powerfully in a collection of poems called *Hymns of the Divine Love*. Unlike the secular poets of Byzantium, religious writers were not constrained to compose in classical Greek, but could write in the demotic, which allowed them to express themselves in a far more spontaneous way.

The Outer Learning, knowledge within the scope of human reason, was studied in secular schools. Elementary schools which taught the fundamental skills of reading and writing were found in most provincial cities, while in important cities, like Thessalonica and Trebizond, there were schools in which classical Greek literature was studied. Constantinople had a university with a fluctuating history which nevertheless persisted until the fifteenth century. The syllabus of studies was that of the seven liberal arts which was also used in the Western schools, and these subjects were seen as the foundation for the study of philosophy. All these courses were based on the study of classical Greek texts and students were taught to write Attic Greek, the language of Athens in the fifth and fourth centuries B.C. Until the dispersal of the great libraries of Constantinople by the Fourth Crusade in 1204, the Byzantines possessed a far wider range of classical Greek works than has subsequently been available. In his *Myriobiblon* the Patriarch Photius (d. 893) recorded extracts from the books in his library together with his comments on them. Many of those books are now only known through those extracts.

Educated Byzantine laymen were trained in this classical tradition and some aristocratic Byzantine women received a parallel training from private tutors. The Outer Learning was also shared by a significant number of the higher clergy who had been educated in the secular schools before they took Holy Orders. The patriarch's academy at Constantinople from the twelfth century onwards provided a good general education in grammar, rhetoric and logic as well as in theology, and laymen often sent their sons there to receive a secular education, although the Academy only taught theology to ordinands. Even so, lay people were often knowledgeable about theology. Everybody was familiar with the Divine Liturgy and those who were literate were able to read the Bible as well as the works of the Fathers and the commentaries on them.

Through studying the classical tradition Byzantine scholars became aware that there were alternative world-views to that of Christianity and a few of them were attracted by this, although they seem to have been rare. John Italus (fl. 1070–1100), who held the chair of philosophy in the university of Constantinople, was among them, and was condemned, among other things, for teaching the eternity of matter, but his heresy was mild compared to that of George Gemistus Plethon (c. 1360–1452). He was deeply influenced by Plato and the Neoplatonists and advocated the rejection of Christianity and a return to the religion and ethics of classical Greece. His practical blueprints for reforming society have been aptly described by Steven Runciman as 'all planned with a superb disregard to actual political conditions and to probable human reactions'.[14]

Men of this kind, who favoured tradition above perfection, were even more rare than those monks who sought perfection and despised tradition. In general, educated Byzantine Christians came to understand their faith in ways which owed much to Plato and the Neoplatonists.

THE EXPANSION OF THE BYZANTINE CHURCH

In the fourth and fifth centuries Greece and the Balkan provinces had become Christian like the rest of the Roman Empire. Bishoprics were established in the main cities, though it is difficult to know how firmly rooted Christianity was in rural areas. Life in parts of the region was disturbed by the influx first of the Visigoths and then of the Ostrogoths, both of whom later moved to Italy (see above pp. 19–21). From the middle of the sixth century the Balkans began to be infiltrated by groups of pagan Slavs who in the seventh century penetrated as far as southern Greece. The Slavs were not politically united, but the pagan Serbs and Croats, settled by Heraclius (610–41) in the western Balkans as a defence against the Avars, formed independent states there. Similarly, the pagan Bulgars were recognized by Constantine IV as sovereign rulers of the lands between the Danube and the great Balkan range in a treaty of 681.

Bulgaria

By the ninth century Bulgaria had expanded to become the dominant power in the Balkans. Some of the population were Christian and were persecuted by the pagan Khans Ormatag (814–31) and Malamir (831–6), but Khan Boris (852–89) was baptized as an Orthodox Christian in 864 and wanted to make Bulgaria a Christian country. He wished the Bulgarian Church to be autonomous and therefore allowed both Byzantine Orthodox and Western Catholic missions to work in his country, seeking to play the two churches off against each other so that he could obtain concessions. In 870 the Patriarch of Constantinople acceded to his request for an independent church with its own archbishop and Byzantine Orthodoxy became the established religion of Bulgaria. Boris was genuinely devout: he founded six bishoprics, together with a number of monasteries, and gave his full support to the work of evangelization. The most significant development in his later reign was his patronage of a school of Old Slavonic translators who came to him from Greater Moravia.

Prince Rastislav, the ruler of this central European Slav state, wanted his people to become Christian and sought help from Byzantium. In 862 the Patriarch Photius sent the brothers Cyril and Methodius to work there.[15] They already had experience of evangelizing Slav settlers in Thessaly and had devised a Slav alphabet, known as

Scenes from the life of St Alexius. An eleventh-century fresco from the church of San Clemente, Rome, where St Cyril, Apostle of the Slavs, is buries.

Glagolitic. In Moravia they translated the Bible into Old Slavonic together with the Western Catholic liturgy, for Moravia was within the pope's sphere of jurisdiction. They had the support of the pope in their use of a vernacular liturgy, but were opposed by the German clergy who came to assist in the evangelization of Moravia after Rastislav was deposed in 870. Cyril had died in 869, and after Methodius's death in 885 his disciples were expelled and Moravia adopted the Latin rite like the rest of the Western Church. The Glagolitic Mass, translated by Cyril and Methodius, was introduced into Catholic Croatia by their followers and came to be used by some Slav congregations there throughout the Middle Ages.

The work of SS. Cyril and Methodius was continued by their disciples, SS. Clement and Nahum, who, when they were expelled from Moravia in 886, were welcomed by Khan Boris of Bulgaria. He founded a monastery for them at Ochrida in Macedonia, which became a centre for the translation and copying of Greek texts into Old Slavonic. The Glagolitic alphabet was modified and given a more graceful form and became known as Cyrillic in honour of St Cyril. An Old Slavonic translation of the Byzantine liturgy was made at Ochrida and priests were trained to use it. In this way Bulgaria obtained a vernacular liturgy and under the direction of its archbishop was able to develop its own distinctive form of Byzantine Orthodoxy.

Boris's son Symeon (893–927) took the title of Emperor, or Tsar, in 913 and perhaps in his reign, but certainly by the beginning of the reign of Tsar Peter (927–72), the Archbishop of Bulgaria was made a patriarch. When Basil II annexed Bulgaria in 1018 he suppressed the patriarchate and appointed an Archbishop of Bulgaria again; but the Bulgarian Empire regained its independence in 1186 and in 1235 the patriarchate was revived. It was based at Trnovo and although the Ottomans conquered the Bulgarian Empire in 1393 the patriarchate was preserved under their rule.

Serbia

The Serbs, unlike their neighbours the Croats who were converted to Catholicism, also became Orthodox and used the Old Slavonic rite. This probably happened while Serbia was under Bulgarian rule in the reign of Tsar Symeon. When it became independent in *c.* 931 under Prince Časlav, Serbia developed close links with Byzantium; Serbian rulers were theoretically vassals of the Byzantine emperors and their church was subject to the Archbishop of Ochrida.

Serbia asserted its independence after the death of Manuel Comnenus in 1180 under the leadership of Stephen Nemanja (1171–95). His son, Stephen II (1196–1228), was able to profit from the political confusion in the Balkans caused by the Fourth Crusade to make himself a king in 1217 and in 1220 his brother Sava was consecrated Archbishop of Peč and made head of the Orthodox Church in Serbia with the consent of the Orthodox Patriarch of Constantinople living in exile at Nicaea.

In the fourteenth century Serbia became a rich country through the development of its silver mines. The royal family were generous patrons of the Church and many fine cathedrals and monasteries were built in the thirteenth and fourteenth centuries and decorated with frescoes designed within the conventions of late Byzantine iconography,

The monastery church of Gracanica, Kossovo, built by King Milutin of Serbia in 1321.

but executed in a distinctive Slavonic style. Under Stephen IV Dušan (1331–55) Serbia became the dominant power in the Balkans and in 1345 he assumed the title of Emperor of the Serbs and Greeks and, with the agreement of a Church synod, raised the archbishopric of Serbia to a patriarchate, a development sanctioned by the Patriarch of Constantinople in 1375. Serbian dominance ended when their army was defeated by the Ottomans at Kossovo in 1389. In the fifteenth century the country became a province of the Ottoman Empire, but the Serbian Patriarchate survived under Turkish rule.

Alania

The Byzantine province of Cherson in the Crimea was an important trading centre, and from the eighth century the emperors allied with the Alans to protect the territory against the Khazars. The Alans, who had their centre in Ossetia to the north of the Caucasus, had spread over the area between the Caspian and the Sea of Azov. The Patriarch Nicholas Mysticus of Constantinople (901–7, 912–25) sent a mission to them led by Euthymius, the Abbot of Bithynian Olympus, who succeeded in converting their ruler, and an Orthodox bishop named Peter was consecrated for Alania. Although the Arab writer Masudi reports that in *c.* 932 the Alans reverted to paganism, this seems to

The thirteenth-century Byzantine church of the Holy Wisdom, Trebizond.

have been a temporary setback. Good relations with Byzantium had probably been restored by the reign of Constantine IX (1042–55) who had an Alan mistress whom the more tactful of his subjects likened to Helen of Troy when she sat in the imperial box at the Hippodrome. Certainly from the late eleventh century onwards Byzantine sources report that there was a metropolitan of the Alans, and in the late Middle Ages his church was made subject to the Archbishop of Trebizond. The last known Metropolitan of Alania, Pachomius, was recorded in 1591.

Russia

In the tenth century Russia had a Slav population and was organized in a number of principalities, from Novgorod in the north to Kiev in the south, ruled by members of a family of Scandinavian descent of whom the prince of Kiev was the senior. By 945 there was a church in Kiev dedicated to St Elias, probably for the use of foreign traders, and in 959 Olga, the widow of Prince Igor of Kiev, was baptized in the Orthodox rite.

At the beginning of his personal rule the young Byzantine Emperor Basil II, faced by a dangerous revolt, asked Olga's grandson, Prince Vladimir of Kiev, for military help. This was given in return for the hand in marriage of Basil's sister Anna, which conferred great prestige on Vladimir because no Byzantine princess born in the purple to a reigning emperor had ever before married a foreign ruler. Before his marriage Vladimir was baptized by an Orthodox archbishop, probably on the Feast of the Epiphany in 988. Yet although he made Orthodoxy the official religion of Russia, the new faith spread slowly and by 1025 there were only about a dozen churches in the whole vast country.

In the reign of Vladimir's son Jaroslav a Russian hierarchy was established under the Metropolitan Archbishop of Kiev. His successors were normally appointed by the patriarchs of Constantinople and were usually Byzantine Greeks, though the rest of the clergy were Russian and used the Old Slavonic liturgy introduced from Bulgaria and Serbia. By the time Jaroslav died in 1055 there were about six bishops in Russia, one of them at Novgorod, and monasteries had begun to be founded, notably that of the Caves at Kiev. Byzantine artists and architects were employed by the princes to build and decorate the new churches, and their influence may clearly be seen in the eleventh-century cathedral of St Sophia, Kiev. The Russian Church adopted Byzantine canon law which influenced the development of social life through its enactments about marriage and rites of passage. Under Church influence Russia began to develop a literature of its own. Theological works translated into Old Slavonic at Ochrida and elsewhere were introduced there, and the Russian Primary Chronicle began to be composed in the late eleventh century. The Russians showed little interest in the Greek classical tradition and those works were not translated.

By the thirteenth century Orthodox Christianity had become firmly established in all the Russian cities, but in 1237–40 the Mongols invaded, causing great devastation and sacking all the cities except Novgorod the

A late fifteenth-century Russian icon of the Crucifixion, with the Virgin and St John.

Great. They then withdrew to the grasslands of the lower Volga, where they became known as the Golden Horde because their khan had a tent of white velvet which glinted in the sunlight. They made the Russian princes tributary, but allowed them a measure of self-government.

Paradoxically, Mongol rule proved beneficial to the Russian Church. Although the Golden Horde were converted to Islam in the late thirteenth century, they gave complete religious freedom to their Christian subjects. Khan Mangu-Temur (1266–80) freed the Church and all its property from payment of tax. The chief source of Russian wealth in the Mongol period was agriculture, for during the invasion the Mongols had carried off skilled craftsmen from the cities to the court of the Great Khan in Mongolia, which made it difficult for urban life to regenerate quickly. It was under Mongol role that monasteries, which had previously been chiefly urban foundations, began to be established in rural areas. Because of their tax-exempt status they had no difficulty in attracting peasants to work their lands, and in this way the Orthodox Church spread into rural areas. Under church auspices new lands were cultivated and settlements were extended in the east almost as far as the Urals.

The western lands of Russia, weakened by the Mongol raids, were threatened by the growing power of the pagan Lithuanians (see p. 41). This led the Metropolitan of Kiev to move his see to Moscow for safety in the early fourteenth century. In 1359 the Golden Horde split into the three khanates of Astrakhan, Khazan and the Crimea, but it was not until 1451 that Vasili III of Moscow stopped paying tribute to them. In 1472 his son, Ivan III (1462–1505), married Sophia Palaeologa, niece of the last Byzantine Emperor, Constantine XI. She introduced the ceremonies of the Byzantine court to Moscow, whose rulers adopted the two-headed eagle as their insignia and accepted Byzantine coronation rituals. Ideologically the Princes of Moscow saw themselves as the heirs of Byzantium, because, apart from the Kings of Georgia, they were the only remaining independent Orthodox rulers.

Archbishop Isidore, the Greek Metropolitan of Moscow, had attended the Council of Florence in 1438–9 as part of the Byzantine delegation and had been a strong supporter of the act of union with Rome (see p. 96). This was very unpopular with the mass of the Russian clergy and people and he was forced into exile. His successors were all Russians, though they continued to be subordinate to the Patriarchs of Constantinople until 1589 when the Metropolitan of Moscow was made a patriarch.

Moldavia and Wallachia

In the fourteenth century two principalities emerged in the area between the Danube and the mountains of Transylvania – Wallachia to the south of the mountains, and Moldavia to the east of them. The population had been converted to Byzantine Orthodoxy, probably from Bulgaria and Serbia, although nothing certain is known about this; and although the people spoke Vlach, a romance language, they worshipped in Old Slavonic. In 1359 Wallachia was granted its own metropolitan archbishop, with his see at Arges, directly subject to the Patriarch of Constantinople, while Moldavia received its own metropolitan archbishop, with his see at Suceava, in 1401.

The Princes of Wallachia became vassals of the Ottoman Sultans in 1462, but Moldavia retained its independence until the death of Stephen the Great in 1504. Even under Ottoman suzerainty these rulers maintained a good deal of independence, for the Ottomans, while garrisoning certain strategic towns, undertook to build no mosques there and to give no lands to Turks, and those promises were observed. The Orthodox princes of Moldavia and Wallachia consciously saw themselves as the heirs of Byzantium and had considerable influence at the court of the Patriarchs of Constantinople. In these Danubian principalities the spirit of Orthodox Byzantium lingered into the early modern world, and, like their Byzantine predecessors, the princes were generous patrons of the Church. In Moldavia the exteriors of many churches in the sixteenth century were covered in frescoes in the late Byzantine style by artists working under princely patronage. This may justly be regarded as a final flowering of Byzantine aristocratic religious art.

THE ALTERNATIVE RELIGION

Paulicianism

The principal challenge to Orthodoxy in the Byzantine world came from the Christian dualist movements. The oldest of these was Paulicianism, founded by an Armenian, Constantine of Mananalis, in the region of Constans II (641–68). He was an absolute dualist, who taught that there were two co-eternal gods. His followers proclaimed:

> We say that the Heavenly Father is one God, who has no power in this world, but who has power in the world to come, and that there is another god who made this world and who has power over the present world.[16]

In all other ways Constantine based his teaching entirely on the New Testament. Christ, he held, was a spiritual being who did not take human nature, or even a human body, from His mother Mary and although He was born and lived among men as a man, this was in appearance only. Similarly, the Church which He had founded had no material sacraments; He, with His arms outstretched, was the cross which had brought salvation; He was the living water of baptism which conferred new life; His word was the eucharist – the four Gospels were His body and the Acts of the Apostles His blood.

It is not known whether the Paulicians had an initiation rite and nothing is known either about their forms of worship. At the head of the sect was a *didaskalos*, or teacher, who was guardian of the faith and was assisted by *synekdemoi*, 'companions in the way', a term used in the New Testament (Acts 19:29; II Cor. 8:18–19), and also by notaries. The *didaskaloi* took the names of New Testament figures associated with the Apostle Paul and gave the congregations which they established the names of churches founded by him. Thus Constantine of Mananalis called himself Sylvanus and the church which he established at Cibossa he called Macedonia. Nevertheless, his followers were not called Paulicians after St Paul. The term Paulicians means 'the followers of little Paul/

contemptible Paul', a term which neither the sect nor the Orthodox would have used of the Apostle. Lemerle is probably correct in supposing that the name was given to the sect by its opponents and refers to Paul, the father of the *didaskalos* Timothy, who virtually refounded the movement in the early eighth century after it had been severely persecuted.[17] Although Orthodox theologians referred to the Paulicians as Manichaeans, there is no evidence of any connection between them and that movement (see pp. 7–8). Despite their beliefs the Paulicians were not world-renouncing. They married and had children, they observed no dietary restrictions, they owned property, they exercised lordship if the opportunity arose and they were renowned as fighting men.

Constantine of Mananalis preached first in Armenia and then moved to the Greek lands around Colonea. The Catholicus John of Ojun complained about the spread of Paulicianism in Armenia at the Council of Dvin in *c.* 719, and also reported how the sect had infiltrated Caspian Albania. Up to that time the Paulicians had been persecuted by the church authorities both in Armenia and Byzantium, but the fortunes of the Byzantine Paulicians improved after the *didaskalos* Timothy was put on trial by the Partriarch of Constantinople in the reign of Leo III (717–41). When asked to subscribe to the Nicene Creed Timothy replied that he believed in 'one holy catholic and apostolic church' and acknowledged 'one baptism for the remission of sins', meaning that he believed in the Paulician Church and in Jesus Christ, the living water. Timothy gave satisfactory answers to all the questions because he interpreted them in a Paulician sense, but the Patriarch, who was not aware of this, pronounced him Orthodox. Thereafter the Paulicians were free to preach wherever they wished and a group of them was brought to Europe by Constantine V in 751 to guard the Thracian frontier against the Bulgarians.

The Emperor Michael I (811–13) began to persecute the Paulicians again and to enforce the death penalty against them. Some of them sought refuge with the Emir of Melitene, where they were later joined by their *didaskalos* Sergius. The persecution was intensified after 843, while the Empress Theodora was regent, and more Paulicians then fled to the emirate of Melitene where by the 850s they had established an independent state centred on the fortress of Tefrike. The *didaskalos* Sergius had been murdered by a rival group in 834/5, and, for reasons which are not known, he did not leave a successor and the *synekdemoi* whom he had trained became the religious leaders of the movement. Under the command of their secular ruler Chrysocheir the Paulicans of Tefrike raided deep into Byzantine territory, on one occasion reaching Ephesus. But in 878 the fortifications of Tefrike were badly damaged by an earthquake and it surrendered to the imperial forces of Basil I.

Thereafter Byzantine policy towards the Paulicians changed completely. They were not persecuted any more, but were allowed to live where they wished in the empire, while their fighting men were recruited into the Byzantine army. When John I Tzimiskes reconquered part of Syria he found Paulicians living there under Muslim rule and deported some of them to garrison Philippopolis, thereby increasing their presence in the Balkans. They remained numerous a century later when Alexius I recruited 2,800 of them to defend Dyrrachium against the Normans in 1081. These later Paulicians seem to have ceased trying to make converts, which may well explain the imperial government's change of policy towards them. Euthymius of Acmonia, an eleventh-century Byzantine monk who was paranoid about the spread of heresy, wrote of them: 'their heresy is obvious and cannot harm anyone except those who hold it as an inherited tradition; no one is upset or grieved on their account.'[18] Despite their lack of proselytizing fervour the Paulicians proved remarkably resilient. They survived the Ottoman conquest, and Pietro Cedolini, the Apostolic Visitor appointed by Pope Gregory XIII to the western provinces of the Balkans in 1580, reported that communities of Paulicians were still to be found there.[19]

The Bogomils

Cosmas, an Orthodox Bulgarian priest, writing probably towards the end of the tenth century, records: 'In the reign of the good Christian Tsar Peter (927–69), there was a priest called Bogomil . . . who started for the first time to preach heresy in the country of Bulgaria'.[20] His followers, the Bogomils, were moderate dualists. They believed that there was only one God, but that he had two sons, Christ and Lucifer, the devil. Lucifer had shaped this world from the elements which his Father had made and had imprisoned angelic souls in the bodies of Adam and Eve, from whom all mankind had inherited material bodies, together with angelic souls that wanted to return to Heaven. Christ, God's elder son, had come to earth with the appearance of a man, though in reality he had been a spiritual being. He had taught men about their true condition and had founded the Bogomil Church as a means of liberating their souls from Lucifer's dominion. The early Bogomils rejected the Old Testament completely, but accepted the New Testament as the authoritative basis of their faith. Unlike the Paulicians the Bogomils were ascetic. They rejected sexual intercourse and would not eat meat or drink wine. Cosmas reports that they prayed frequently together by day and by night and confessed their sins to each other, but that the only set form they used was the Lord's Prayer.

Neither in their theology nor in their way of life were the Bogomils at all like the Paulicians. As R.C. Zaehner pointed out, the Bogomil concept of a godhead, consisting of a Father and two sons, one good and one evil, is found in Zurvanite Zoroastrianism, the dominant religion of Sassanian Persia (AD 226–651), and Yuri Stoyanov has suggested that the Bulgars may have become familiar with this system while they were still living on the Russian steppes. The asceticism which Pop Bogomil enjoined on his followers was almost certainly inspired by the Orthodox monastic ideal, and he used the Old Slavonic translation of the New Testament made by the Orthodox. Some of the texts translated into Old Slavonic at Ochrida by the successors of St Clement were Gnostic apocryphal works from the early Christian centuries and, as Stoyanov has pointed out, many of the legendary elements which came to characterize later Bogomil teaching derive from these sources.[21]

Bogomilism was able to spread quickly in Bulgaria because the Orthodox Church had only recently been established there and many people had received little instruction in that faith. After the death of Tsar Peter in 969 Bulgaria was much fought over until, in 1018, it was annexed by Basil II; and during those troubled years Bogomilism spread into the Byzantine Empire. The Byzantine Bogomils were prepared to attend Orthodox services, to which they attached no significance, and, like the Paulicians, to make orthodox professions of faith which they understood in an unorthodox sense. They were more sophisticated than the primitive Bogomils of Bulgaria; they had a *Ritual*, or service-book of their own, and a class of initiates. These were men and women who had been fully instructed in the faith and then received baptism in the Holy Spirit, which was conferred by placing a Gospel book on each candidate's head. Bogomil initiates looked very like Orthodox monks. Anna Comnena, daughter of the Emperor Alexius I, described them in this way:

> You would never see a lay hairstyle on a Bogomil; the evil is hidden under a cloak or a cowl. A Bogomil has a grave expression; he is muffled to the nose, walks bent forward and speaks softly, but inwardly he is an untamed wolf.[22]

Her father, who was worried about the way in which Bogomilism was spreading among some of the great aristocratic families, arrested the leader of the sect in

The church of St Saviour in Chora, Constantinople, restored by Theodore Metochites, c. 1315–21.

Constantinople. He was an elderly doctor named Basil, who was trapped into revealing his beliefs by Alexius's ungenerous claim that he wished to become a Bogomil himself. Basil was examined by the emperor's private theologian, Euthymius Zigabenus, who was writing a compendium about heresy, *The Dogmatic Panoply*. The account which he gives of Bogomil beliefs and practices is by far the most detailed and coherent that we have. One of the most valuable parts of his work consists of the substantial extracts he cites from a Bogomil commentary on St Matthew's Gospel, for this is the only known example of Bogomil exegesis. The trial of Basil took place between 1097 and 1104 and many of his fellow Bogomils were also arrested. The emperor made considerable efforts to convert them to Orthodoxy and succeeded in some cases, but Basil, who refused to recant, was burnt at the stake in a great public spectacle at the Hippodrome in Constantinople, while those of his followers who stood fast in their faith were condemned to life imprisonment.

There is a widely held opinion that the Byzantine Church very rarely used the death penalty for heresy and in this was unlike the Catholic Church of the West, but this seems to be a complete myth. Unrepentant heretics, particularly dualist heretics, were regularly put to death and Byzantine churchmen often urged the secular authorities to enforce the death penalty for heresy, as enacted in the law codes.

Bogomilism spread to Western Europe where it was known as Catharism, and Western sources show that Bogomils began to appoint bishops in the twelfth century. These sources also indicate that a division occurred among the Bogomils at that time. The Bulgarian Bogomils remained moderate dualists of the kind described by Cosmas the Priest, but those of the school of Drugunthia were absolute dualists, who combined that faith with the traditional asceticism, forms of initiation, worship and organization associated with the Bulgarian school. Drugunthia is a western form of the name Dragovitia, a province near Philippopolis, which since the tenth century had been home to a strong Paulician settlement. It therefore seems probable that the Drugunthian form of Bogomilism had evolved under the influence of Paulicians who were absolute dualists.

Papal sources reveal that Bogomilism spread to Bosnia in the twelfth century. Bosnia was part of Catholic Christendom and its ruler, the Ban, was technically a vassal of the King of Hungary. In 1203 the latter forced the seven priors of 'those who up until now have been uniquely privileged to be called Christians in the land of Bosnia', to sign the Agreement of Bolino-Polje drawn up by the legate of Pope Innocent III, in which they undertook to bring their beliefs and practices into conformity with those of the Roman Church. It seems clear from the assurances which were required of them that these men were heads of Bogomil communities whose members styled themselves 'good Christians', just as some of the southern French Cathars did. The Agreement proved difficult to implement and fresh attempts were made by the Papacy with the support of the kings of Hungary to suppress Bosnian Bogomilism until the Mongol invasion of Hungary in 1240–2 brought such intervention to an end. Soon after this the Bosnian Church seceded from communion with Rome. Although it appears to some scholars, including myself, that this happened because Bogomilism had become the established religion of Bosnia by the mid-thirteenth century, other scholars hold that the Catholic Church of Bosnia, wishing to remain independent of Hungarian control, went into schism at that time, while remaining in other ways Catholic in faith, and that Bogomilism did not play any significant role in the country's history. Yet whether as the established Church, or as a dissident group, the Bogomils remained active in Bosnia until the Ottoman conquest of 1463.[23]

The political fragmentation in Byzantine lands consequent on the Fourth Crusade of 1204 made concerted action against the Bogomils impossible, although the Patriarch Germanus II of Constantinople (1222–40), living in exile at Nicaea, did preach vigorously against them, while in 1211 Tsar Boril of Bulgaria, perhaps acting under papal pressure, legislated against them at a Synod at Trnovo. Bogomilism continued to exist in many parts of the Byzantine world throughout the later Middle Ages. In *c.* 1350, for example, another Bulgarian synod at Trnovo condemned a group of absolute dualist Bogomils led by Cyril the Bare-footed, who had been expelled for heresy from Mount Athos. The fate of the Bogomils under Ottoman rule has yet to be determined.

BYZANTIUM AND THE WESTERN CHURCH

Although the popes ceased to be political subjects of the Byzantine emperors in 751 and claimed to be sovereign rulers in the Papal States with the kings of the Franks as their protectors, this did not damage relations between the Churches of Rome and Constantinople. Moreover, although Byzantine opinion was outraged by Pope Leo III's coronation of Charlemagne as Emperor of the West in 800, since this implied that there could be more than one legitimate emperor of Rome, in practice this factor seldom proved ecclesiastically divisive. It was ecclesiastical competition which created new tensions between Rome and Constantinople in the ninth century. When Khan Boris of Bulgaria invited Latin missionaries to work in his country, he asked Pope Nicholas I to advise him about the differences between the usages of the Latin and Greek clergy. In his very detailed reply the pope was critical of the Greeks, which led Photius, Patriarch of Constantinople, to summon a council in 867 to defend the Orthodox tradition. It criticized the Latins for minor differences, such as omitting *alleluia* from the liturgy during Lent, fasting on Saturdays, and celebrating the eucharist with unleavened bread, but the only serious criticism offered was that German clergy working in Bulgaria had made an unauthorized addition to the section of the Nicene Creed defining belief in the Holy Spirit. The text ratified by the Council of Chalcedon had read: 'I believe in the Holy Spirit, the Lord, the giver of life, who proceedeth from the Father'. The Council had anathematized anyone who added to the creed, yet the practice had grown up in the Western Church during the early Middle Ages of adding the words 'and from the Son' (in Latin *Filioque*) to the clause about the Holy Spirit. The Council of Constantinople objected to this addition, not because it was untrue, but because it was unauthorized.[24] It condemned the addition and excommunicated the pope for allowing it to be used in the Western Church, even though at that time it was not used in the papal liturgy.

Pope Nicholas died in 867 before news of the excommunication had reached him and Photius made his peace with Rome, but the issues raised in 867 became part of the standard polemic used in later quarrels between the two churches. Good relations were maintained between Rome and Constantinople until Pope Sergius IV in 1009 included the word *Filioque* in the text of the Nicene Creed, which he sent as a statement of his faith when he wrote to tell the eastern patriarchs of his election. They refused to commemorate him when they prayed for the leaders of the Church at Mass and this marked the beginning of a formal schism between the Catholic Church of the West and the Orthodox Churches.

Relations between the churches became more strained because of events in southern Italy. In 1050 Pope Leo IX held a synod at Siponto in Apulia to enforce his reform programme on the clergy. The Normans had recently conquered this region from the Byzantines and the pope tried to make the Greek clergy acknowledge him as their canonical superior, in place of the Patriarch of Constantinople, and to conform to Latin Catholic norms of discipline and worship by accepting a celibate priesthood and using unleavened bread at Mass. The Patriarch of Constantinople, Michael Cerularius, one of the most autocratic men ever to hold that office, wrote to the Orthodox bishops living in the parts of Apulia still under Byzantine rule criticizing Latin practices. In 1054 Leo IX sent an embassy to Constantinople to demand that the patriarch retract his criticisms. It was led by Cardinal Humbert, who did not consider tact a virtue and, when Cerularius refused to apologise, excommunicated him. The Emperor Constantine IX had no wish to quarrel with the pope, whom he hoped might act as a restraining influence on the Normans. It was no doubt at his suggestion that Cerularius assembled a synod which, while refuting the charges contained in Humbert's bull, adopted the fiction that the legate and his party had not been sent by the pope, but had been acting on their own initiative. No criticism was made, therefore, of the Western Church as a whole. The polemical issues raised by Humbert and Cerularius were not very different from those aired between Nicholas I and Photius 200 years earlier, except in one regard. Cerularius complained to the Patriarch Peter III of Antioch:

> What is the most serious matter of all and the least bearable, and what affords clear evidence of their feeble-mindedness, is this: they say that they have not come here to learn or to discuss anything, but rather to teach us and to persuade us to hold their doctrines.[25]

The monarchical role adopted by the reformed Papacy, however necessary it may have been as an instrument of reform in the Western Church, was something the Byzantine Church was not prepared to accept.

Diplomatic relations were maintained between the Papacy and the Byzantine Empire, and in 1089 Urban II sent an embassy to Constantinople asking for full relations to be restored between the two Churches. This met with a friendly response from Alexius I, who in 1095 asked the pope to appeal for western knights to serve as mercenaries in his armies against the Turks. Urban II developed this request into an appeal for a crusade to liberate the Church of God in Jerusalem and although it was not what Alexius had asked for, the First Crusade was of considerable benefit to him, for with its help he recovered

Christ the Pantocrator, Byzantine mosaic in the apse of the Latin cathedral of Monreale, Sicily, 1180–9.

a large part of western Asia Minor from the Turks at no cost to himself. Yet in the long term the crusades led to a deterioration in relations between Catholics and Orthodox. The problems this caused in the Crusader States will be examined in Chapter Three, but it is necessary here to consider the impact of the crusades on relations between Byzantium and the West. The need to defend the kingdom of Jerusalem led to the launching of new crusades in the West, and the passage of large Western armies through Byzantine territory inevitably caused friction and generated ill will. Moreover, the Byzantines, because of their other commitments, did not always present a common front against Islam with the crusaders. Thus, at the time of the Second Crusade (1147–8), Manuel I made peace with the Turks of Iconium, while at the time of the Third Crusade (1188–92) Isaac II remained allied to Saladin and this led the West to regard the Byzantines as traitors to the Christian cause.

The degree of hostility felt by the Byzantines towards the West was made apparent in 1182 when a revolution, headed by the strongly anti-western Prince Andronicus Comnenus, led to a spontaneous uprising by the people of Constantinople who massacred all the westerners in the city, irrespective of age, sex or status. Western hostility to Byzantium found expression in the sack of Constantinople by the Fourth Crusaders.

The crusade had been launched by Innocent III to attack Egypt. Its leaders had commissioned Venice to provide ships, but they overestimated the number of troops they would need to transport and ended up heavily in debt to the Venetian senate. When the Byzantine Prince Alexius approached the leaders, offering to pay the crusaders' debts, to restore full Venetian commercial privileges in the Byzantine Empire, and to support the crusaders with men and money in their attack on Egypt, if they would first place him on the Byzantine throne, the Doge of Venice and the crusade leadership found the offer attractive. The wealth of the Venetian Republic was largely based on the exemption from payment of tariffs which Alexius I had granted their merchants in 1081 in return for their naval help in his war against the south Italian Normans. Alexius was conscious that in order to deal with that emergency he had given Venice a stranglehold over Byzantine trade and he and his successors throughout the twelfth century tried to restrict or totally rescind those privileges. The Venetians therefore welcomed the possibility of placing a pro-western emperor on the Byzantine throne, who would end this vacillation and safeguard their economic interests.

In 1203 the crusade reached Constantinople and forced the people to enthrone Prince Alexius, but he proved unable to fulfil the extravagant promises he had made.[26] When it became clear that the crusaders and Venetians would not be paid for their help, on 23 April 1204 they forced their way into the city and put it to the sack for three days. They were able to breach its defences because their ships had been allowed to anchor in the Golden Horn. The spoils were immense and part of them may still be seen in the treasuries of many western cathedrals, but particularly in that of St Mark's at Venice. Innocent III was horrified when he learned of what had happened and excommunicated the Venetians for their part in it, but made no attempt to uphold the rights of the Byzantine emperor or the Orthodox Church.

THE LAST CENTURIES OF ORTHODOX BYZANTIUM

The leaders of the Fourth Crusade elected Baldwin of Flanders as Latin Emperor of Constantinople, and he and his vassals soon went on to conquer Thrace and most of mainland Greece. The Venetian doge received part of Constantinople, some important ports and many of the Greek islands, including Crete. He was a sovereign ruler and styled himself 'lord of a quarter and a half of a quarter of the Roman Empire'. The Byzantines founded three independent states in the ruins of their empire: Alexius Comnenus declared himself Emperor of Trebizond; Michael Ducas seized Epirus, where his descendants took the title of Despot; but the chief centre of opposition to the crusaders was at Nicaea in Asia Minor and was led by Theodore Lascaris. He supervised the election of a new Orthodox Patriarch of Constantinople, Michael IV, in 1208 when the see fell vacant, and in return Michael crowned him emperor. Because of this close association with the Orthodox Church the rulers of Nicaea came to be regarded as the legitimate successors of the Byzantine Emperors of Constantinople.

The Venetians had appointed one of their citizens, Thomas Morosini, as Latin Patriarch. Pope Innocent III confirmed this and ignored the rights of the Orthodox Patriarch John X (d. 1207), thereby alienating the Orthodox Church. In Frankish Greece Orthodox bishops were required to recognize papal authority, but the majority refused to do so and went into exile at one of the independent Byzantine courts and their places were filled by Latins. The Frankish settlers formed a new landowning class. They had their own Catholic chaplains and took over a few city churches for their own use, but on the whole the Orthodox priests in the towns and villages were undisturbed: they were placed under the authority of Latin bishops but in other ways their life was unchanged. If they were married they were allowed to keep their wives, and no liturgical changes were imposed on them; they could, for example, continue to use leavened bread at Mass and recite the creed without the addition of the *Filioque*.

Abbots were given the same choice as bishops, of acknowledging the pope or going into exile. Some monastic communities did leave and the Frankish rulers invited monks from the West to take over such houses. The Cistercians, for example, settled in the Orthodox monastery of Daphne outside Athens and the Mendicant Orders set up some new houses in Frankish Greece, but many Orthodox monasteries, particularly small rural ones, accepted papal authority and remained undisturbed.

Although many of the Frankish settlers married Greek wives, their male children kept their fathers' religion and their legal status, so that the Frankish ruling class, while being of mixed blood and often speaking Greek, always remained Catholic.

The Latin Empire of Constantinople proved ephemeral. In 1259 the Emperor of Nicaea, Michael VIII, defeated the Franks and their allies, the Kings of Sicily and Serbia, at the Battle of Pelagonia, and in 1261 he recaptured Constantinople. On 15 August of that year he made a solemn entry and was crowned again in the church of the Holy Wisdom by the Orthodox Patriarch Arsenius. Among the prisoners he had taken at Pelagonia was William II of Villehardouin, Prince of the Morea (as the Latins called the Peloponnese), together with most of his chief vassals. Michael offered to ransom them in return for the cession of four key fortresses in the Peloponnese. The proposal was considered in 1262 by a meeting of the High Court of the Morea which was known as the Parliament of Ladies because only two men were present; all the other participants were the wives or widows of Frankish lords who were administering the fiefs for their imprisoned husbands or minor heirs. They agreed to the terms and as a result a new Byzantine province was established in southern Greece, known as the Despotate of Mistra, since it was there that the governor established his capital.

Michael VIII controlled the former Empire of Nicaea, together with Constantinople, Thrace, northern and central Greece, Mistra and a few Greek islands. The rest of the Morea remained in Frankish control, as did Athens, while Venetian rule in the islands and some ports was unaffected. The problem with the restored Byzantine Empire was that it had extremely long frontiers and comparatively slender financial resources with which to provide for their defence. Michael VIII preserved the integrity of his state by being an unusually capable diplomat. This involved him in relations with the Papacy. When the Byzantines reconquered territory from the Franks they expelled the Latin clergy and restored the Orthodox hierarchy. The Papacy was therefore anxious to restore the Latin Empire, and Charles of Anjou, King of Sicily (1266–85), who being ambitious to build an empire in the eastern Mediterranean, was very willing to support such an enterprise, bought the reversion of his rights from the last Latin Emperor, Baldwin II.

Michael VIII pre-empted an attack by negotiating the union of the Byzantine and Latin Churches at the Second Council of Lyons held by Pope Gregory X in 1274. By this act Byzantium declared itself to be a Catholic power, and Gregory X forbade Charles of Anjou to attack it, for there was no longer any need to restore the Latin Empire if the Greek Empire was Catholic. The union, though successful as a political expedient, produced deep divisions among the Byzantines, who had not forgotten the events of 1204, and it was revoked by Michael's son, Andronicus II, when he became emperor in 1282.

During Andronicus II's long reign (1282–1328) the empire was faced by a revival of Turkish power under the leadership of the Sultan Osman, founder of the Ottoman dynasty, but at that time the ruler of a small principality on the Byzantine frontier in Asia Minor. He was an able general and attracted Turks from other states to serve in his armies. By 1337 the Ottomans had conquered the lands of the former Empire of Nicaea and in 1354 they gained a foothold in Europe by seizing the ruined fortress of Gallipoli. From this base they conquered much of Byzantine Thrace and Macedonia and in 1366 set up their capital at Adrianople. By 1393 Ottoman forces had reached the Danube, thereby alarming Catholic Europe.

Although the Western Church was divided by the Great Schism (see p. 54), both popes supported the launch of a crusade against the Ottoman Turks. It was immensely popular with the chivalric nobility of France, many of whom set off in 1396, led by the son of the Duke of Burgundy whose entourage was equipped with tents of green velvet embroidered with Cyprus gold thread. They were joined by contingents from Italy, England, Castile and Aragon, the German principalities, Bohemia, Poland and Hungary; but this huge Christian army was disunited in leadership, and when it met the professional Ottoman forces at Nicopolis on the Danube on 26 September the crusade was routed.

The Ottomans blockaded Constantinople and in 1399 the Emperor Manuel II came to the West to appeal for aid. He visited Venice and Paris and spent Christmas 1400 at the court of Henry IV of England at Blackheath. Yet although he was received with great sympathy he received no practical help. On that occasion Constantinople was delivered by the intervention of Tamerlane, ruler of Samarkand, who, in the process of creating a world empire, in 1402 attacked Anatolia, where he defeated the Ottoman army at Ankara and took the Sultan Bayezid prisoner. Although Tamerlane died in 1405 and his empire soon disintegrated, Ottoman power was not fully restored until Murad II became sultan in 1422.

Manuel's son John VIII (1425–48) realized that the Ottoman attack on Constantinople would be renewed and that his only possible allies were the Catholic Western powers, whose help would be conditional on the unity of the Churches. He therefore began negotiations with the Papacy which culminated in 1438 when he and the Orthodox Patriarch, Joseph II, led a large Byzantine delegation to the Council of Ferrara/Florence convened by Pope Eugenius IV. After prolonged debate the terms of union were agreed and on 6 July 1439 the act of Union, *Laetentur Caeli (Let the Heavens Rejoice)*, was sung in Latin and Greek by deacons standing in the great pulpit of Florence cathedral. In return the Pope attempted to organize a crusade to relieve Constantinople, but it was decisively defeated by the Ottomans at Varna on the Black Sea coast in 1444.

The city of Constantinople had never recovered from the sack of 1204, while its population had been further reduced by the Black Death in 1347 and there were many ruined buildings inside the walls, including the Great Palace. The later emperors lived in the more modest palace of Blachernae. The wealth of Constantinople, dispersed in the sack of 1204, had never been replenished, and even the crown jewels had been pawned to the Venetians in the fourteenth century. Yet as Bertrand de la Brocquière, envoy of the Duke of Burgundy, found when he visited the city in the early years of John VIII's reign, the court still preserved its ancient rituals with considerable dignity, though with less magnificence than in earlier centuries. He saw the imperial family ride to the liturgy in the church of the Holy Wisdom, the public games held in the Hippodrome to celebrate the state visit of the emperor's brother, the Despot of Mistra, and he attended solemn vespers in the chapel of the Blachernae palace, sung in the presence of the emperor on the feast of Candlemas.

Although imperial power was restricted to the capital and to the principality of Mistra, in theory the emperor was still considered by the Orthodox Church the sole divinely constituted secular ruler on earth and the temporal head of the Christian commonwealth of nations. When in *c.* 1394 Prince Vasili I of Moscow learned that Manuel II was paying tribute to the Ottoman Sultan, he forbade prayers to be made for him in the churches of Russia. This led the Patriarch of Constantinople, Anthony IV (d. 1397), to remonstrate:

My son, you are wrong in saying, 'We have a Church but not an Emperor.' It is not possible for Christians to have a Church and not to have an Empire. Church and Empire have a great unity and community; nor is it possible for them to be separated from one another . . . Our great and holy *autocrator* . . . is most orthodox

The ruins of Mistra, former Byzantine capital of the Peloponnese.

and faithful: he is the champion, defender and vindicator of the Church; and it is not possible that there should be a primate who does not make mention of his name.[27]

The patriarch's powers remained considerable, for he was recognized as their religious leader not only by the Byzantines, but also by the Orthodox in his patriarchate living under Turkish rule, as well as by the Emperor of Trebizond, the Princes of Moldavia and Wallachia, and the Church of Russia. The Church enjoyed the patronage of the imperial family and remained vigorous until the fall of the empire. At Mistra, in particular, fine new churches were built in the fourteenth and fifteenth centuries and were richly decorated with frescoes in the late Byzantine style, while the scholarly

Mistra, the palace of the Despots.

Orthodox clergy who accompanied John VIII to Florence were greatly admired there, in the home of the Italian Renaissance, for their classical learning.

The Union of Florence did not command wide support, and when John VIII died childless in 1448, his brother Constantine XI, who succeeded him and remained faithful to the union, had to be crowned in Mistra, where he was Despot, because it was feared that if the coronation took place in Constantinople most people would boycott the ceremony.

In the fifth year of Constantine's reign the new Sultan, Mehmet II (1451–81), laid siege to Constantinople. He possessed cannon, which rendered the city's defences obsolete, and although the Byzantines resisted bravely for six weeks, the walls were finally breached early on the morning of 29 May 1453. The Emperor charged into the line of advancing Janissaries and was cut down, while the clergy sang the Divine Liturgy in the church of the Holy Wisdom until the Turks broke down the great bronze doors and seized the worshippers.

In Mistra the emperor's brother, Thomas, continued to hold court as Despot until the Ottomans annexed the principality in 1460. Then only Trebizond remained of the Byzantine successor states. The Emperor David Comnenus had been crowned there in 1458 and tried to preserve his independence by allying with Turkish princes in eastern Asia Minor who were hostile to the Ottomans. This policy misfired, for it made him seem dangerous to the Sultan, and in 1461 Mehmet attacked Trebizond in a joint land and sea campaign and the last Byzantine Empire fell on 15 August.

The sultan had a huge number of Christian subjects. In the Asian provinces Christians still made up just under 10 per cent of the population, while the former lands of Trebizond remained almost entirely Christian. In the European provinces, although there was some Turkish settlement, and although some of the subject peoples were converted to Islam, Orthodox Christians remained predominant. In 1453 the Patriarchate of Constantinople was vacant because the pro-unionist Gregory III had already withdrawn to the West. Mehmet nominated in his place the learned George Scholarius, who took the name Gennadius II. He was well versed in Latin as well as in Greek theology and admired the work of St Thomas Aquinas, but he was strongly opposed to the Union of Florence. In 1454 Mehmet issued a Concordat for the Orthodox Church. This enacted that the patriarch should continue to be elected by the Holy Synod in the traditional way, and that the Synod alone should have the power to depose him, though in either case the Sultan's confirmation was needed. The patriarch was made the ethnarch, responsible to the sultan for the obedience of his Orthodox subjects. The Church was granted many legal and fiscal privileges and Mount Athos became in effect a self-governing monastic republic under the sultan's protection.

The quest for perfection which had characterized the Byzantine world was maintained by the patriarch and his court and by the monks of Athos, but its link with the classical Greek tradition, which had given Byzantine religious culture its distinctive character, came to a sudden end with the Ottoman conquest.

CHAPTER THREE

CHRISTIAN RIVALRY IN THE LEVANT AND THE CAUCASUS

The area which stretches from the Sinai peninsula to the Taurus Mountains, bounded to the south-east by the Syrian desert and extending to the north-east through northern Mesopotamia to the Caucasus Mountains, is a region of great ethnic diversity. Throughout the medieval centuries it was also subject to frequent political changes. These factors, though they did not cause Christian divisions, certainly helped to perpetuate them. Consequently, a number of independent churches coexisted there and it is that which makes a separate study of this area essential.

The Patriarchate of Antioch in Late Antiquity

Christianity was already well established in Palestine, Syria and northern Mesopotamia by Constantine the Great's reign. There is evidence to suggest that Abgar VIII of Edessa (177–213) was the first ruler to accept that faith.[1] Nevertheless, there were strong centres of paganism in the region as well, notably at Harran, where the population remained pagan until the Arab conquest, when they began to call themselves Sabians, the name of a people mentioned in the Koran, thereby ensuring that they were tolerated by their new rulers.

The sixth canon of the Council of Nicaea in 325 had named Antioch as the third main see in the Christian Church, after Rome and Alexandria, and in the fifth century the Bishop of Antioch was given the title of patriarch. His jurisdiction in theory extended to all the Christian communities of Asia. Antioch in the fourth century was an important centre of theological studies. In contrast to the theology schools of Alexandria, which emphasized the use of allegory in biblical exegesis (see pp. 138–9), those of Antioch stressed the primary importance of the literal and historical senses of scripture, although they did not exclude other levels of interpretation. This emphasis may have developed as a response to Arianism and was certainly characterized by an insistence on the full humanity of Christ. The most distinguished alumnus of the Antiochene schools was St John Chrysostom (c. 347–407), who was ordained priest in 386 and derived his name, Chrysostom, the golden-tongued, from his eloquence in the pulpit. The Orthodox Church considers his commentaries on the scriptures, mostly first delivered as sermons, as the greatest

8 *Reliquary statue of Ste Foy de Conques, France, tenth century.*

9 *The fall of Lucifer and the rebel angels from Heaven, from the Très Riches Heures of Jean, Duc de Berry, fifteenth century.*

10 *Christ feeding the five thousand, from the Très Riches Heures of Jean, Duc de Berry, fifteenth century.*

11 A sixteenth-century fresco illustrating a scene from the Apocalypse of St John, in the Dionysiou monastery, Mount Athos.

12 Benozzo Gozzoli's fresco of the journey of the Three Holy Kings, Palazzo Medici-Riccardi, Florence, 1459–61.

13 Scenes from the life of St Mark. A thirteenth-century mosaic in the basilica of San Marco, Venice.

works of exegesis that the Church has ever produced. St John spent most of his adult life in Antioch, until he was appointed Patriarch of Constantinople in 398.

The Church of Antioch worshipped in Greek and its scholars taught and wrote in that language, but already a different tradition was developing among the Christians of Mesopotamia. St Ephraem the Syrian (306–73) spent most of his life at Edessa and wrote religious poetry in which he meditated on the Scriptures and explored the ways in which Christians experienced God and His creation. St Ephraem wrote in Syriac, a form of Aramaic which in his day was the vernacular speech of the Edessa area. He used vivid and unusual images to explain God's dealings with men. In one poem he likens God to a man who is teaching a parrot to speak by using a mirror: the parrot will not speak to a man, but he will speak to the other parrot that he sees in the glass. In the Incarnation, God, who is Other, appears among men as a man, like the parrot in the glass, so that men will understand and speak to Him:

> This bird is a fellow creature with the man,
> but although this relationship exists, the man beguiles and teaches
> the parrot something alien to itself by means of itself; in
> this way he speaks with it.
> The Divine Being that in all things is exalted above all
> things
> in His love bent down from on high and acquired from us our
> own habits;
> He laboured by every means so as to turn us all to Himself.[2]

The whole region had a vigorous monastic life. Tradition said that this had begun, as it did in Egypt, with solitaries like St Hilarion of Gaza, who withdrew to the desert before the Peace of the Church and gathered disciples round them. The Judaean Desert proved particularly attractive to monks from the fourth century onwards because of its strong biblical associations, but large numbers of monasteries were also to be found in northern Syria and Mesopotamia. Like the monks of Egypt, many of those in Syria cultivated an austere lifestyle, but in the view of his contemporaries none surpassed St Symeon Stylites. He was born in *c.* 385 in northern Syria and in his youth entered the monastery of Teleda. In 412 he felt a vocation to the solitary life and went to Telanissus, now called Deir Sim'an after him, where he practised great austerities. Then in 423 he had a pillar made, said to have been more than fifty feet high, which he mounted and where he remained for twenty-six years until he died in 459. Standing on his pillar Symeon performed penitential devotions, bending down to pray so that his forehead touched his toes, and his biographer describes how, 'During the public festivals . . . after the setting of the sun until it came again to the eastern horizon, stretching out his hands to heaven he stands all night, neither beguiled by sleep nor overcome by exertion.'[3] St Symeon was considered a holy man whose prayers would be favourably received by God, and people from all over the Levant came to ask him to pray for their needs: some wanted healing, others the gift of children; litigants brought disputes for him to settle; and sometimes envoys came from the imperial court to ask his advice about some

The basilica of St Symeon Stylites, built around the saint's column.

religious controversy. Symeon was credited with oracular powers, the capacity to predict droughts and plagues of locusts and even foreign invasions.

The Church of Antioch was disturbed in the fifth century by disputes about the way in which the divine and human natures of Christ coexisted. These were in part produced by the different kinds of theological speculation fostered by the schools of Antioch and Alexandria and were certainly exacerbated by the rivalry between those sees and the new Patriarchate of Constantinople. In 431 the third General Council of Ephesus deposed Nestorius, Patriarch of Constantinople, for allegedly teaching that there was a division between the divine and human natures in Christ and certainly for refusing the title of *Theotokos*, Mother of God, to Christ's mother, Mary. The decision of Ephesus was a victory for St Cyril of Alexandria and therefore an implied criticism of the schools of Antioch, where Nestorius had been trained. Nestorius's condemnation did not have much direct effect on the Church of Antioch, but indirectly it helped to shape the way in which eastern churchmen responded to the Council of Chalcedon.

This Council, which met in 451 to debate the teaching of Eutyches, that there was only one nature in Christ after the union of his divinity and humanity, accepted the definition of Pope Leo I that Christ was fully God and fully man and that his two natures were united in one person. The word Leo used for 'person' was *hypostasis*, and this doctrine is known as the Hypostatic Union. Eutyches was condemned as a Monophysite, someone who held that there was only one nature in Christ, and that therefore He did not fully share our humanity. Nevertheless, the decision of Chalcedon was viewed with misgiving by many churchmen in the East, because the emphasis which Leo's definition placed on the two natures seemed to imply a Nestorian view of Christ, which had been condemned by the Council of Ephesus. In fact the doctrine of the Hypostatic Union was no different from St Cyril of Alexandria's teaching that Christ had 'one nature after the union', but the western vocabulary in which it was expressed was unfamiliar to theologians in the eastern patriarchates. The majority of the opponents of Chalcedon were 'moderate Monophysites', that is, they were orthodox in their belief that Christ was perfect God and perfect man united in one nature, but they did not consider that the Chalcedonian definition defended that truth. In Syria they found a spokesman in Peter the Fuller, Patriarch of Antioch (470–88). Initially the emperors attempted to remove from office senior clergy who did not subscribe to Chalcedon, but that failed to end the dispute and in 482 the Emperor Zeno issued a formula of union, the *Henoticon*, which was used as an alternative test of Orthodoxy. It consisted of the Nicene Creed, together with condemnations of both Nestorius and Eutyches, but did not contain the Chalcedonian formulae. In the eastern patriarchates many clergy, both Orthodox and moderate Monophysites, were willing to subscribe to this, though it was rejected by the Papacy as a betrayal of Chalcedon, and the Western Church broke off relations with the other partriarchates because of it.

The eastern compromise lasted until Justin I became emperor in 518. He wished to restore full communion with the Western Church and therefore attacked members of the hierarchy who would not subscribe to the decrees of Chalcedon. Among them was Severus, Patriarch of Antioch, who was a gifted theologian and made one of the most lucid defences of the moderate Monophysite position. Justin deposed him in 518, but he

The heavily fortified Orthodox monastery of St Sabas near Jerusalem.

did not die until 538 and the Monophysites continued to regard him, rather than the patriarchs appointed by the emperors, as the true patriarch. In 543, Theodosius, the deposed Monophysite Patriarch of Alexandria, consecrated Jacob Baradeus as Bishop of Edessa and he organized an independent Monophysite hierarchy in Syria and Egypt (see p. 147). The division between the two Churches has never been healed. The followers of Severus call themselves the Syrian Orthodox Church, but are often referred to as Jacobites because their hierarchy was organized by Jacob Baradeus.

The Council of Chalcedon had agreed to the request of Bishop Juvenal of Jerusalem that his church, the mother-church of Christendom, should also be given patriarchal status. It became the smallest of the five patriarchates, with jurisdiction only over Palestine.

The schisms of the sixth century had no apparent harmful effect on the quality of the religious life of the region. Monasticism continued to flourish and new communities were established, such as that of St Sabas near Jerusalem, founded in 478. In the sixth century there were about thirty monasteries in the Judaean desert alone, some of which were huge, like that at Tekoa which had 600 monks.

In *c.* 600 John Moschus, a monk of St Theodosius in Judaea, set out with his friend Sophronius to visit the monasteries of the Levant and wrote a record of their journey called the *Pratum Spirituale, The Spiritual Meadow*. This provides an account of the state of the religious life of the region in the last years of Christian rule there and is full of charming anecdotes. Among them is a cautionary story about class consciousness told by a woman solitary, Lady Damiana, who had persuaded a well-to-do kinswoman to accept alms from a poor woman who gave away what little spare money she had for the love of God. The rich lady had taken two small coins reluctantly, but had bought and eaten vegetables with the money and had found them the best she had ever tasted.[4]

Very soon after John Moschus made this journey war broke out between Persia and Byzantium. The Persians overran all the eastern provinces, capturing Antioch in 611. In 614 they captured Jerusalem and carried off the relic of the True Cross to Ctesiphon. The Persians went on to conquer Eygpt and it was not until 629 that the Emperor Heraclius was able to force them to withdraw and to restore the frontier to where it had been before the war. On 21 March 630 Heraclius brought the Holy Cross back in triumph to Jerusalem, carrying the reliquary into the city on his own shoulders.

Yet the Christian restoration was short-lived, for in *c.* 633 the Arab invasion of Syria began. By 635 Damascus had fallen and in 636 the Arabs defeated a large Roman army at the River Yarmuk. In 638 John Moschus's companion, the monk Sophronius, who had become Patriarch of Jerusalem in 634, wept as he admitted the Caliph Omar to the city. The Arabs' advance into Syria and Palestine may not have been so orderly as their historians, writing much later, claimed it had been, but by the time Heraclius died in 641 their victory was almost complete. Antioch had fallen, as had much of Egypt, and the Taurus Mountains had come to mark the effective south-eastern frontier of Byzantium.

Antioch and Jerusalem from the Arab Conquest to the First Crusade

The Arabs, newly converted to Islam, were willing to tolerate the adherents of other religions which, like their own, believed in one God and had a written revelation. As Garth Fowden has commented, they had '[a] readiness to accept that the Earthly City could not wholly anticipate the Heavenly City's austere Muslim character . . .'.[5] They organized their non-Muslim subjects in accordance with their religion and made the religious leaders responsible for the obedience of their followers. As a result of this policy the schism between the Orthodox and the Jacobites was perpetuated and both communities enjoyed equal rights in the Arab Empire. Indeed, the Arabs preferred the Jacobites (Syrian Orthodox), who had no links with Byzantium, and referred to the Orthodox as Melkites, a term meaning 'the Emperor's men'. Both communities were allowed to elect their own patriarchs freely, but their appointments had to be confirmed by the Caliph and that normally entailed the payment of a large gratuity.

The population of Antioch was strongly Hellenized and had remained predominantly Orthodox; the Orthodox Patriarch therefore retained control of the cathedral and of most of the churches in the city. At first the patriarchs had to live in exile in Constantinople, but in 742 the Caliph Hisham allowed the Patriarch Stephen III to return. There were Orthodox populations in many of the other cities of northern Syria, including Damascus, and some communities in rural areas as well. An Orthodox hierarchy was preserved there, but the Orthodox were far outnumbered by the Jacobites who had a huge following, particularly in rural areas and in the mountains which stretched from the anti-Taurus north of Antioch across to the Tur Abdin on the Tigris frontier. Their patriarch did not have a fixed see: he claimed the throne of St Peter at Antioch and lived in exile in one of the many Jacobite monasteries. At the height of its power in the seventh and eighth centuries the Jacobite Church of Antioch had twenty metropolitans, 103 bishops and a large number of monasteries.

In Jerusalem the patriarchate remained in Orthodox hands, and, indeed, most of the Christian population of Palestine remained Orthodox as well.

The Orthodox and the Jacobites shared a common heritage. Both accepted the Nicene Creed as their profession of faith and although the Jacobites rejected the Council of Chalcedon their Christology was not heretical. They called themselves Syrian Orthodox, because their worship was conducted exclusively in Syriac, which,

The interior of the St Sabas monastery in 1839, painted by David Roberts.

when they first adopted it, was the vernacular of many people in north Syria. During the Middle Ages Arabic came to be spoken almost everywhere, except in a few villages, so Syriac became a learned language known only to the clergy. The Byzantine Orthodox, or Melkites, worshipped in Greek, although during the Middle Ages their rural clergy too came to use Syriac. This sometimes makes it difficult to know whether sources which describe congregations as 'Syrians' are referring to Jacobites or Melkites. Despite the fact that many of their clergy used Syriac, all senior officers in the Melkite churches, bishops, abbots and cathedral canons were Greeks.

In 661 the Caliph Muawiya I founded the Umayyad dynasty and fixed his capital at Damascus. The Umayyads caused very little disturbance to the social order over which they presided, which, as Peter Brown remarks, they described as 'a garden protected by our spears'.[6] They did not encourage conversions to Islam and at that time restrictive laws against Christians probably did not exist but certainly were not enforced. Of course, non-Muslims had to pay additional taxes, but monks were sometimes exempted from the poll tax by the Umayyads. The art and learning of the Christians was esteemed by their new rulers, and Christian architects and artists were employed to build some of the cult centres of the new faith, like the Dome of the Rock at Jerusalem and the Umayyad mosque at Damascus. An example of the degree of freedom which Christians enjoyed at this time is afforded by St John of Damascus. Born in c. 675 he held a post at the Umayyad court which had previously belonged to his father, then in c. 725, when he was about fifty years old, retired to the Orthodox monastery of St Sabas in Judaea, where he spent the rest of his life writing a prodigious number of theological works in Greek. Not only was he the chief apologist for the cult of the icons in the Orthodox Churches (see, p. 67), he also discussed the problem which Islam constituted for Christians. If, as St Paul had held, 'God was in Christ reconciling the world to Himself', then there was no room for any further revelation, yet the Prophet Muhammad claimed to have received a direct revelation from God. St John argued that Muhammad had misunderstood Christianity and that therefore Islam was a Christian heresy. It is remarkable that this argument should have been advanced by a former servant of the caliph writing in the Islamic Empire.

St John of Damascus died in c. 750 at a time when a great change was taking place in the Muslim world. The Abbasid revolution, which originated in Persia, brought a new dynasty of caliphs to power who had a different understanding of Islam and a different attitude to the conversion of subject peoples. The Umayyads had considered that Islam was a religion for Arabs and there had thus been no advantage to non-Arabs in accepting it. The Abbasids regarded it as a universal religion and granted equal rights to converts. This meant that the tax burden was reduced for converts and that in theory equal social opportunities were available to them. In the reign of the Abbasid Caliph al-Mutawakkil (847–61) the first evidence is found of restrictions on the religious and social freedom of Christians: they might not build new churches, they needed special permission to repair existing churches; they should not practise their faith publicly in places where Muslims lived; and they should wear distinctive clothes and not ride horses. Moreover, when in 762 the caliph moved his capital from Damascus to Baghdad, the Melkites and Jacobites were no longer naturally present at the centre of power. All these factors, together with the attraction of the new faith, may have contributed to the large number of conversions to Islam which occurred among both the Melkite and Jacobite communities in the period c. 800–950. Thereafter Christians ceased to be a majority in Syria and Palestine, though they remained a very substantial minority and in some areas were still dominant. The restrictive laws were not uniformly enforced. Christians, for example, continued to hold public processions in many parts of Syria on great feast days, which the Muslim rulers often came to watch.

During the later ninth century Abbasid power began to fragment. In 909 the Hidden Imam of the Ismaili Shi'ites appeared at Kairouan in Tunisia and declared himself caliph, and by 969 his descendants had gained control of all Muslim Africa and had fixed their capital at Cairo. They were known as Fatimids because they claimed descent from the Prophet's daughter, Fatima. Concurrently the Byzantines launched a new offensive in the East. In 934 they captured Melitene, and attacks on Edessa were only abandoned when in 944 the Muslim governor forced the Christians there to surrender the Mandylion to the Byzantines. This was a cloth which bore the likeness of Christ; it was said that Christ himself, during his life on earth, had imprinted his features on it and sent it as a present to King Abgar. There was no relic more highly revered in the Christian world except that of the True Cross, and when the Emperor Romanus I brought it in triumph to Constantinople in 944 this added greatly to the prestige of Byzantium as defender of the Christian world.[7] In 965 the Emperor Nicephorus II captured Cilicia and Cyprus and that was a prelude to the recapture of Antioch in 969. In 975 John I Tzimiskes campaigned in the East and reached Nazareth, but died in the following year before he could build on this victory.

Instead the Fatimid Caliphs took over Palestine and all the lands as far north as Damascus in 978. The Emperor Basil II in 1001 made a treaty with the Fatimid Caliph al-Hakim (996–1021), by which the frontier between the two powers was fixed to the south of Latakia. al-Hakim's mother was an Orthodox Christian and his father, al-Aziz (975–96), had appointed her brother Orestes as Orthodox Patriarch of Jerusalem when the see fell vacant in 986. al-Hakim, unlike the rest of his dynasty, was violently anti-Christian and in 1009 ordered all Christian churches in his dominions to be destroyed, including the Holy Sepulchre. These orders were only partially effective, and the policy was certainly abandoned later in al-Hakim's reign, for he allowed a new patriarch of Jerusalem, Theophilus, to be appointed in 1012. Basil II was unable to intervene in Syria at this time because he was in the middle of a war with Bulgaria, and he merely renewed the treaty with Egypt when it expired in 1011. al-Hakim vanished in 1021. The circumstances of his death are not known, but the Druzes of Lebanon, who regard him as their founder, consider that he was taken up living into paradise.

After 969 the Byzantines were able to exercise direct control over the Patriarchate of Antioch once more, and they tried to force the Jacobites to conform to Byzantine Orthodoxy. This led the Jacobite patriarchs to spend most of their time in Muslim territory, where they were not liable to Byzantine harassment.

The Orthodox of Jerusalem, who were in communion with Constantinople, welcomed Byzantine protection. Hakim's successor, the Caliph az-Zahir (1021–36), renewed his father's treaty with Byzantium, and his son, al-Mustansir (1036–94), allowed

The entrance to the grotto of the Nativity, the Church of the Holy Nativity, Bethlehem.

the Emperor Michael IV (1034–41) to send Greek craftsmen to rebuild the church of the Holy Sepulchre at Byzantine expense (see p. 219). It was probably at this time that other Orthodox churches were built or rebuilt in Fatimid territory, among them the convent of Our Lady of Saidnai'a to the north of Damascus. The township was, and remains still, an Orthodox Christian enclave. The fortified convent of Saidnai'a is served by a community of Orthodox nuns, and a small Orthodox monastery of monks is attached to the same complex. The earliest sources state that it was founded in 1059 and it became an important pilgrimage centre because the nuns' chapel contained a miraculous icon of the Blessed Virgin, which on her feast days exuded oil which had healing properties and was distributed in phials to pilgrims. From the beginning it attracted Muslim as well as Christian pilgrims, for among Muslims there is a devotion to Mary the Mother of Jesus, arising from what is said of her in the Koran.

The favourable conditions which existed for Christians in the patriarchates of Jerusalem and Antioch in the mid-eleventh century were changed by the Turkish invasions. The Turks were a central Asiatic people, many of whom in the late tenth century were converted to Islam and took service in the armies of the Muslim rulers of the eastern Islamic lands. Under the leadership of princes of the house of Seljuk the Turks staged a number of successful military coups and took over the government of much of eastern Islam, and, in 1058, led by Toghril Beg, they entered Baghdad where the caliph recognized Toghril as the Sultan, or temporal administrator, of the caliphate. Toghril's successors consolidated their power in Iraq and then moved west, defeating the Byzantine field army at Manzikert in 1071, thereby opening up Asia Minor to their incursions. They also took over the inland regions of Syria and Palestine; by 1079 Jerusalem had a Turkish governor. In 1086 Antioch, together with much of Byzantine north Syria, was conquered by the Turks. The Turks were not in principle hostile to Christians, but they were not familiar with them, and they tended to treat them harshly. Symeon II, Orthodox Patriarch of Jerusalem, went into voluntary exile in Byzantine Cyprus in 1095 because of the harassment he suffered from the Turkish garrison of the city. It was this growth of Seljuk power which led the Byzantine Emperor Alexius I to make an appeal to Pope Urban II in 1095 for western troops to serve in his armies. This was the catalyst which led to the preaching of the First Crusade.

Antioch and Jerusalem from the First Crusade to the Ottoman Conquest

As a result of the victorious campaigns of the First Crusade, four Frankish states were established in the early years of the twelfth century, extending in an arc from northern Mesopotamia to the Sinai peninsula: the County of Edessa, the Principality of Antioch, the County of Tripoli and the Kingdom of Jerusalem. Part of Urban II's motivation in organizing the Crusade seems to have been a desire to restore good relations between the Holy See and the Orthodox Churches (see p. 91) and when Antioch was captured in 1098 his legate, Bishop Adhémar, recognized the Orthodox Patriarch, John IV as having canonical authority over all Latin Catholics as well as Orthodox Christians in his jurisdiction. This decision was not challenged at the time, for John IV was a war-hero because the Turks had suspended him from the walls of Antioch in an iron cage during the long siege. But Adhémar died a few weeks later during an epidemic, Pope Urban died in July 1099 and his successors did not share his vision of Church unity in which the Orthodox hierarchy enjoyed parity of rights with Catholics.

Indeed, when Jerusalem was captured in 1099 the first decision which the crusader leaders made was to appoint a Latin patriarch. The Orthodox Patriarch, Symeon II, was known to them; he was living in exile in Cyprus and had cooperated with Adhémar in appealing to the West for reinforcements. He died at about the time Jerusalem was taken, but the crusaders ignored the Greek canons of the Holy Sepulchre, who were still in Cyprus, to whom the right of choosing a new patriarch canonically belonged. The crusader princes found it natural to appoint western Christians to church offices in the newly founded states, and even John IV did not last long at Antioch. The Byzantine Emperor Alexius I claimed that Antioch should be restored to him as part of the former lands of his empire and made war on Prince Bohemond I when he refused to hand over the city. John IV was a Byzantine Greek and Bohemond was unwilling to keep him in a position of power while he was at war with Byzantium. In 1100 he forced John to leave and appointed a French Catholic, Bernard of Valence, as patriarch; John went to Constantinople, where he resigned his office and retired to a monastery.

The Crusader leaders established the Catholic Church in all the territories they conquered. They regarded their Orthodox subjects as members of the same church as themselves but this worked to the disadvantage of the Orthodox. In the patriarchate of Antioch, for political reasons, the Franks evicted all the Orthodox bishops and replaced them by Latins. In the Kingdom of Jerusalem, which was not at war with the Byzantines, the crusaders were willing to allow Orthodox bishops to remain if they were prepared to accept the authority of the Latin Patriarch, though in such cases they were reduced to the rank of coadjutors, or assistants, to the Latin bishops in whom all real power was vested. The Orthodox parish clergy were left in peace. They had to accept the authority of Latin bishops, but otherwise were allowed to keep their churches and property, to celebrate public worship either in Greek or Syriac in the customary way, and to observe Orthodox rites and practices. The Orthodox therefore continued to have married priests and to celebrate Mass with leavened bread. Orthodox monasteries were left undisturbed and the Abbot of St Sabas became the most important representative of the Orthodox community in the Crusader Kingdom.

At the time of the First Crusade Orthodox bishops had only been found in dioceses where substantial Orthodox communities had survived, so the crusaders could not simply take over the existing Orthodox organization. Instead, they established a Catholic hierarchy throughout their lands, under the authority of the two Latin Patriarchs, and absorbed the Orthodox population into this new form of organization. The Latin Patriarchs were not merely in communion with the pope, but were made subordinate to him. Only one Latin patriarch in the Crusader States challenged this assumption: Ralph of Domfront, the second Latin Patriarch of Antioch (1135–40), claimed that he was a colleague of the pope; but this merely shortened his career by ensuring that his political opponents received the full support of the Papacy in securing his deposition.

Although the Frankish population was not large, they built a huge number of Catholic churches and chapels not only in the cities, but in the villages of the Latin states as well, as the recent work of Denys Pringle has shown. They also established Catholic monasteries, chiefly in Jerusalem, to serve the Holy Places, but some elsewhere, such as the royal convent of Bethany, a house of Benedictine nuns in Judaea, the Cistercian monastery of Belmont in the County of Tripoli, and the Benedictine monastery of St Pauls at Antioch. In addition, as recent work by Benjamin Kedar and Andrew Jotischky has shown, many Catholic solitaries settled in the Crusader States. Some lived in cells on the walls of Jerusalem, others among the ruined tombs outside the city; large numbers lived in the woods on the slopes

The keep of Chastel Blanc (Safita) in northern Syria, built by the Knights Templar.

The castle of Marqab in Syria built by the Knights of St John.

of Mount Tabor in Galilee, and others on the Black Mountain of Antioch which was already the site of many eastern–rite monasteries and hermitages.

The Crusader States also produced a new kind of monasticism, that of the Military Orders. The Knights Templar were recognized as an independent religious Order in 1128 through the support of the leading Cistercian abbot, St Bernard of Clairvaux. Its members took the three traditional vows of poverty, chastity and obedience, but instead of devoting their lives to contemplative prayer, they were dedicated to fighting for the defence of the faith. Initially their chief work was that of patrolling the pilgrim routes in the Holy Land to keep them free from bandits, but as their numbers grew they came to form an important part of the army of the kingdom and to be responsible for garrisoning certain key fortresses.

The Knights of St John, or Knights Hospitaller, evolved from a hospital which had been founded before the First Crusade to care for western pilgrims in Jerusalem. It grew in wealth and popularity and in 1112 was recognized by the Papacy as an independent religious Order, and at some point in the second quarter of the twelfth century it developed a military wing, probably in imitation of the Templars. The Order of St John continued to perform charitable work as well, founding a number of hospitals. The Order's mother-house at Jerusalem was responsible for one of the largest hospitals in the Christian world, which had over a thousand beds and also regularly distributed free food and clothing to destitute pilgrims. But the military functions of these Orders became increasingly important, and by the second half of the twelfth century the Templars in their white mantles with red crosses and the Hospitallers in their black mantles with white crosses came to form an important component of crusader armies.

In the thirteenth century the Teutonic Knights, founded in 1198, came to share in the defence of the Holy Land, as did other, smaller Orders, like the English Order of St Thomas of Acre, founded at the time of the Third Crusade.

The Byzantine Emperors were not prepared to accept the latinization of the churches of Jerusalem and Antioch, and appointed to both sees titular patriarchs who lived in Constantinople. This was chiefly because the Byzantines did not wish to lose the dominant position which they had held for centuries in the pentarchy of patriarchs in whom they believed that authority in the Church was vested. The appointment of titular patriarchs may also have been a pastoral necessity, because Orthodox communities in places such as Damascus were the subjects of Muslim rulers who would not have allowed them to recognize Latin Patriarchs. In 1165 the Emperor Manuel succeeded in

The crusader cathedral of Our Lady of Tortosa in Syria.

restoring the Orthodox Patriarch Athanasius Manasses of Antioch to his see in return for paying the ransom of Prince Bohemond III, who had been taken prisoner by Nur ad-Din of Damascus. Athanasius was enthroned in St Peter's cathedral and his Catholic rival, Aimery of Limoges, was forced to live in exile in the castle of Cursat. But the change was not popular with the Franks, who were relieved when Athanasius was killed in an earthquake in 1170 and Aimery was able to return. Manuel also attempted to restore the Orthodox Patriarch Leontius II of Jerusalem in 1177–8, but was unsuccessful and in 1180, in order to preserve good relations with Catholic rulers in the West, agreed to accept the Latin incumbents as the rightful patriarchs of Antioch and Jerusalem.

Manuel upheld the rights of Orthodox Christians living in the Crusader States by other means. For example, he paid for the church of the Holy Nativity at Bethlehem to be embellished with mosaics executed by Byzantine craftsmen, which may still be seen in the nave. They represent the General Councils of the Church and are an assertion of Orthodoxy, because the text of the Nicene Creed is displayed in Greek in its original form, without the addition of the *Filioque* clause, even though these mosaics were made for display in a Catholic cathedral. Manuel also restored some of the Orthodox monasteries in the Judaean desert.

The Jacobites fared rather better under Frankish rule than the Orthodox. The crusader leaders had been unprepared for the variety of Christian confessions which they encountered when they conquered Antioch in 1098 and wrote asking the pope to come and deal with the religious problems in person. When he failed to do so, they took a pragmatic approach, tolerating all forms of Christianity among their subjects. Michael III, Jacobite Patriarch of Antioch (1166–99), was amazed by Frankish tolerance which contrasted so markedly with the doctrinal intransigence of the Byzantines:

> The Franks never raised any difficulty about matters of doctrine or tried to formulate it in one way only for Christians of differing race and language, but they accepted as Christian anybody who venerated the cross, without further examination.[8]

Because they did not consider the Jacobites part of their own Church, the Franks allowed them complete freedom to choose their bishops and respected their property rights. They sometimes went to unusual lengths to do so. When the First Crusade reached Jerusalem in 1099 the Jacobite community fled and two of their estates were granted to a Frankish knight named Geoffrey. Soon after this he was captured in battle by the Fatimids and imprisoned in Egypt and the Jacobite Bishop of Jerusalem, who had returned, received his estates back. Then, in 1137, during an armistice, Geoffrey was released by the Egyptians and returned to Jerusalem, where he was fêted as a surviving companion of Godfrey of Bouillon. Yet when he tried to recover his estates, King Fulk and Queen Melisende were unwilling to antagonize the Jacobite community by sequestering them and arranged for the Jacobites to give him a money compensation instead.

When the Franks attempted to conquer Egypt in the reign of King Amalric (1163–74) they became even more friendly towards the Jacobites, whom they considered might prove useful allies because they were in full communion with the

Coptic Church of Egypt. Michael the Syrian, who became Jacobite Patriarch in 1166, visited Jerusalem twice and was honourably received by the Franks, and he was also on excellent terms with Aimery of Limoges, the Latin Patriarch of Antioch, even though he claimed to be the lawful Patriarch of Antioch himself. He stayed in the city twice, in 1168–9 and again in 1178, and on the second occasion Aimery invited him to attend the Third Lateran Council in Rome in 1179. Although he declined to go, Michael sent a tract against the Cathar heresy (which has sadly not survived) which was on the council's agenda. This invitation suggests that Aimery of Limoges, who was a well-trained theologian, did not consider Michael the Syrian unorthodox.

Although the Franks had large numbers of Muslim subjects they made no attempt to evangelize them. Despite their massacre of Muslims in Jerusalem in 1099, the Franks were thereafter remarkably tolerant of their Muslim subjects. While they evicted most of them from the cities, because they considered them a security risk, rural Muslim communities were allowed to be self-governing under their own headmen and to worship freely. They were required to pay a religious tax to the crown, but in other ways had considerable freedom; some villagers from the Nablus region, for example, were able to make the pilgrimage to Mecca.[9] Consequently there was no decline in the number of Muslims in rural areas under Frankish rule.

In 1187 the Franks were defeated by Saladin at the Battle of Hattin and despite the best efforts of the Third Crusade commanded by Richard I of England were unable to recover most of their former territories. By the treaty between Richard and Saladin which ended the war in 1192 the Crusader Kingdom was reduced to a strip of coastal territory stretching from Jaffa to Tyre, though most of the County of Tripoli remained in Frankish hands, together with the city of Antioch and its environs. The Latin Patriarch of Jerusalem went to live in the new crusader capital of Acre and an Orthodox Patriarch returned to the Church of the Holy Sepulchre in Jerusalem although Saladin allowed a few Latin priests to stay there to minister to Western pilgrims. The Latin Patriarch remained at Antioch, and Latin clergy stayed in those areas which were still under Western control, but non-resident Orthodox Patriarchs of Antioch continued to be appointed, while in places with Orthodox populations which had reverted to Muslim rule an Orthodox hierarchy was re-established.

Relations between Latins and Orthodox in the Crusader States in the thirteenth century were embittered by events elsewhere. On his way to the Holy Land in 1191 Richard I had annexed Cyprus, a Byzantine island, which became a Frankish kingdom ruled by the Lusignan family. Frankish families from the mainland, dispossessed by Saladin, emigrated to Cyprus, ejected the Greek nobility, and came to form the new landowning class. The people of Cyprus were all Orthodox Christians of the Byzantine rite, and although at first the Orthodox Church was left in peace, in 1222 the Papacy insisted that a Latin hierarchy should be set up there. Only four Orthodox bishops were allowed to remain as coadjutors to the Latin bishops, and they were required to accept papal primacy. This caused widespread unrest, because relations between the Orthodox Church of Constantinople and the Papacy had been embittered by the events of the Fourth Crusade and consequently many Cypriots were unwilling to recognize bishops who had submitted to Rome (see pp. 93–4).

The Court of the Chain, or royal customs house, in the crusader city of Acre, now the Khan al-Umdan.

These events made the Orthodox still living under Frankish rule in the Crusader States hostile to the Latin hierarchy in ways which they had not previously been. James of Vitry, Catholic Bishop of Acre (1216–28), complained that the Orthodox in the city did not believe that Latin consecrations of the eucharist were valid, which is a classic symptom of schism. Pope Innocent IV (1243–54) attempted to solve the problem by empowering his legate, Lorenzo da Orte, in 1246 to free the Orthodox of Antioch, Jerusalem and Cyprus from the authority of Latin bishops. Under this plan the Orthodox Patriarchs of Jerusalem and Antioch and the Orthodox Archbishop of Cyprus should have control over their own clergy and people and be directly responsible to the pope. This common-sense solution was welcomed by David, the Orthodox Patriarch of Antioch (1245–58), but in the long term failed because it was opposed by the Latin hierarchy who were not willing to undergo the loss of revenue and prestige that such a policy would entail.

In 1268 Antioch was captured and sacked by the Mamluks who had come to power in Egypt in 1250 (see p. 150). An Orthodox Patriarch was restored, while the Latin Patriarch Opizo went to live in the West and appointed vicars to administer the parts of his diocese which remained in Frankish hands. In 1274 the Council of Lyons brought all the Orthodox Churches officially into communion with Rome (see p. 95). Because the Patriarchate of Antioch was vacant the Byzantine Emperor Michael VIII appointed Theodosius of Villehardouin to that office. He was a member of the Frankish princely family of the Morea, who had been converted to Orthodoxy and was living as a monk on the Black Mountain of Antioch. Michael thought rightly that he would favour the union, but his adhesion was short-lived because the new Emperor Andronicus II revoked the agreement of Lyons in 1282 and the eastern patriarchs followed his lead.

Frankish relations with the Jacobites grew distant after the death of their pro-Western Patriarch Michael III in 1199. Very few Jacobites lived under Frankish rule in the thirteenth century and their leaders were concerned to remain on good terms with the Muslim rulers of north Syria. But in 1236, at a time when Jerusalem had briefly been restored to crusader control, the Jacobite Patriarch Ignatius II came there on pilgrimage and was officially received into the Catholic Church by Philip, prior of the Dominicans, who had recently established a house there. Similar conversions were subsequently made among other Jacobite clergy, and Pope Gregory IX (1227–41) gave permission for Catholic prisoners of war held at Aleppo to receive the sacraments from Jacobite priests if no Latin clergy were available. Yet the majority of Jacobites had not entered into communion with Rome and these conversions could have seriously divided their Church. This did not happen because Pope Innocent IV gave those converts a faculty 'to dwell among their own people and be in communion with them'. This illustrates the important difference which existed between medieval Catholic rulings about the

Acre, thirteenth-century capital of the crusader kingdom. The walls were rebuilt in the nineteenth century.

reception of separated Christians into the Church and the policies of the post–Tridentine Papacy: in the Middle Ages popes were concerned to establish corporate reunion, whereas in modern times the emphasis has been on individual conversions. The Patriarch Ignatius was very well disposed towards the Latins. He had a palace built at Antioch and lived there from 1238 until his death in 1252. Thereafter, perhaps partly because of the Frankish loss of Antioch, Jacobite relations with the Franks became more distant, and they ceased altogether when the Mamluks seized the remaining crusader strongholds in 1291.

A permanent Catholic presence in the Holy Land was permitted once again in 1336 when, in response to requests from King Robert of Naples, the Sultan of Egypt allowed the *Custodia Terrae Sanctae*, administered by the Franciscan Order, to set up its headquarters in Jerusalem to minister to western pilgrims. Like all Muslim authorities the Mamluks extended toleration to their Christian subjects, but they did not view them at all favourably, because they had supported the Mongols when they invaded Syria in 1260 (see p. 150). During the centuries of Mamluk rule there was a marked decline in the strength of the Christian communities of Syria and Palestine. Orthodox Patriarchs continued to be appointed to Jerusalem and Antioch and to preside over their diminished flocks. In 1439 Dorotheus of Antioch and Joachim of Jerusalem assented to the act of union with the Western Church negotiated at the Council of Florence; but four years later, at a synod in Jerusalem attended also by the Orthodox Patriarch of Alexandria, the oriental patriarchs withdrew from communion with the pope.

In 1517 the Ottoman Sultan, Selim I, conquered the Mamluk Empire and all four Orthodox patriarchs were, for the first time since the seventh century, once again subject to the same secular authority.

The Maronites

When the First Crusade advanced down the Syrian coast in 1099 it was joined by Christians from Mount Lebanon. These good fighting men were Maronites. There are conflicting accounts of their origins. The Maronites themselves claim that they received the Orthodox faith from the followers of St Maron (d. *c.* 410), a hermit who lived near Aleppo, and whose followers founded an important monastery, dedicated to the saint, at Apamea. They claim that they chose a patriarch of their own in the late seventh century at a time when there was no resident Orthodox Patriarch at Antioch after the Arab invasions (see p. 106) and that most of them had later migrated to Lebanon in order to maintain their independence. However, all non-Maronite sources suggest that in the seventh century the community later known as Maronite had supported the *Ecthesis* issued by the Emperor Heraclius in 638 in an attempt to heal the Monophysite schism. The emperor had worked out this formula in consultation with Monophysite leaders. It asserted that in Christ there were two natures, human and divine, but only one divine will. This doctrine became known as Monotheletism and met with strong opposition from some Orthodox Christians as being contrary to the teaching of the Council of Chalcedon. It was condemned at the sixth General Council held at Constantinople in 680–1, but the Maronites refused to accept that ruling and seceded from the Orthodox

The Maronite monastery of Mar Kozhaya in Lebanon.

Church, appointing their own patriarch whom they claimed was lawful Patriarch of Antioch.

There is no doubt that by the time of the crusades the Maronites formed an independent Church, most of whose members lived in the mountains of Lebanon. Like the Jacobites they worshipped in Syriac and used a version of the Orthodox liturgy of Antioch. They were unusual among Christians living under Islamic rule in being warriors, which was a consequence of the independence they enjoyed in their mountain strongholds.

Most of the Maronites lived in the Latin Patriarchate of Antioch and in 1181 the Patriarch Aimery of Limoges held discussions with the Maronite Patriarch Peter, which led to the Maronite Church entering into communion with the Papacy.[10] William of Tyre, the contemporary historian of the Crusader States, reports this and although the union was less total than he makes it appear, his account does seem to be substantially accurate. In 1183, when a new Maronite Patriarch, Jeremiah al-Amshitti, was appointed, he went to Rome, presumably to receive papal confirmation. Saladin's conquests interrupted the negotiations between the two churches, but by the treaties of 1192 the Maronites remained under Frankish rule, so that relations with the Papacy could be resumed. In 1203 Pope Innocent III sent a legate, Cardinal Peter of S. Marcello, to discuss the implementation of the union with the Maronite leaders. The Patriarch Jeremiah was still in office and in 1215 attended the Fourth Lateran Council in Rome at which Innocent issued the bull *Quia Divinae sapientiae* (so called from its opening words 'Because, through the Divine Wisdom . . .') which set out the conditions of the union.

The Maronites were to profess full doctrinal agreement with the Catholic Church and they also undertook to bring certain rites and usages into conformity with Catholic norms, for example, by standardizing the ingredients used in making the oil of the chrism. The patriarch should receive a *pallium*, to signify that he was in communion with the pope, and should owe obedience directly to the pope and not to the Latin Patriarch of Antioch. The patriarch should continue to have jurisidiction over the Maronite hierarchy and his church should preserve its liturgy, organization and canon law in so far as these were compatible with Catholic principles. In other words, the Maronites became a uniate Church, that is, a Church in full communion with Rome which retained its own autonomy and traditions.

As K.M. Salibi has argued, the Maronite Union was at first divisive. It was welcomed by those Maronites who lived in the coastal cities and had close dealings with the Franks, but was viewed with suspicion by the Maronites in the mountains who had little contact with their Frankish rulers. Some Maronite bishops refused to accept the union, and a schism persisted within the Church throughout the time of Frankish rule. But after the Mamluks conquered Tripoli in 1289 they treated the Maronites very harshly and this had the effect of making all of them view the union with Rome more favourably, as a means of enlisting Western protection. Communications with the Western Church were conducted through the Franciscan priory established at Beirut in the early fifteenth century and in 1439 the Maronite Patriarch John appointed the Franciscan prior of Beirut as his representative to the Council of Florence. There the Maronite Union was ratified and the prior returned with a *pallium* for the patriarch. The Franciscans of Beirut worked among the Maronite clergy, seeking to bring their practices into conformity with Catholic usage. The union was preserved and in 1514 Pope Leo X described the Maronite Church as 'protected in the midst of infidelity and heresy as the roses are protected among the thorns'.[11]

Although the full implementation of the changes desired by Rome was not effected until after the Synod of Lebanon in 1736, there was never any wish on the part of the Maronites to abandon the union after the Council of Florence. The Maronites are unusual in being the only Eastern Church which has entered into communion with the Holy See as a body; there are no Maronite separatist groups.

The Mount Sinai Monastery

In the early Christian centuries Mount Sinai, where God had given the law to Moses, was identified with Jebel Musa in the south of the Sinai peninsula. In the fourth century this became a place of pilgrimage; chapels were built there and it and the surrounding region attracted many monks and hermits. They were vulnerable to attack by beduin, which led Justinian towards the end of his reign to build a great fortress monastery at the foot of the mountain, around the chapel of the Burning Bush. The monastery was dedicated to the Mother of God and a large garrison was stationed nearby, not only to protect the monks, but also to monitor beduin movements.

During the Christological controversies of the sixth and seventh centuries the Sinai monastery remained firmly Orthodox. It produced some notable writers, such as St John Climacus (d. *c.* 649), the author of *The Ladder of the Divine Ascent*, a treatise on the spiritual discipline of the monastic life. At some point the bishops of Pharan went to live in the monastery, and after a time their office merged with that of abbot of the house.

When the Arabs conquered the Sinai the community was treated with great respect because the Muslims recognized Moses as a prophet and held in reverence the burning

The Mount Sinai monastery, fortified by Justinian I (527–65).

bush where God had first called him and Mount Sinai where God had given him the law. The monks of Sinai were protected by the caliphs and were allowed not only to keep their estates, but also to retain lordship over the peasants who worked them.

At some time, perhaps in the ninth century, a new cult grew up in the monastery, that of St Catherine of Alexandria. She was said to have been a Christian philosopher, who defeated many learned pagans in public debate and was martyred at Alexandria on the orders of the Emperor Maxentius (306–12). Her body was carried to Sinai by angels and centuries later was found by the brethren resting on top of a nearby mountain. They placed it in a sarcophagus and translated it to the choir of their church. On occasions when the tomb was opened the saint's bones were found to have exuded oil which had healing properties and phials of it were given to pilgrims. St Catherine of Alexandria was probably unique among saints in becoming the major patron of a monastery which had originally been dedicated to Our Lady, but she gave her name to the Sinai monastery. The enormous prestige which she came to enjoy in the churches of East and West was expressed iconographically by giving her three haloes, white for her virginity, green for her learning and red for her martyrdom.[12]

The West came to know about her early in the eleventh century when the community sent brethren there to collect alms and found a generous patron in Richard II, Duke of Normandy (996–1026). Symeon, a monk from Sinai, presented a phial of the wonder-working oil of St Catherine to the Duke's foundation, the monastery of the Holy Trinity at Rouen, and Western Christians began to want to visit her shrine. Paradoxically, it became more difficult for them to do so after the First Crusade had conquered the Holy Land. The Fatimid Caliphs of Egypt were naturally anxious to exclude the Franks from the Sinai, and the Caliph al-Amir commissioned a mosque to be built inside the compound of St Catherine's monastery. His commander, al-Afdal, presented it with a pulpit in 1106 and as Moritz has suggested, this mosque was almost certainly not built for the convenience of Muslim pilgrims but for the use of Egyptian troops stationed in southern Sinai to fend off Frankish attacks.

As Fatimid power grew weak in the 1160s the Frankish lords of Transjordan established a protectorate over the southern Sinai and encouraged pilgrims to visit the monastery. This came to an end when Nur ad-Din's lieutenant, Shirkuh, became master of Egypt in 1169, thus uniting Damascus and Egypt under a single ruler. The importance which Shirkuh attached to controlling the Sinai monastery may be gauged from the fact that one of his first acts as ruler of Egypt was to confirm its privileges and abolish the new taxes which had recently been imposed on the community. Yet although St Catherine's then became more difficult of access for western pilgrims, throughout much of the rest of the twelfth century relics of the saint continued to reach Europe by a variety of routes and devotion to her shrine was kept alive.

In the thirteenth century, after the Franks had lost control of Transjordan, western pilgrims to Sinai were no longer perceived as a threat by the Muslim authorities. Among those who went there was the German pilgrim Thietmar in 1217, and he reports how he saw the chapel of the Burning Bush which contained a golden replica of the bush, surmounted by an image of Christ, with a golden statue of Moses kneeling beside it. This shrine was venerated by Muslims as well as Christians and all the worshippers

The west end of the church of the Mount Sinai monastery, built c. 550. The bell-tower was added later.

removed their shoes before entering the chapel. The Abbot of Sinai opened the sarcophagus of St Catherine so that Thietmar might venerate her relics and receive some of the holy oil. Thietmar also climbed the many hundred steps to the top of Jebel Musa, traditionally revered as the place where God had given Moses the tablets of the law.

Unlike most Orthodox in the thirteenth century, the Sinai community was anxious to remain on good terms with the Western Church because it owned extensive estates in Venetian Crete and in other parts of Frankish Greece. The Papacy took those lands under its protection and throughout the Middle Ages considered the Mount Sinai monastery as the one part of the Orthodox Church which had remained in continuous communion with Rome. The abbots of Sinai did indeed have western sympathies: in the final years of crusader rule, for example, they commissioned a substantial number of icons from painters trained in the western tradition, working at Acre.

When the Mamluks came to power in Egypt in 1250 they also treated the Sinai community with respect, which contrasted with the hostility they showed to most of their Christian subjects. This seems to have been because the community possessed a letter of commendation which purported to have been written by the Prophet Muhammad himself. It appears to have been forged by the community as an instrument of protection, possibly in the reign of the anti-Christian Caliph al-Hakim (996–1021). It was regarded as genuine by later Muslim rulers, and perhaps by that time by the monks as well, and led to their being well treated.

Pilgrims from the West continued to visit the monastery although they had first to obtain permission from the Mamluk Sultan, and a special chapel was set aside for the use of Catholic clergy. Some of the Western noble pilgrims had copies of their coats-of-arms placed in the monastery compound where they may still be seen. One of the pilgrims was the very talkative German Dominican, friar Felix Fabbri from Ulm. He records how in 1483, as his party was about to leave the house, the abbot sent a message to say, 'A piece of the tomb of St Katherine had been broken off by an iron instrument; if we delayed to restore it, the Arabs, into whose hands he would put the matter, would see to it that we did so without delay.'[13] The desire for relics clearly remained strong among western pilgrims throughout the Middle Ages.

When the Ottomans conquered Egypt in 1517, the Sinai community presented Muhammad's letter of protection to the Sultan Selim I, who kept it and had a copy made for them. As a result they continued to enjoy the favour of the Islamic rulers. In 1575 the Holy Synod of Constantinople recognized the Archbishop-abbot of Sinai as head of an autocephalous church, that is, of one which has no religious superior. The St Catherine's monastery in that way became the smallest autonomous church in the Orthodox communion.

The Armenian Church

In late antiquity Armenia was an independent kingdom sandwiched between the empires of Persia and Rome. Christianity probably first reached the region of Taron from Edessa in the third century, but it did not reach the court until St Gregory the Illuminator was consecrated Bishop of Armenia by the Archbishop of Caesarea and converted King Tiridates III. This event was traditionally dated to 301, but it is now generally accepted that it happened in 314. That is, it occurred after the conversion of Constantine and may have been inspired by it, but it does not materially alter Armenia's claim to be the first state to become Christian, for although in the Roman Empire Christianity was tolerated after 312, it did not become the established religion until eighty years later, whereas Tiridates made it the religion of his kingdom when he was baptized and proscribed pagan cults, although, of course, it took time to enforce that decree. In 387 Armenia lost its independence and was partitioned between Rome and Persia. Initially client kings were allowed to rule there, but the Romans imposed direct rule in 389 and the Persians in 428.

By that time Christianity was firmly established throughout Armenia and the Church was a major force in preserving the identity of the Armenian people. St Sahak (*c.* 390 – *c.* 440) secured permission from the Byzantine Emperor for the Armenian Church to be freed from the control of the Archbishops of Caesarea and be placed directly under the authority of the Patriarchs of Constantinople. He and his successors fixed their see at Ejmiazin and took the title of Catholicus. One unique feature of Armenian Church government was that all the Catholici down to the death of Gregory VI in 1203 were members of the family of St Gregory the Illuminator. During the fourth century the Armenians had worshipped in Greek, but between 392 and 406 St Mesrob, with the help of a team of Syrian and Greek scholars, devised an Armenian alphabet. It then became possible to translate the Bible and service books of the Church into the vernacular and work was also begun on translating the works of the Greek Fathers. Many of these translations were made in monasteries which in Armenia, as everywhere else in the Christian world, occupied an important place in the life of the Church.

The Armenians took part in the first three general councils of the Church and accepted their rulings but they were not represented at Chalcedon in 451 because at that time the Shah of Persia, Yazdigerd II (439–57), was seeking to impose Zoroastrianism in Armenia, which led to the persecution of Christians and widespread revolts there. The Catholicus of Ejmiazin was a Persian subject and the Armenian Church's lack of interest in Chalcedon is readily comprehensible. Like many other Christians in the Near East the Armenians refused to accept the canons of Chalcedon, but their initial reasons for this were that they had had no part in formulating them. In the sixth century the Armenian Church aligned itself more positively with the moderate Monophysites. In 506 a Church Council at Dvin accepted the *Henoticon* of the Emperor Zeno, designed as a conciliatory measure acceptable both to the Orthodox and to the opponents of Chalcedon (see p. 103); but at a second Council of Dvin in 555 the Armenian Church specifically rejected the Council of Chalcedon. Like the moderate Monophysite churches of the Syrian Jacobites and the Egyptian Copts, with whom it had good relations, the Armenian Church was suspicious of the terms in which the definitions of Chalcedon had been formulated, which they all thought verged on Nestorianism.

Byzantine rule was established in most of Armenia in the reign of the Emperor Maurice (582–602), who tried to impose Chalcedonian Orthodoxy on the Armenian Church. This caused great discontent and may have been one of the factors which enabled the Arabs to gain control of the Armenian provinces between 641 and 661, since they were uninterested in the kind of Christianity their subjects professed. Until *c.* 700 the Arabs allowed the Armenians a large measure of self-government, but after that they began to place garrisons there in order to defend their empire against the attacks of the Khazars from north of the Caucasus. When the Abbasid revolution took place in 750 the Armenians revolted against Arab rule and ejected their garrisons. This independence movement was suppressed in 772 and large numbers of Muslims were settled in Armenia by the Abbasids, which led many Armenians to emigrate to Byzantine territory.

Some Armenians did support Chalcedon; they were found chiefly in the provinces which bordered on north Syria and those along the Georgian frontier. But there was no schism in the Armenian Church at that time, and no rival hierarchies were set up by pro- and anti-Chalcedonians as happened in Syria and Egypt. A large number of Armenians lived in the Roman provinces of Eastern Anatolia and Armenian groups were found throughout the Byzantine Empire, but they preserved their cultural and religious identity, building churches in which the liturgy was celebrated in the Armenian rite. For many centuries they did not have a separate hierarchy in Byzantine lands, but were subject to Orthodox bishops. Likewise, the Byzantines did not appoint Orthodox bishops when they recovered Armenian territory, but accepted the Armenian hierarchy. Clearly both sides hoped that it might be possible to unify their churches and talks to that end were regularly, though unsuccessfully, held.

In the second half of the ninth century, as the Abbasid Caliphate grew weaker and as the Byzantines began to expand towards the east, the Armenians were able to play off the two powers against each other and regain their independence. In 884–5 the Bagratid King Ashot I was recognized both in Constantinople and Baghdad. He made Ani his capital and the Catholicus of Ejmiazin lived in his dominions. In 908 a southern Armenian Kingdom was founded at Vaspurakan, with its capital at Aghthamar. The new rulers in both kingdoms were generous patrons of the Church and much new building was undertaken. In this period a formal schism developed between the Armenian and Byzantine Churches; the Byzantine authorities expelled non-Chalcedonian communities of Armenian monks from Anatolia and they went to live in Vaspurakan, while other Armenians living in the Empire renounced the authority of Greek bishops and set up an independent Armenian hierarchy.

Armenian independence came to an end as a result of Byzantine eastward expansion under Basil II, who annexed Vaspurakan in 1021–2. By 1045 the whole of Armenia had been annexed by the Byzantines. The emperors, in an effort to weaken Armenian opposition, transferred some of the noble families to Anatolia, particularly to the province of Cilicia. Armenian troops were also enlisted in the Byzantine armies and were used to garrison some of the cities of northern Syria. Byzantine dominance was very short-lived, for in 1071 the Turkish victory over the main Byzantine army at Manzikert led the Byzantines to lose most of their Asian provinces. Since Armenian commanders, some of them holding office in the Byzantine administration, were in key positions and since the Turkish occupation of Asia Minor was a very piecemeal affair, what were in effect independent Armenian principalities came into being after 1071 in an arc of territory stretching from Edessa through Melitene and Marash to the Taurus Mountains.

When the First Crusade reached eastern Anatolia in 1097 it was greatly helped by the Armenian lords who guarded some of the chief approach roads to Antioch. Relations between the Franks and the Armenians were often ambivalent in the twelfth century. In one way the Armenians were natural allies: they were Christians and good fighting men and the Franks intermarried with members of their aristocracy. Queen Morphia of Jerusalem, the wife of King Baldwin II (1118–31), was the daughter of the Armenian Prince Gabriel of Melitene. On the other hand the Franks quarrelled with the Armenians over possession of land: they seized Edessa from its Armenian ruler during the First Crusade and throughout much of the twelfth century the princes of Antioch struggled with the Armenian lords in the Taurus for control of the Cilician plain and its cities.

By contrast, relations between the Armenian Church and the Catholic Church were on the whole very cordial. Like other Eastern Christians the Armenians living in the Crusader States were allowed complete religious freedom by the Franks. The Armenians had not had very close dealings with the Western Church before the crusade, but they had a tradition that a pact had been made between the two Churches by St Gregory the Illuminator and St Sylvester of Rome. St Nerses the Gracious, in his *Elegy on the Fall of Edessa,* written after 1144, apostrophized the Roman See:

> And you, Rome, Mother of Cities,
>   Brilliant above all and honourable,
> You throne of the great Peter,
>   first among the apostles;
> You immovable church,
>   built on the rock of Cephas,
> Invincible at the doors of hell,
>   and breaker of the seals of heaven,
> Becoming vine of many branches,
>   and Paul's firmly-rooted tree,
> Besprinkled with his blood
>   like paradise, which is in Eden . . .[14]

St Nerses became Catholicus in 1166, but he wanted union with the Orthodox rather than with the Latins. The Catholici had abandoned their traditional see at Ejmiazin because of Turkish raiders in 1065, and in 1150 the Catholicus Gregory III bought the great castle of Hromgla on the Euphrates from Beatrice, Countess of Edessa. The Catholici remained there after the Turks conquered the area and in that way enjoyed some measure of independence from the political pressures exerted by Armenian rulers. Discussions about church unity were held at Hromgla in 1170–2 between the Armenians and a Byzantine delegation led by the theologian Theorianus. These proved inconclusive, because St Nerses died before they had been completed. His successor, Gregory IV, negotiated directly with the Patriarch of Constantinople who stipulated that union could only be restored if full dogmatic agreement was reached. In 1179 a synod was held at Hromgla, attended by thirty-three Armenian bishops, which drew up a profession of faith acceptable to the Orthodox, but this only reached Constantinople after the Emperor Manuel's death in 1180 and because of the political turmoil which ensued it was never followed through. Thereafter Byzantine military influence waned in the eastern frontier region and the Armenians began to look towards Rome as a source of help.

Prince Rupen III (1175–87) was the real founder of the Armenian state of Cilicia. Armenian princes had controlled the mountain area since the 1070s, but Byzantine garrisons were only finally evicted from the coastal cities in Rupen's reign. He opened negotiations with Pope Lucius III, to whom he sent an embassy in *c.* 1184. The pope clearly considered this a token of recognition of his authority and in return sent the Catholicus Gregory IV a *pallium* and a copy of the *Rituale Romanum*, implying that the Armenian Church was now in communion with the pope and that it should bring its customs into conformity with Catholic usage. The *Ritual* was translated into Armenian by St Nerses of Lampron, Armenian Archbishop of Tarsus. He was one of the younger Armenian prelates, who has had close dealings with the Franks and favoured union with Rome. He had been trained as a monk in an Armenian monastery on the Black Mountain of Antioch, where he has learned Latin, Greek and Syriac. He had then stayed in Antioch and been invited by the Latin patriarch to preach in the Catholic and Orthodox churches there, and had come to admire the orderly way in which the Latins performed the liturgy and also the charitable organizations which they had set up to feed the poor and care for the sick.

Negotiations with Rome were interrupted by the conquests of Saladin and the events of the Third Crusade, but Cilicia remained independent and grew in importance in Western eyes because of this. Rupen's successor, Leo II (1187–1219), wished to make himself king. It was generally supposed in Christian countries in the Middle Ages that only an emperor could create a king, and in 1195 Leo opened negotiations with the Western Emperor, Henry VI, who was about to come on crusade. Henry welcomed this overture, which would strengthen his own position in the Levant, and although he died in 1197 and his crusade did not take place, the creation of the Cilician kingdom went ahead. Henry VI had stipulated that the coronation of Leo should be conditional on the union of the Armenian Church with the Papacy, and so on 6 January 1198 the pope's legate, Conrad, Archbishop of Mainz, set out the terms of the union, and this declaration was signed by twelve Armenian bishops who undertook to convene a council and secure the assent of all their colleagues. The imperial chancellor, Bishop Conrad of Hildesheim, then crowned Leo II. The union existed on paper, but proved impossible to implement. The majority of bishops, who lived in old greater Armenia, had no contact with the Franks and no interest in union with the pope, particularly since it involved accepting changes in traditional practices. Although the difficulties of convening a representative council of the Armenian Church when its hierarchy were the subjects of different and antagonistic rulers were undoubtedly considerable, the impression is given by some sources that there was no will among most Armenians for reunion on the terms which the pope envisaged. Whereas the Papacy in the thirteenth century thought of its role in the Church in monarchical terms, the Armenians, even those who, like St Nerses of

Jonah is thrown to the whale. An Armenian manuscript miniature of 1286.

Lampron, were sympathetic to Western Catholicism, thought that the Church universal was made up of independent regional churches (the Church of the Latins, the Church of the Greeks, the Church of the Armenians), bound together by a common faith and reverencing the pope as successor of St Peter, the senior bishop and elder brother of the universal episcopate. So the years passed and the Armenians made no attempt to fulfil the conditions laid down by the pope in 1198.

A crisis developed as a result of the intervention of the Mongols in the affairs of the Near East. In 1243 their victory over the Turks in Asia Minor made them the near neighbours of the Armenians in Cilicia. King Hethum first sent his constable to offer his submission to the Great Khan and then in 1253 himself went to the court of the Great Khan Möngke at Karakoram. The Mongols were delighted by this, for although they always demanded the submission of all the kings of the earth, Hethum was the first king who had ever voluntarily come to their court. Möngke therefore freed the Armenian Church throughout his dominions from all payment of tax. Consequently, when in 1260 the Mongols invaded Syria, King Hethum joined with them and persuaded his son-in-law, Prince Bohemond VI of Antioch, to do the same. The Mongol general, Kitbuka, was a Christian and having defeated the Egyptian governor he entered Damascus in triumph in 1260 flanked by King Hethum and Prince Bohemond. The Papacy objected to Christian rulers, particularly those like Hethum who were officially in communion with the Holy See, giving allegiance to the pagan Great Khan. The confrontation between the Armenian Church and the Papacy was conducted in religious terms, even though the real issues at stake were political ones. The pope's legate in Acre, Thomas of Lenton, convoked a synod to which the Armenians were invited, to consider why they had failed to fulfil the conditions of the union. King Hethum sent a representative who was hostile to Catholic claims, the doctor Mekhitar, who complained that Rome wished to sit in judgement on other churches, but refused to be judged by them, and this caused the discussions to break down. It appeared at that stage that the Armenian union with Rome was at an end.

Yet as the power of the Egyptian Mamluks increased later in the century, the Cilician kings looked once more to the West for help. In 1292 the Mamluks captured the fortress of Hromgla, siezing the Catholicus Stephen VI, who died in captivity. His successor, Gregory VII, moved his see to Sis, the capital of Cilicia, and in 1307 convoked a synod there, which agreed to accept all the changes required by the Papacy as conditions of unity with the Western Church: that the Armenians should accept as canonical the seven General Councils and in particular their Christological teachings and that they should also make various liturgical and disciplinary changes. The Church and the crown could see that it was essential to have western aid and that submission to Rome was the price which must be paid for this. That view was not shared by Armenians already living under Muslim rule, who refused to implement these changes. Indeed, the Armenian Bishop of Jerusalem was made a Catholicus in 1311 as a protest against the westernizing tendencies of the Catholicus at Sis.

As the fourteenth century progressed western influences became stronger in Cilicia. In 1342, as the result of intermarriage between the Armenian royal family and the Lusignan kings of Cyprus, Guy of Lusignan, the cousin of the previous king, Leo IV, succeeded to the throne of Cilicia, and although in deference to his subjects he took the name Constantine II, he had a French-speaking court. Cilicia became very isolated after the Mamluks captured the last Armenian-held port, Ayas, in 1347, but the Armenians continued to control the Taurus Mountains. In 1375 King Leo V withstood a long Mamluk siege in his capital, Sis, but was finally forced to surrender. Initially he was held prisoner at Cairo, but was later freed and went to Paris, where he died in 1393.

The Catholic Mendicant Orders came to work among the Armenians in the fourteenth century, trying to promote union with Rome. The Franciscans established a province in Cilicia in 1292, and the Dominicans worked in Greater Armenia, where in 1356 they established an Order called the Brethren of Unity. These were Armenian monks who had come into communion with Rome and used the Catholic liturgy in an Armenian translation. For their benefit the works of the Dominican scholars, St Albert the Great and St Thomas Aquinas, were translated into Armenian. In 1438 Constantine, Catholicus of Sis, licensed a group of Armenian clergy to represent his Church at the Council of Florence, where in November 1439 they and Pope Eugenius IV reached an agreement which reiterated, though in more detail, the points made by the Synod of Sis of 1307 about the adoption of doctrinal and ritual changes by the Armenian Church. Like all previous attempts it produced no lasting result, and indeed seems to have precipitated the restoration of the Catholicusate of Ejmiazin in 1441 as a protest against the unionist policies of Constantine of Sis.

During the medieval centuries the Armenian Church came to develop a very distinctive character. Its liturgy derived from the ancient Greek rite of Caesarea, with some Antiochene influence, but its vernacular language and distinctive chant and ritual have made it into something very different from the Orthodox liturgy. The Armenian Church has certain features which differentiate it from other Eastern churches; it celebrates the eucharist, as the Western Catholic Church does, with unleavened bread; it does not mix water with the wine in the chalice at Mass; and it has no separate commemoration of Christ's birth – Christmas Day and the Epiphany are kept as a single feast on January 6th, which is a very ancient Christian observance. Monasticism occupied a central place in the medieval Armenian Church, with communities founded in large numbers throughout Old Great Armenia and also in the Taurus Mountains of Cilicia and on the Black Mountain of Antioch. The Armenian hierarchy developed an office not found elsewhere in the Christian world, that of vardapet; this term designated a learned monk, who was in Holy Orders and who was entrusted with a teaching office in the Church. He might instruct boys in the monastery schools, but he might also preach to lay people. Armenian religious culture found expression in the building of fine churches, in manuscript illumination, of which a wide range of examples has been preserved, and also in the production of theological and poetical works by scholars like St Gregory of Narek in the tenth century and St Nerses the Gracious and St Nerses of Lampron in the twelfth.

Western people who came to know them were very impressed by the austere piety of some of the Armenian clergy. Burchard of Mount Sion, a Catholic pilgrim who visited the court of the Catholicus at Hromgla in *c.* 1280, relates:

I stayed with him for fourteen days . . . In his diet, his clothes and his way of life he was so exemplary that I have never seen anyone, religious or secular, like him . . . all the clothes that he wore were not worth . . . [fifty pence] and yet he had exceeding strong castles and great revenues and was rich beyond any man's counting. He wore a coarse, red sheepskin pelisse, very shabby and dirty, with wide sleeves, and under it a grey tunic, very old and almost worn out. Above this he wore a black scapular and a cheap rough black mantle. . . He and all his prelates used to fast all Lent on bread and water, and so did the king and his nobles.[15]

The Armenian Church also developed its own forms of piety. One distinctive example of this is a prayer to be said for men who 'are addicted to rash swearing', by which is meant not profanity, but the impulsive taking of oaths which cannot, and perhaps should not, be observed, such as oaths to be avenged on one's enemies:

O God who knowest the nature of man to be changeable and weak, and dost truly know the designs and intentions which issue from our understanding, that they are the result of our fraud and deceitfulness; as thou art not vindictive, do thou make worthy of forgiveness those who have presumed to contaminate themselves with an oath. For thou alone dost know the secret things of our hearts. We beseech thee to afford remission of sin unto them and unto us, through thy unspeakable benevolence. For praised is thy name and glorified the kingdom of Father and Son and Holy Spirit, now and ever and to eternity of eternities. Amen.[16]

The Church of Caspian Albania

King Unayr of Caspian Albania is said to have been baptized by St Gregory the Illuminator. The Albanians had their own language and St Mesrob is said to have devised an alphabet for them, with the help of an Albanian called Benjamin. The liturgy could then be celebrated in the vernacular. Although the Albanian alphabet is known, none of the works written in the language have survived. The chief source for the history of the kingdom is an Armenian work, traditionally attributed to Moses Dasxurançi, a tenth-century scholar, but which appears to have been compiled and re-edited between the early eighth century and c. 1100. From this it is known that, probably as early as the fifth century, the Albanian Church had its own Catholicus. His see was initially at Derbent, but was transferred to Partaw in 552 to escape the raids of the pagan Khazars.

The Albanian Church rejected the Council of Chalcedon, and when the Georgian Church accepted that Council in 608 the Albanians supported the Armenians in severing communion with them. Armenian influence there was clearly strong, for when the Catholicus Nerses showed pro-Chalcedonian sympathies, the Armenian Catholicus Elias (703–17) came to Albania and presided at a synod at which Nerses was deposed. The rulers of Albania were pro-Byzantine. At the time of the Arab invasions Prince Jvañser offered his submission to the Emperor Constans II (641–68) who gave him the honours of a consul but during the eighth century Albania came under Islamic control.

The church of Mtskheta, Jvari in Georgia, built between 586 and 606.

The Albanian Church retained its vitality in these troubled years. In 682 an Albanian Bishop, Israel, led a successful mission to the Khazars, and in the early eighth century the Albanian Church outlawed the Paulician heretics who had appeared there (see pp. 85–7). The *History of the Caucasian Albanians* ends with a list of their Catholici and the lengths of their reigns. The last of them is Moses, prior of the monastery of P'arisos, who reigned from 983–9. In the following centuries the whole area of Albania became islamicized and the Albanian Church, with its distinctive language and liturgy, died out completely.

The Church of Georgia

In late antiquity there were two Georgian kingdoms, that of Iberia in the east and in the west the kingdom of Lazica on the Black Sea coast. Tradition, recorded by the church historian Rufinus writing in *c.* 380, credits the conversion of Iberia to a woman, St Nino. She is said to have been a Christian slave who by her miraculous powers of healing and prediction converted King Mirian and his wife, who then sent to Constantine the Great for priests to baptize them. She is, I think, the only woman to whom the courtesy title of Apostle has ever been given. Françoise Thelamon has called

The tenth-century church in the citadel of Kvetera, Georgia.

the historicity of this story into question and her views have gained general acceptance.[17] It is now agreed that Christianity reached Iberia from Antioch, probably in the reign of Constantine the Great, and that the court was converted then and a cathedral built in the capital, Mtskheta. In *c.* 400 the versatile St Mesrob devised an alphabet for Georgian, a non–Indo-European language. This made it possible to begin translating the Bible and the works of the Greek Fathers into the vernacular. King Vachtang of Iberia (d. 522) gave his support to the *Henoticon* of Zeno, thereby avoiding involvement in the controversies about the Council of Chalcedon. During his reign, in 486–8, the head of the Iberian Church was made a Catholicus, and it was at this time that the Greek liturgy was translated into Georgian and used in public worship. Vachtang also moved the capital to Tiblisi (Tiflis), together with the cathedral. The kingdom of Lazica had become largely Christian by 500, though the king was not baptized until 522. Conversion is, of course, a relative term. Large areas of both kingdoms were still pagan in the mid-sixth century when thirteen priests came to Iberia from Antioch to carry out an intensive programme of evangelization. In 608 the Catholicus Cyrion I accepted Chalcedonian Orthodoxy and this caused the Churches of Armenia and Albania to sever communion with the Georgian Church.

The Iberian monarchy was abolished by the Persians in the late sixth century, and thereafter the Georgian people were ruled by local princes under the hegemony of foreign powers. Although the frontiers varied a good deal because of almost constant warfare, broadly speaking the western Georgian provinces remained under Byzantine control while the eastern provinces were ruled first by the Persians and, after 653–4, by the Arabs. The Georgian Church, with its vernacular liturgy, undoubtedly helped to keep alive a sense of Georgian identity in those centuries. Western Georgia became virtually independent under King Leo II in 767–8, but it was not until 888, when the Abbasid Caliphate had grown weak, that the Iberian kingdom was revived under Adarnase IV. In 1008 Bagrat III, who claimed to be descended from King David of Israel, united both realms and for the first time there was a single Georgian kingdom.

King David III (1089–1125) was ruling at the time of the First Crusade and was able to profit from the problems which the Crusade caused to the Turkish princes of Syria in order to expand his own kingdom. In 1117 he forced the ruler of Shirvan to become his vassal, thus extending his power to the Caspian, and in 1123–4 captured the old Armenian capital of Ani and pushed his border southwards. During the twelfth century Georgia consolidated her dominions and continued to expand until the reign of Queen Thamar (1184–1212), whose armies captured Kars in 1209 and even attacked Tabriz in northern Persia in 1210. Queen Thamar also helped David and Alexius Comnenus, who had grown up as refugees at her court, to establish an independent Greek Empire at Trebizond in 1204.

The twelfth century was the golden age of Georgian civilization. The Church was very strongly influenced by Byzantium. An important link between the two traditions was the Georgian monastery of Iviron, founded on Mount Athos in *c.* 971, the recipient of many benefactions from the Georgian kings. The Georgian Church had, by the central Middle Ages, adopted the Byzantine liturgy, but used it in a Georgian translation and had a distinctive form of chant. From the start there was a strong monastic tradition,

The early thirteenth-century church of Tinotesubani, Georgia.

and Georgian rulers had made foundations not only in their own kingdom, but also on the Black Mountain of Antioch and in Jerusalem and its environs, where the monastery of the Holy Cross, founded in *c.* 1040, was particularly important. The Georgian kings were generous patrons of the Church in their own lands. David III built the cathedral of Ghelati and a monastery attached to it, which had a notable school, headed by John Petritzi (d. *c.* 1125), a Neoplatonist scholar who had been trained in Constantinople by John Italus. There was also a flourishing school of secular poets in twelfth-century Georgia, the most remarkable of whom was Shota Rustaveli. His epic *The Knight in the Panther Skin*, written in *c.* 1200, is contemporary with the work of some of the best Provençal troubadours and shares with them a similar convention of courtly romance, but shows a far higher degree of sensibility.

This period of Georgian history came to a sudden end in 1222 when the kingdom was attacked by a large Mongol army. Although they did not occupy Georgia, the Mongols caused immense damage and wrecked its prosperity. In the reign of Queen Rusudan (1223–45) the Mongols returned. They imposed the same settlement on

Georgia as they were to do on Christian Russia a few years later: the ruling house was left in power, but was required to pay an annual tribute in money and also in men to serve in the Mongol army. The Mongols encouraged rivalries within the royal family as well, so that for much of the thirteenth century Georgia was once again divided into several principalities.

By the early fourteenth century the power of the Mongols in western Asia was growing weak and King George VI (1314–46) of Georgia was able to unite his country once again and to begin to restore its prosperity and civilization. The work proved short-lived, for in 1386 Georgia was invaded by Tamerlane, who sought to make himself ruler of the whole of Asia. He sacked Tiblisi and took King Bagrat V captive. After Tamerlane's death in 1405 Georgia once more asserted her independence. As the power of the Ottoman Turks grew greater, so the Georgians strengthened their links with Byzantium and in 1438 a metropolitan and a bishop from the Georgian Church formed part of the Byzantine delegation to the Council of Florence at which they represented King Alexander I (1412–42) and assented to the union with Rome.

King George VIII (1446–65) joined with the Emperor David of Trebizond to support the crusade against the Ottomans preached by Pope Pius II at the Congress of Mantua in 1459. It had not achieved adequate support by the time of Pius's death in 1464 and his successor Paul II abandoned the plan. By that time Trebizond had fallen to the Ottomans (1461). Georgia was weakened by internal struggles in the later fifteenth century and split into three kingdoms, Georgia/Iberia, Imeretia and Kakhetia, and five independent principalities. Remarkably, most of these survived until they were absorbed by the Russian Empire in the nineteenth century. The Georgian Church, of course, still survives, as an autonomous branch of the Orthodox Church.

CHAPTER FOUR

THE CHURCHES OF MEDIEVAL AFRICA

In the early Christian centuries all the Mediterranean provinces of Africa from Egypt to Morocco were part of the Roman Empire. Christian communities were well established throughout this area before the reign of Constantine the Great, but they were culturally divided. Churches from the Atlantic seaboard to the eastern borders of Tripolitania worshipped in Latin, whereas those of Cyrenaica and Egypt worshipped in Greek. This linguistic distinction was to have wide-ranging effects on the way in which those churches developed during the Middle Ages, and for that reason it is necessary to consider them separately.

The Egyptian Church

Egypt had an integral place in Christian history from its very beginning, for it was there that the Holy Family had sought refuge from Herod. The Church of Alexandria has traditionally claimed St Mark as its founder. Its bishops were styled popes from the third century, and since the sixth century have been known as patriarchs. Their authority over Egypt and Cyrenaica was recognized by the first General Council of Nicaea in 325. At that time there were proportionally more Christians in Egypt than in any province of the empire.

The Church in Roman Egypt influenced the development of medieval Christianity in two important ways. The catechetical school of Alexandria had a profound influence on the development of early Christian thought, under the direction of St Clement (c. 200–15) and Origen (c. 215–31), who succeeded in showing that there was no inherent conflict between the Christian religion and the Hellenistic intellectual tradition. Origen promoted the allegorical interpretation of the Bible (a method used by the writers of the New Testament), in a radical way, to explain the spiritual meaning of passages which, if taken literally, were repugnant to human reason. For example, he comments on the Fall of Man in Genesis:

> And who is so foolish to suppose that God, after the manner of a husbandman, planted a paradise in Eden towards the east, and placed in it a tree of life, visible and palpable, so that one tasting of the fruit by the bodily teeth obtained life, and that again one was a partaker of good and evil by masticating what was taken from the [other] tree. And if God is said to walk in the paradise in the evening, and Adam to hide himself under a tree, I do not suppose that any one doubts that these things

figuratively indicate certain mysteries, the history having taken place in appearance and not literally.[1]

The medieval Church was also indebted to Egypt for a central element in its spirituality, since the monastic movement originated there. A vocation to the contemplative and celibate life was envisaged for some of Christ's followers by the writers of the New Testament, and in third-century Egypt some Christians withdrew to the desert to live as solitaries. The earliest of them is said to have been St Paul of Thebes, who retreated to the western desert to escape the persecution of Decius (249–51) and remained there until on his death-bed he was visited by St Antony, some hundred years later. St Paul may have been a pious fiction, symbolizing the hermits who preceded the monastic movement, but St Antony undoubtedly existed and was known to St Athanasius,

St Antony the Great, shown in a seventeenth-century icon.

who is traditionally credited with writing his biography. Antony withdrew as a solitary to the eastern desert in *c.* 287, where disciples came to him seeking instruction in the eremitical life. By the time he died in 356 a large community had grown up around his hermitage at Mount Clysma, and he gave the brethren a rule of life. He did not regard community life as an end in itself, but as a training for the solitary life.

True communal monasticism was initiated by Antony's contemporary, St Pachomius, who had grown up a pagan and had been a professional soldier before he was converted to Christianity. In 323 he founded a monastery at Tabennessi to the north of Thebes. Unlike Antony he saw the monastic community as a school of perfection in which its members would spend the whole of their lives. In his Rule he established the threefold division of time adopted in all later rules: time set aside for communal liturgical prayer; time devoted to manual labour, and time given to religious study which, since most of Pachomius's monks were illiterate, meant private prayer and meditation. This new kind of monasticism proved very popular, and by 346, when Pachomius died, it had been adopted by eleven monasteries.

Given its strong intellectual tradition, it is not surprising that the Egyptian Church became centrally involved in the doctrinal controversies which convulsed the Christian world in the fourth and fifth centuries. The earliest and most radical of these originated with Arius, a priest of Alexandria, who taught that Jesus Christ the Son of God was inferior to God the Father. What was at issue here was the truth of Christ's claim 'I and my Father are one' (John 10:30). Many fourth-century Christians, trained in the Graeco-Roman tradition of philosophy and logic, found it difficult to reconcile the absolute and infinite nature of God the Creator with the limitations accepted by God the Son when he became incarnate as Jesus of Nazareth. Arius held that God the Son was a created being, even though he partook of the godhead to a far greater degree than any other of God's creatures. Although the first Council of Nicaea, convoked by Constantine in 325, condemned this teaching and affirmed that no distinction could be made between the godhead of the Creator and that of Jesus Christ, this did not put an end to the dispute, for Arius's followers advanced modified forms of his teaching, which gained favour with Constantine's successor Constantius. One of Arius's chief opponents was the long-lived Bishop of Alexandria, St Athanasius (328–73), who defended the faith of Nicaea and consequently spent much of his life either in exile or in hiding, while bishops favourable to Arianism were intruded in his see by the emperor. It was not until 381 that the second General Council of Constantinople, convened by the Emperor Theodosius I, condemned all schools of Arianism and upheld the teachings of the Council of Nicaea. (see p. 17). Thereafter Arianism ceased to be an important force in the eastern provinces and unity was restored to the Egyptian Church.

The acceptance by the Church in 381 of the full divinity of Christ almost inevitably led to disputes about the relationship between his divine and human natures. This issue had a resonance in the late Roman Empire beyond the interests of professional theologians because of Christian Gnostic movements, which were particularly strong in Egypt. Basilides, whom some scholars consider the most subtle of Gnostic thinkers, had taught at Alexandria in the period 117–60. He still had followers in fourth-century Egypt, and by that time many other schools of Gnosticism had grown up there and were attracting wide support, and Greek Gnostic writings were being translated into Coptic to meet the needs of this wider audience. All Gnostics challenged the claims of the Catholic Church to be the guardian of the apostolic teaching. The Gnostics claimed knowledge (*gnosis*) of the esoteric meaning of the Christian faith. They wrote treatises to expound their teaching, which they attributed to well-known biblical figures like Seth, Isaiah and the Apostles, or to oral traditions received from Christ himself. *Pistis Sophia*, a Coptic Gnostic text of the late third century, is a work of this kind, which begins:

> It came to pass that when Jesus had risen from the dead, that he passed eleven years discoursing with his disciples, and instructing them only up to the regions of the First Commandment and up to the regions of the First Mystery, that within the Veil, within the First Commandment, which is the four-and-twentieth mystery without and below – those four-and-twenty which are in the second space of the First Mystery which is before all mysteries – the Father in the form of a dove.[2]

Although Gnostics and Catholics were in some measure addressing the same problem – how to understand the cosmic significance of the life and teaching of Jesus of

Nazareth – their approaches to it were fundamentally different. For although the various Gnostic schools of Egypt differed a good deal between themselves about matters of detail, they all agreed that the material world had come into being as the result of a cosmic accident and that the demiurge who had fashioned it was not the true God. They also agreed that the spirits of men and women had become trapped in material bodies but belonged by nature to the spiritual world, which was perfect, and they used the vivid metaphor 'gold in the mud' to describe the human condition. Christ was a totally spiritual being, an aeon or emanation of the supreme God, who had sent him into the world to make men aware of their true spiritual state. In order to be understood by them, Christ entered into the man Jesus of Nazareth. Those who were willing to receive the knowledge (*gnosis*) that Christ imparted obtained salvation. When they died their enlightened spirits could return to the realm of the supreme God where they belonged. The Gnostics were not interested in the human body because it was a part of the imperfect material creation.

Upholders of the Catholic tradition could not be so dismissive of the material world, which they believed had been created by God, even though it was now flawed by evil. Christ, God's Son, in their view became a man, not just as a way of communicating with mankind, but as a means of restoring the whole creation to a rightful relationship with God. His humanity was therefore integral to his mission: he lived a fully human life, he died as all men do, and he rose bodily from the dead as the firstborn of the new creation. Given this centuries-long debate between Gnostics and Catholics about the importance of Christ's humanity, it was inevitable that strong feelings should have been aroused in Egypt by the theological disputes about the relationship between the divine and human natures of Christ.

Initially they centred on the role of the Blessed Virgin Mary in Christ's incarnation. Nestorius, Patriarch of Constantinople (428–31), objected to her being called *Theotokos*, literally 'the God-bearer', a term usually translated in English as 'Mother of God', claiming that she was only the mother of Christ's humanity. St Cyril, Patriarch of Alexandria (412–44), accused Nestorius of trying to separate the divine and human natures of Christ and the dispute was resolved at the third General Council of Ephesus in 431, at which Nestorius's teaching was condemned, Mary was declared to be indeed the *Theotokos* because she bore the Son of God, and Nestorius was deposed for heresy. It should be noted that although he undoubtedly opposed the use of the title *Theotokos*, Nestorius denied that he held the more radical views about the two natures of Christ attributed to him, a matter which will be considered in more detail in the next chapter.

The decision of the Council of Ephesus about the status of Mary marked a victory for the Catholic tradition that the material creation is important. God the Son had taken human nature fully and been born of a human mother. This was the mystery of the Infant Christ which Lancelot Andrewes later expressed in the paradox, '[He was God] the Word, and not able to speak a word'. A Gnostic saviour, who was entirely spiritual, could not have been reduced to such dependence on a human mother.

The Council of Ephesus had a considerable impact on Church politics as well as on Christian doctrine, because although St Cyril and the Church of Alexandria had won the argument at Ephesus, they had humiliated the Patriarchate of Constantinople by deposing Nestorius and had also antagonized the Patriarchate of Antioch in whose theological schools Nestorius had been trained.

Later speculation focused on how the two natures of Christ were united in one person. Cyril's successor, the Patriarch Dioscorus (444–51), was attracted by the teaching of Eutyches, a theologian of Constantinople, that Jesus had only one nature, which was divine, and that he therefore did not fully share in our humanity. This was condemned by Flavian, Patriarch of Constantinople, but a Church Council at Ephesus in 449, at which Dioscorus played a leading role, vindicated Eutyches and deposed Flavian. Eutyches's opponents complained that that Council had been unrepresentative of the Church and persuaded the new Emperor Marcian (450–7) to summon the fourth General Council, which met at Chalcedon in 451. The assembled fathers annulled the acts of the 449 council and reversed its decisions, condemning Eutyches and vindicating Flavian, who had died. They also deposed Dioscorus of Alexandria. The Council pronounced that Christ is fully God and fully man, and proclaimed the Hypostatic Union, that is the union of the divine and human natures in one person (*hypostasis*) in Christ. In formulating this doctrine they were strongly influenced by a letter from Pope Leo I of Rome, who pointed out that the New Testament writers use the terms Son of Man and Son of God almost interchangeably when speaking about Jesus. The doctrine defined at Chalcedon was binding on all Catholic Christians and the Council labelled those who opposed it Monophysites, that is, those who, like Eutyches, believed that Christ had only one nature.

The opponents of Chalcedon in Egypt, and they were numerous, do not for the most part seem to have been Monophysites in any meaningful sense. They rejected Chalcedon because they misunderstood the theological terminology used by the Council to express the Hypostatic Union, and mistakenly saw in it a resemblance to the teaching attributed to Nestorius by the Council of Ephesus.[3]

While these Christological disputes were taking place, Egypt became an almost entirely Christian society. This was mainly due to the monasteries, and to the less numerous convents of nuns, which attracted large numbers of vocations in the fourth and fifth centuries. Many of these new communities were founded in populated areas, like the city of Alexandria and its environs, the Fayum, where there were at one time thirty-five monasteries, and the whole length of the Nile Valley as far as St Symeon's monastery near Aswan on the Nubian frontier. Nevertheless, many monks continued to seek solitude, and new clusters of monasteries sprang up in the western desert on Mount Nitria, at Cellia, and in the Wadi Natrun (then known as Scete).

Although some of these monks and nuns came from great landowning families or from the prosperous urban classes, the majority were peasants. There are no statistics of monastic profession in late Roman Egypt, but all sources indicate that there were a large number of monks: there are said to have been 6,000 in the monastery of St Arsenius at Gebal Tura alone. Edward Gibbon was horrified by the popularity of asceticism in Egypt and elsewhere in the late Roman period and believed that this hastened the fall of the Empire. There is no evidence to support this: only a minority of the male population, albeit a substantial minority, enrolled as monks in late Roman Egypt. As wartime casualties and epidemic diseases show, stable societies in the Middle Ages could

A fish and a cross surrounded by vine-leaves. Coptic, fifth century.

absorb a considerable degree of population loss without being undermined. There is no way of determining why most of these people chose to become monks and nuns, though genuine religious commitment must have been important to many of them, for the monastic life involved sacrifice. In the case of the rich this is self-evident: they gave up the comforts of an affluent life to devote themselves to austerity and prayer. The poor, while they may have welcomed the status that monastic profession conferred on them, also had to make a sacrifice, that of the emotional security provided by family life and the extended kin group.

Although many monks may have been unreflective, some of them became acknowledged masters of the spiritual life. Long periods of silence and solitude, coupled with the regular discipline of mental self-examination, made them aware of human psychology in all its irrational complexity. They expressed their internal conflicts as battles between devils and angels for control of the human soul, but the mental processes they described are common human experiences. Many people will recognize the symptoms associated by John Cassian with the noonday demon:

> When this besieges the unhappy mind it begets . . . boredom with one's cell and scorn and contempt for one's brethren . . . Also, towards any work that may be done we become listless and inert . . . we lament that in all this while, living in the

same spot, we have made no progress, we sigh and complain that bereft of sympathetic fellowship we have no spiritual fruit . . . We praise other and far distant monasteries . . . as more helpful to one's progress . . . Towards . . . midday [the demon] induces such lassitude of body and craving for food as one might feel after the exhaustion of a long journey . . . Finally, our malady suggests that in common courtesy we should salute the brethren and visit the sick, near or far . . .[4]

Monastic settlements along the Nile Valley ensured that Christianity spread among the Egyptian peasants. Many of the monks were unlearned men, fanatical in the defence of their own faith and intolerant of any other. Although after 392 the public practice of pagan cults was forbidden by imperial decree, the enforcement of this law depended very much on the attitude of provincial officials, who in turn deferred to powerful local men. In Egypt the monks were often more powerful on a local level than anybody else because of their sheer numbers, and by the middle of the fifth century no pagan temples remained open in Egypt apart from that of Isis at Philae, which served the tribes of Nubia. Christians soon moved into these deserted sites. The monastery of the Metanoia outside Alexandria was built in the ruins of the temple of Serapis; at Thebes a church was built in the second court of the temple of Ramses III; the great festival hall of Thutmosis III in the temple at Karnak was also used as a church, while Christian anchorites went to live in the Valley of the Kings, as is known from the Coptic graffiti found on the walls of the tomb of Ramses IV.

While the monks were able to exercise their influence over the Egyptian laity and incite them to riot on behalf of church leaders like Athanasius during the Arian controversy, the subtleties of Christological definition which preoccupied the hierarchy must have been beyond the grasp of most lay people and probably of many simple monks as well. The piety of most Egyptian laymen was shaped not by theologians but by monks like St Shenute, who became Abbot of the White Monastery at Sohag in 385. He wrote in Coptic, and translated the liturgy into Coptic for his monks, who did not know Greek, a practice which was later to spread to the whole Coptic Church. Shenute's writings show a deep reverence for the humanity of Christ. He wrote what may be the earliest example of devotion to the Holy Name:

> If you celebrate a feast and are joyful [say] Jesus.
> If you have worry and suffering [say] Jesus.
> If the sons and daughters laugh [say] Jesus. . . .
> [Let] those who have pain or illness [say] Jesus . . .
> [Let] those who were unjustly judged and suffer injustice [say] Jesus.[5]

A high proportion of Egyptians supported their bishops in refusing assent to the decrees of the Council of Chalcedon, but the reasons for the bishops' opposition were not solely doctrinal. Not merely had their own patriarch been deposed at Chalcedon, but canon 28 of the Council had given precedence in the universal Church, after the Bishop of Rome, to the Patriarch of Constantinople, 'the new Rome', despite its being a position traditionally belonging to Alexandria.

The strength of popular resentment soon became apparent when the Patriarch Proterius of Alexandria, appointed by the Emperor Marcian to replace Dioscorus, was lynched by the mob in 457. In his place the Egyptian clergy chose the anti-Chalcedonian Timothy II, known by the nickname of Aeluros, the Cat. Although he was deposed in 460 by the Emperor Zeno and replaced by a Chalcedonian, he continued to be regarded by most Egyptians as the true patriarch until he died in 477.

The imperial authorities were anxious to restore religious unity in the eastern provinces and in 482 the Emperor Zeno published his *Henoticon* (formula of unity), a decree which affirmed the faith of the first three General Councils, condemned Nestorius and Eutyches, but did not explicitly endorse the Council of Chalcedon. It was a compromise which was widely welcomed in the eastern provinces, including Egypt.

By the sixth century Gnosticism as a conscious alternative form of Christianity seems to have faded out of Egypt. The Gnostic library of texts found in 1945 at Nag Hammadi, some sixty miles from Thebes, consists of codices and papyri mostly written in the fourth century, but apparently quite deliberately hidden in the fifth. It is not entirely clear whom they had been written for: the most plausible hypothesis is that they belonged to a Gnostic community, though it is also possible that they may have been produced for the use of heterodox brethren in a Pachomian monastery. Their concealment implies that attempts were made to suppress Gnostics during the fifth century, just as attacks were made at that time on surviving pagan cults. The enforcers of Orthodoxy were probably the same in both cases, the monks who wielded such great local power in Egypt.

Copies of some Gnostic texts, or of works influenced by Gnosticism, continued to be read by Egyptian Christians during the Middle Ages, but had only a very limited effect because they no longer formed part of a living tradition. Popular religious practice, however, shows the continued influence of both Egyptian pagan religion and Gnostic Christianity, as may be seen from this example of a Christian amulet, dating from the sixth century, designed to be placed over a door to protect the house against vermin:

+ The door, Aphrodite

Phrodite

Rodite

Odite

Dite

Ite

Te

Te

E

Hor Hor Phor Phor, Yao Sabaoth Adonai, I bind you, artemisian scorpion. Free this house of every evil reptile [and] annoyance, at once at once. St Phocas is here. Phamenoth 13, third indiction.[6]

The people who used charms of this kind were members of the Coptic Church of Egypt, not of some syncretistic sect. By the sixth century the Church had defeated its

A Coptic icon of Christ with St Menas, sixth to seventh centuries.

religious rivals and had absorbed fragments of their cosmologies into its own thought-world, but the Church itself was becoming divided.

The Chalcedonians and the anti-Chalcedonians lived together in Egypt as members of a single church and were ruled by a succession of anti-Chalcedonian patriarchs from 482 until the reign of the Emperor Justinian (527–65). A staunch supporter of Chalcedon, he sought to reconquer Italy and he therefore needed the support of the

Catholic West. In order to heal the schism between Rome and Constantinople (see p. 103) he ordered eastern church leaders to subscribe to the Council of Chalcedon, and when Theodosius of Alexandria refused to do so, he deposed him in 536 and replaced him by a Chalcedonian named Paul. Theodosius was exiled to Constantinople, but not only did he continue to be regarded as lawful patriarch by many of his clergy, he also enjoyed the support of Justinian's wife, the Empress Theodora, who had strong anti-Chalcedonian sympathies. It is difficult to believe, as contemporary sources on both sides imply, that Justinian was ignorant of his wife's attempts to subvert his religious policies. It seems more probable that he connived at her initiatives on behalf of his non-Chalcedonian subjects, and that Theodora's intervention helped to pacify the eastern provinces, while Justinian could disclaim any knowledge of her activities and thus keep his Orthodox subjects and the Western Church contented.

In c. 543 the suspended Patriarch Theodosius consecrated Jacob Baradeus as a bishop and he effectively set it up an anti-Chalcedonian hierarchy in Egypt and Syria, so that when Theodosius died in 566 it was possible to appoint a successor. From that time until the present day a schism has existed in the Egyptian Church. Pro-Chalcedonian patriarchs were appointed by the emperors, and their followers therefore came to be known as Melkites, the emperor's men. Their anti-Chalcedonian opponents were called Copts, the name of the indigenous population of Egypt.

The Melkites enjoyed a privileged position and had the support of the Greek-speaking population of Alexandria and the other cities of lower Egypt, but the mass of the people were loyal to the Coptic Church. From 619–26 Egypt was occupied by the Persians, who were hostile to Christianity of all kinds, but when the Emperor Heraclius restored Roman rule he failed to capitalize on this anti-Roman sentiment among his Coptic subjects. In c. 630 he appointed a new Melkite Patriarch, Cyrus, whom he also made civil governor of Egypt. Cyrus supported the Monothelete doctrine, promulgated by the emperor in an attempt to promote religious unity, (see p. 118), and used his civil powers to prosecute Coptic bishops who refused to subscribe to it. This persecution was ended by the Arab invasion of Egypt. In 642 Cyrus surrendered Alexandria and retired to Cyprus where he died, while the Coptic Patriarch Benjamin made his submission to the Arab commander al-'Amir, who allowed him to live in Alexandria.

The Arab conquest perpetuated the schism in the Egyptian Church because the new rulers organized their non-Muslim subjects in accordance with their religious affiliations and made their ecclesiastical leaders responsible for the behaviour of their flocks. Perhaps for that reason the Melkites retained an organized hierarchy, even though no patriarch was appointed for ninety years after the death of Cyrus's successor, Peter III, in 651. Their representatives attended the sixth General Council at Constantinople in 680–1 at which Monotheletism was finally condemned, as well as the Council in Trullo of 692. The Melkite Church was nevertheless clearly weakened by this long interregnum, for when a new Patriarch, Cosmas I, was finally appointed in 742, he had to be consecrated by Syrian Melkite bishops in Tyre because the three Melkite bishops required by canon law were not to be found in Egypt. The Muslim authorities allowed Cosmas to live in Alexandria, no doubt because he was potentially a useful diplomatic link between them and Byzantium and the Christian West. In the eighth century the Melkites were still quite numerous. Most of them lived in the cities of lower Egypt, but there were some Melkite centres elsewhere, such as Cyrenaica, and also the monastery of St Antony in the eastern desert, which seems to have remained Melkite until the late ninth century.

Although the Copts initially welcomed the substitution of Arab for Byzantine rule, this did not last. There were six unsuccessful Coptic uprisings between 725 and 773. This discontent was partly caused by heavy taxation, for while the Arabs tolerated Christians they imposed both a poll tax and a land tax on them. When the Caliph Umar I (717–20) exempted converts to Islam from the poll tax, there was a significant number of conversions, but it would be wrong to ascribe all conversions to self-interest. Some Egyptian Christians may well have found the Islamic religion more attractive than their own, while, as G.C. Anawati has pointed out, in the early Islamic period intermarriage between Christian women and Muslim men was encouraged by allowing the wives to keep their own religion, though all children of such marriages automatically became Muslims.[7] Probably the most powerful secular incentive for conversion to Islam was that this was the way of attaining full parity in the dominant culture. Thus for a variety of reasons Christians had become a minority in Egypt by c. 950, albeit a very substantial minority.

Once they were no longer a threat to the Islamic establishment, the Arabs allowed the Copts some share in power. The Tulunid Sultans (868–905) were the first to do so, and this policy was continued by their successors, particularly by the Shi'ite Fatimid Caliphs, who made Cairo their capital in 969. Although the Caliph al-Hakim (996–1021) persecuted his Christian subjects, his intolerance was exceptional and his successor, az-Zahir (1021–36), not only allowed Christians to rebuild their churches, but even ruled that Christians forcibly converted to Islam under al-Hakim should be free to resume the practice of their former faith. The Copts responded favourably to such good treatment and in 1077 their Patriarch Christodoulus signalled the support of his church for the Fatimid Caliphs by moving his see from Alexandria to Cairo.

Of course, under even the most favourable conditions, the Christian population of Islamic Egypt gradually became second-class citizens. They were segregated in certain quarters of the main cities, they were not allowed to ride horses and were supposed to wear distinctive dress. They were not officially allowed to build new churches and had to obtain special permission to repair existing ones. Although many of these rules were not strictly applied, they remained the official law, and as Anawati has pointed out, 'When, for example, the Byzantine enemy had gained military success at the borders, the fanatic populace would invade the Christian quarters, burn the churches, and demand that the government enforce the regulations concerning the *dhimmis*'.[8] But for much of the time relations between Christians and Muslims were reasonably cordial. Christians were allowed to practise their faith openly, not just inside their churches. For example, they continued to go on pilgrimage to the shrines of saints on their feast days: the liturgy would be celebrated in the shrine church, pilgrims would make offerings at the shrine, and healing miracles were said to take place. Such pilgrimages were occasions for feasting and conviviality and Muslims often joined in, not merely because they

The 'Hanging Church' of our Lady in the citadel of Cairo, cathedral of the Coptic Patriarchs since 1077.

enjoyed the party atmosphere, but also because they too hoped for some share of supernatural aid. Although Coptic was still spoken in some villages in upper Egypt, by the late eleventh century most Christians and Muslims spoke the same language, Arabic. Nevertheless, church services were still conducted in the traditional way: the Melkites worshipped in Greek and the Copts in Coptic.

If, during the Middle Ages, many monasteries had to be abandoned owing to a lack of new vocations from a dwindling Christian community, even so a substantial number survived: in 1088 there were still 712 monks and seven monasteries in the Wadi Natrun, for example. As society became less Christian, so the desert monasteries became vulnerable to attack by the beduin, who were mostly Muslim: the Coptic Patriarch, Shenute I (859–80), provided for all the monasteries of Wadi Natrun to be walled and fortified. Such measures may have reduced the problem, but they did not eliminate it, for in the fifteenth century the great monastery of St Antony in the eastern desert was sacked and burnt by its beduin servants, although it was subsequently rebuilt.

Saladin, who seized power in 1170, abolished the Fatimid Caliphate and restored Egypt to the obedience of the Caliph of Baghdad. At first he excluded Copts from holding posts in the Egyptian treasury, but later relented, probably because he found that there were not enough Muslims with the right training to carry out this work. Saladin also became well-disposed towards the Egyptian Melkites, for the Syrian Melkites had helped him to capture Jerusalem in 1187.[9]

Until the thirteenth century the Coptic community enjoyed a large measure of prosperity and some degree of power, and the Coptic Church was rich enough to patronize a distinctive form of religious art. This, like Coptic architecture, had its roots in the late Roman period. Many of the Coptic churches and monasteries were decorated with frescoes which have an affinity with, but are quite different in style and feeling from, Byzantine wall-paintings. Moreover, although it used to be thought that no medieval icons from Coptic Egypt had survived, some important examples have recently come to light.[10] Some fine figured textiles made for Coptic use have also been preserved. Medieval Coptic scholars produced a considerable body of theological writing, but their outstanding literary achievement is *The History of the Patriarchs of the Egyptian Church*. The part of this work covering the period before 1092 was compiled by Mawhub Ibn Mansur and a group of collaborators, who searched the monasteries for materials relating to Coptic history, translated them into Arabic, edited them, incorporated new and relevant information, and wrote a section on events from 1047–92. This became the standard history of the Coptic Church, and was brought up to date by the additions of later writers, and it is evidence of a community which was aware of the dignity of its own place in the Christian dispensation.[11]

In the late Middle Ages there was a steep decline in Coptic fortunes and therefore in Coptic culture, which came about in this way. In the first half of the thirteenth century two major crusades were launched against Egypt by the Western powers in an attempt to force Saladin's successors to restore the Holy Land to the Franks. Although it was unsuccessful, the Fifth Crusade (1217–21) led the Egyptian government to view the Copts with suspicion as a possibly subversive element in their state. The Crusade of St Louis (1249–50), though itself defeated, was the catalyst for a revolution in Egypt which overthrew Saladin's family, the Ayyubids, and brought the Mamluk Sultans to power.

In 1260 the Mamluks defeated the pagan Mongols, who had overrun much of the Near East, at the battle of Ain Jalut in Galilee, but the Mamluks remained afraid for many years that the Mongols might ally against them with the Western crusading powers. This led to anti-Christian feeling in Egypt. The Copts continued to control the financial administration, and some Christian families had become very rich as a result of this. Muslim resentment against them flared up in 1293 and again in 1301 when there were widespread anti-Christian riots: churches and monasteries were looted and burned, treasury officials were threatened with loss of office if they did not apostatize, and the strict laws governing the dress and behaviour of Christians in an Islamic state were enforced. Although some Copts were pressurized into becoming Muslims, their sincerity was widely called in question, and in any case the Mamluk Sultans continued to run the treasury with the help of Copts who had remained Christian, because there was nobody else competent to do the work. Nevertheless, after Sultan al-Nasir Muhammad (1310–41) arrested some of the most important of these treasury officials and confiscated their fortunes, the Coptic community began to lose social and economic power.

The Mamluks had no wish to suppress the churches of Egypt completely. They were aware that any sustained persecution might antagonize the Western powers who were important trading partners. In the fourteenth century the sultans were also concerned to promote good relations with Byzantium in order to ensure the regular supply of white slave boys from the Russian steppes, who were shipped to Egypt by way of Constantinople to be trained as professional soldiers. This involved preserving the Melkite Patriarchs whom the Byzantines recognized as lawful heads of the Egyptian Church. The sultans themselves considered that the Coptic Patriarchs were even more important, because they were also recognized as the religious heads of the Churches in the independent Kingdoms of Ethiopia and Nubia.

In the Mamluk period some Western powers made treaties with Egypt and were able to establish merchant colonies in some of the cities there, while many western pilgrims travelled to Mount Sinai and the Holy Land by way of Egypt where some of them became interested in Coptic shrines, particularly those connected with the Holy Family.

The Papacy, too, tried to form links with the Egyptian Churches. Innocent III (1198–1216) corresponded with the Melkite Patriarch Nicholas I (1210–43), whom he regarded as lawful head of the Egyptian Church, and met with a cordial response. Nicholas was represented at the Fourth Lateran Council in 1215. Then in 1237 Philip, prior of the Dominicans in the Holy Land, sent an embassy to the newly elected Coptic Patriarch Cyril III (1235–43), who welcomed this overture, although the Melkites were upset by it, and thereafter the popes had dealings with both churches.

The Council of Florence (1438–44), called to heal the schism between the Western and Byzantine Churches, was attended by representatives of the other Orthodox Patriarchs, including Philotheus, Melkite Patriarch of Alexandria, whose legate signed the act of union with Rome in 1439. In August 1441 Andrew, Abbot of St Antony's monastery and representative of the Coptic Patriarch John XI (1428–53), reached Florence and addressed the council in Arabic. After lengthy discussions between the Coptic delegation and a group of Roman cardinals the unity of the Coptic and Roman Churches was declared in the bull *Cantate Domino (O sing unto the Lord)* of 4 February 1442. For the first time for almost a thousand years there was official unity between the Melkite and Coptic Churches, in the sense that both of them had entered into communion with the Catholic Church of the West. The Melkite Union proved ephemeral, for in 1443 Philotheus of Alexandria met the Orthodox Patriarchs of Jerusalem and Antioch and they jointly renounced the Union of Florence. Yet although the Coptic Church adhered to the union, political circumstances made it almost impossible to implement. The Mamluk Sultans did not welcome the prospect of popes exercising spiritual authority over Egyptian Christians and put obstacles in their way.

By 1500 the Melkite community was very small: Cyrenaica seems to have become completely Muslim by the twelfth century, and thereafter Melkites were found chiefly in Alexandria and some of the cities of lower Egypt. By contrast the Coptic Church, although it had declined in power and numbers under Mamluk rule, remained a sizeable minority in 1500. It still had a great deal in common with the Orthodox Churches of the East from which it had separated in the sixth century. The hierarchy, the sacraments, the Divine Office were recognizably very similar. The Coptic liturgy of St Basil, which was in daily use, and of St Gregory Nazianzes, used at Christmas, Epiphany and Easter, resembled the Greek liturgies of late Roman Alexandria, from which they had been translated, in structure and content. Some well-known liturgical formulas, such as 'Peace be with you all' (*eirene pasis*) and the communion invitatory, 'Holy things for the holy' (*Ta agia tois agiois*), had been left in Greek. Even the vestments which the clergy wore were recognizably similar to those of the Byzantine rite. Moreover, although the Copts rejected the Council of Chalcedon and all later general councils, their beliefs did not differ in substance from those of the rest of the Catholic-Orthodox world.

There were of course, many minor differences. The Copts observed a different church calendar, and not only honoured local saints, but also kept some universal feasts on different days from other Christians; for example, they observed the Feast of the Annunciation, Lady Day, on 7 March not 25 March. Although they had the same canon of scripture as the rest of Catholic Christendom, the Copts frequently included *The Shepherd of Hermas* in the New Testament as a work which might be read with profit. During the Middle Ages they adopted certain new ceremonial practices: cymbals were used to accompany the chant, while ostrich eggs were quite commonly hung in churches.

These were all minor matters. Nevertheless, the Coptic Church developed a distinctive character, quite different from that of any other part of medieval Christendom. This was partly because its members worshipped in Coptic, but also because, unlike the rest of Egypt which had adopted the Islamic dating system, the Copts continued to use that of the fourth-century Egyptian church. This took as its Year 1 the accession of Diocletian on 29 August AD 284, which inaugurated the era of the martyrs. The Copts also continued to use the ancient Egyptian calendar, consisting of twelve months, each of thirty days, with an additional month of five days (six in a leap year), and they preserved the traditional names of those months, Tut, Babah, Hatur and so on. The Coptic Church in 1500 thus remained a living link with the world of St Antony the Great and St Athanasius.

The Ethiopian Church

The Kingdom of Aksum, from which the empire of Ethiopia later evolved, was an important centre of trade and a strong military power in the early fourth century. The church historian Rufinus (340–410) reports how Frumentius of Tyre, captured and

The cathedral of St Mary of Zion at Aksum, said to house the Ark of the Covenant.

enslaved while on a voyage in the Red Sea, ended up holding high office in the kingdom of Aksum. Finally he was freed, and was later consecrated bishop by St Athanasius of Alexandria to minister to the many Christians living in Aksum – almost certainly a reference to the expatriate merchant communities there.

Frumentius's mission was presumably licensed by King Ezana of Aksum (325–52), and an inscription found in 1970 shows that the king himself became a Christian in later life. Unlike earlier inscriptions from his reign which use pagan or neutral terminology, this begins, 'In the faith of God and the power of the Father, the Son and the Holy Spirit, to Him who preserved for me the kingdom through faith in His Son Jesus Christ . . . I, Ezana, King of the Axumites . . .' [12]

Aksum is famous for its monumental sculpture: funerary stelae, the greatest of which weighs 517 tonnes and is 97 feet high, are the most notable surviving examples of this, but it is known from the descriptions of travellers that the city also once contained impressive stone palaces. The present cathedral of Our Lady of Sion at Aksum dates from the seventeenth century, but the huge stepped plinth on which it stands is Aksumite, and Phillipson has plausibly suggested that it may well have been the foundation for a large basilica built by Ezana himself or one of his successors. [13]

Although Christianity became the religion of the court in the fourth century there is little archaeological evidence to suggest that it was more widely diffused before the fifth century. Ethiopian tradition attributes the evangelization of the population at large to the Nine Saints of Rome (a reference to the Roman Empire, not its capital city), and also credits them with founding some of the most ancient monasteries in the country, like Debra Damo and Debra Libanos.

The Christian Kings of Aksum came to be regarded as potential allies by the Byzantine Emperors. In *c.* 520 King Kaleb, with the help of a fleet sent by the Emperor Justin I, invaded the Himyarite kingdom in the Yemen, whose ruler had persecuted his Christian subjects. Kaleb made the Yemen a province of Aksum and his son built a cathedral at Sa'na as an act of thanksgiving:

> He built this church, and decorated it with gilding and beautiful paintings, and paved it with coloured marble and [set up] marble pillars . . . He adorned it with the most beautiful ornaments of gold and silver . . . and he overlaid the doors with plates of gold studded with silver nails . . . and on the doors leading to the altars he put broad plates of gold . . . and in the midst of each plate he set a golden cross, in the centre of which was a red, transparent carbuncle; and around these jewels were flowers of open work in various colours, so that spectators were astonished at it.[14]

The other peoples of western Arabia were impressed by Aksumite power. The threat of a viceroy of Yemen in *c.* 570 to attack Mecca, the centre of a pagan pilgrimage, passed into folk memory and is recorded in the Koran, where the King of Aksum is likened to a war elephant:

> Hast thou not seen how thy Lord dealt with the army of the Elephant?
> Did he not cause their strategem to miscarry? (Sura CV).

At the end of the sixth century the Persians conquered southern Arabia and Aksumite rule there came to an end.

The seventh century in the Near East was dominated by the rise of Islam and the growth of the Arab Empire. Early Muslims on the whole thought well of Aksum because in 615 some companions of the Prophet had been kindly received when they sought refuge there from persecution by the Meccan authorities. Warfare between the two powers did not occur until 702, when Aksumite pirates sacked Jiddah, the port of Mecca, and the Muslims retaliated by sacking Aksumite ports and annexing the Dahlak islands.

But Aksum was indirectly weakened by the Arab conquest of Egypt, which closed the Red Sea to Byzantine shipping and made it a commercial backwater. Trade flowed away from Aksum, which abandoned its gold coinage and after *c.* 750 stopped importing prestigious foreign goods. An Aksumite war-fleet was maintained in the Red Sea until the mid-eighth century, but then gradually declined, probably because the Zanafaj, an independent and warlike people related to the Blemmyes, took over much of Aksum's coastal territory, making it in effect an inland power.

The period 700–1100 is at present a dark age in Ethiopian history and the development of the kingdom has to be reconstructed from random evidence. An inscription from Aksum, probably of the ninth century, records how the *Latsani* Danael had protected the city from attack, but by then it seems to have become a religious capital rather than a centre of government. All the fragmentary evidence implies that in the early Middle Ages the kingdom of Aksum expanded southwards into Amhara and the area round Lake Hayq. Ibn Hawqal, writing in or before 977/8, reports that power had recently been seized by a pagan queen, probably an Aksumite vassal in the province of Shoa, who successfully rebelled against her Christian overlord.[15] Her power was short-lived for in 977 a new Aksumite claimant overthrew her with the help of the Church and restored Christian rule.

Aksumite kings continued to rule until the Zagwe dynasty came to power, traditionally in 1137, although that date is disputed. Although the Zagwe were portrayed as usurpers by the historians of the later Solomonid dynasty, they restored the international prestige of their kingdom, as Tamrat has rightly observed.[16] From this time it is customary to call that kingdom Ethiopia. In 1209 an embassy from the Zagwe King Lalibela reached Cairo, bringing a crown of pure gold for the Coptic Patriarch John and an elephant, a giraffe, a hyena and a wild ass for the sultan, Saladin's brother, al-Adil, who was impressed by the wealth of Ethiopia.[17]

The Zagwe consolidated their power in the province of Lasta, but in 1268 were overthrown by Yekunno Amlak, who claimed descent from the former kings of Aksum and founded the Solomonid dynasty, under which Ethiopian expansion continued. King Amda Sion (1312–42) made the Muslim emirate of Ifat tributary and subdued the neighbouring Islamic states. This enabled the Ethiopians to expand southwards into Shoa and beyond, and they also gained control of the western regions around Lake Tana. This huge area remained under Solomonid rule for the rest of the Middle Ages.

Amda Sion's conquests gave him control of the main trade routes in the Horn of Africa and this led foreign writers to form an exaggerated impression of his power. The Egyptian historian al-Umari wrote: 'It is said that he has ninety-nine kings under him and that he makes up the hundred.'[18] The Dominican missionary, Jordan Catalani de Sévérac, Bishop of Quilon in South India, concluded that Amda Sion must be Prester John who had been sought in vain throughout much of Asia in the previous eighty years. The identification was made easier because the Horn of Africa was commonly known as the Third India by medieval western writers. In his *Book of Marvels*, written in 1324, Jordan relates how in Ethiopia there are many dragons which have the jewels called carbuncles on their heads. The inhabitants cut these stones from the skulls of dead dragons and carry them 'to the Emperor of the Aethiopians, whom you [Western Christians] call Prester John'.[19] This identification gained general acceptance in Western Europe in the later Middle Ages.

The Zagwe and Solomonid Kings of Ethiopia identified themselves as rulers of the new Israel. It is a commonplace in Christian thought that the Church is the new Israel, but the rulers of Ethiopia understood this role in a very special way. King Lalibela is the first ruler who is known to have been associated with this ideology because of the complex of rock-churches built in his capital of Roha, which is now called Lalibela in his honour. The site is divided by a river known as the Jordan, and at the beginning of the pilgrimage there stands a monolithic cross. On the left bank of the river is the

The tallest stele still standing at Aksum.

church of the Redeemer of the World, a five-aisled basilica 100 feet long. Beside this stand the chapel of the Holy Cross and the church of St Mary. Next come three interlinked buildings, the church of Mount Sinai, the church of Golgotha, and the chapel of the Holy Trinity. On the right bank of the Jordan, on the site of what may once have been the palace of the Zagwe kings, is the church of Emmanuel, perhaps once the palace chapel, and the churches of St Aba Libanos, St Mercurius and SS. Gabriel and Raphael. Standing apart from the rest is the church of St George, where the hoofprints of his horse are shown in the courtyard.

These churches are hewn out of the rock, and, as Gerster rightly remarks, 'the work demanded of the architect an astonishing degree of ability in visualizing space'.[20] The churches show continuity with the building styles of Aksum, which have been reproduced to include features which have no structural function in the rock churches. King Lalibela may perhaps justly be credited with the overall plan of this site, but some of the churches were probably not completed in his reign, while others may have been there already and have been incorporated in the complex. Lalibela is sometimes called the African Zion, and was certainly designed to be a pilgrimage centre, but it was also intended to symbolize the legendary origins of the Ethiopian crown and people.

King Lalibela is also associated with the Ethiopian national epic, the *Kebra Nagast* (*The Glory of the Kings*). This work relates how the Kings of Ethiopia are descended from Menelik, son of King Solomon and the Queen of Sheba, who, with a great company of young men, had brought the Ark of the Covenant from Jerusalem to Aksum. The colophon of the only early manuscript of this text records that it was translated into

Geeze in the reign of King Amda Sion (1312–42) from an Arabic version made in the reign of King Lalibela, which was itself based on a Coptic original. It was certainly believed in Egypt during Lalibela's reign that the Ark was in Ethiopia. Abu Salih (d. 1208) writes:

> The Abyssinians possess also the Ark of the Covenant, in which are the two tables of stone inscribed by the finger of God wth the commandments . . . The Ark of the Covenant is placed upon the altar, but is not so wide as the altar; it is as high as the knee of a man and is overlaid with gold; and upon it there are crosses of gold . . . The liturgy is celebrated upon the Ark four times a year, within the palace of the king; and a canopy is spread over it when it is taken out from [its own] church to the church . . . in the palace of the king.[21]

In its present form the *Kebra Nagast* would seem to have been edited to support the claims of Amda Sion and his family to the Ethiopian throne by demonstrating their descent from King Solomon. Yet it is evident that it is based on far older material. Indeed, as Shahid has pointed out, the world picture which it gives is pre-Islamic and reflects the political situation of *c.* AD 600.[22]

It is not only Ethiopian royal ideology which bears strong marks of Old Testament influence in the later Middle Ages, the same is also true of some features of the Ethiopian Church. Some scholars, notably Edward Ullendorff, have argued that these influences were present from the earliest days of Christianity there, and derived from the Jewish communities already established in the Yemen and Aksum.[23] It could alternatively be argued that these customs were first adopted in the Zagwe period as the rulers began consciously to identify themselves and their people as the new Israel. It is, in my view, impossible in the present state of knowledge to determine this issue satisfactorily, because of the absence of written records between the classical Aksumite period (when they are rare) and the late twelfth century. Even liturgical manuscripts for the pre-Zagwe period have not been found, although they may come to light as a result of the systematic cataloguing of monastic manuscript collections which is now in progress.

What may be said with certainty about the evolution of the Ethiopian Church is that it was founded in the fourth century as a province of the Patriarchate of Alexandria, and when the schism occurred in the Egyptian Church in the sixth century the Ethiopians, for reasons which are not known, acknowledged the Coptic Patriarch as their canonical head and rejected the Council of Chalcedon. The Coptic Patriarchs exercised firm control over this distant province. The metropolitan of the Ethiopian Church, known as the abuna, was always an Egyptian, appointed by the Coptic Patriarch: this remained the case until 1958. The patriarch also consecrated all other Ethiopian bishops, whose number was restricted to seven for the whole vast kingdom by Coptic canon law. This system enabled the Islamic government of Egypt to impose spiritual sanctions on Ethiopia if there were ever political tensions between the two powers and this could have serious consequences for the Ethiopian Church. Thus when the abuna died in 1458 the Mamluk sultans would allow no successor to be appointed until 1481. During that time all the Ethiopian bishops died, so that towards the end of this period no new priests could be ordained. It is an index of how venerable this system was that the Ethiopians continued to accept it and did not seek to set their church free from control by Cairo.

Before their conversion the Ethiopians had a written language, Geeze, which is an unusually difficult script to master as it has 267 characters. The Ethiopian Church at first worshipped in Greek, but by the seventh century the liturgy had been translated into Geeze. The first part of the Ethiopian eucharistic rite, which never varies, is a translation of the Greek liturgy of St Mark, used at Alexandria in the fourth century, but many of the eighteen anaphoras (prayers of consecration) found in liturgical manuscripts seem to have been composed in Ethiopia during the Middle Ages. The Bible was translated into Geeze between the fifth and seventh centuries. The Ethiopian text is based on a Greek recension used in the Church of Antioch. St Frumentius had been a Syrian, and that may explain this link. Like other newly converted peoples, the Ethiopians were interested in apocryphal as well as canonical texts, and a significant number of them, some showing strong Gnostic influences, was translated into Geeze. The complete texts of *The Ascension of Isaiah, The Book of Enoch* and *The Book of Jubilees,* now exist only in the Geeze versions.

There is now a general consensus among scholars that in the Middle Ages most Ethiopian churches were square, and that the round church, which is now almost universal, is a modern development. This is exemplified by the church of Bethlehem in Gayent, where the modern church is circular and roofed with straw, but is built over a square medieval church. The rock churches of Lalibela, which are also rectangular, are modelled on the ancient basilicas of Aksum, but they are not unique. There are said to be hundreds of smaller rock churches of a similar type in Tigré province which have not yet been scientifically examined and recorded.

The Ark of the Covenant is now believed to rest in St Mary of Zion at Aksum, but there is no known evidence about the Ark's being there, or elsewhere in Ethiopia, before Abu Salih wrote in *c.* 1200. Since the later Middle Ages every Ethiopian church has possessed a *tabot,* an altar slab which symbolizes the Tables of the Law kept inside the Ark. When a new church was built the *tabot* was taken to the abuna for consecration, a ritual which fulfilled the same function as the consecration of a church by a bishop in the rest of the Christian world. It is possible that the *tabot* was originally simply a portable altar. Ernst Hammerschmidt has suggested that it was only 'later, apparently in connection with a strong movement which tried to make Ethiopia to be the true Israel [that] the altar slab [was] interpreted as a copy of the Ark of the Covenant'.[24] If this hypothesis is true, this association must first have been made during the Zagwe period when it came to be believed that the true Ark rested in the cathedral at Aksum.

There are replicas of the Ark in all Ethiopian churches and the clergy perform liturgical dances whenever the *tabot* is carried in procession, following the example of King David who danced before the Ark (2 Sam. 6:14). The Ethiopian liturgy has its own musical tradition, attributed to St Yared, who lived in the Aksumite period. It is distinctive because of its use of sistrums and drums, and although these are said to have been revealed to the saint in a vision of the worship of Paradise, it seems likely that they were also in secular use in the Aksumite kingdom and were adapted to liturgical needs. Another distinctive feature of the Ethiopian rite is its use of brightly coloured liturgical umbrellas during processions, made necessary by the equatorial climate.

The Ethiopian Church was unique in the late medieval world in observing the Jewish sabbath as well as the Christian Sunday. This 'double sabbath' was first advocated by the reforming abbot Ewostatewos (Eustathius) (c. 1273–1352). Some scholars would argue that he was simply urging that a well-established practice should be universally observed, but there is no clear evidence to support this view. His teaching caused a dispute which was referred to the Coptic Patriarch Benjamin (1327–39) who ruled against this practice; but Eustathius's followers continued to keep the double sabbath and in 1450 the synod of Debra

The traditional approach to the monastery of Debra Damo, Tigré province, Ethiopia.

Mitmaq enacted that this practice should be adopted by the whole Ethiopian Church.

Kings could exercise considerable power in the church and even influence devotional practices. The devout King Zara Jacob (1434–68), for example, is credited with promoting devotion to the Blessed Virgin Mary, by increasing the number of her feasts to thirty-two each year, that is one every ten days, and also by persuading the clergy to incorporate passages from the Geeze text of *The Miracles of Mary* into the Sunday lectionary, and by commissioning icons of the Virgin to be placed in churches, a form of religious art new to Ethiopia.

The Ethiopian Church in the later Middle Ages had considerable vitality. This was seen particularly in its monasteries, which followed the Geeze translation of the Rule of St Pachomius. Monasteries and convents of nuns regarded communal worship as their primary function, but some were also centres of study, where religious texts were translated, copied and commented on, and where the arts of manuscript illumination and liturgical music as well as calendrical science were practised. Although some monasteries were lax in their observance, nevertheless, the Ethiopian Church kept alive, and even in some degree intensified the austere ascetic traditions of the monks of Egypt. Many monasteries were in extremely remote locations, some were built on the tops of inaccessible hills or on ledges high up on mountainsides and some were only accessible by rope pulleys. A few monks habitually abstained not only from meat, but also from bread, living exclusively on dried vegetables; others were recluses, and were voluntarily walled up to avoid distraction; others sought to subdue the flesh by wearing heavy iron chains; while a technique of mortification, unique to the Ethiopian Church, consisted in standing on one leg for long periods of time while praying or meditating.

Because the abuna and all the bishops were Egyptians, the most able Ethiopian clergy tended to become monks, for the abbots of great monasteries could exercise considerable social and political power. Until the mid-twelfth century almost all the monasteries were situated within the boundaries of the old kingdom of Aksum. The incorporation of vast new territories into the kingdom meant that many pagans as well

Brethren at Debra Damo watch the ascent of a guest.

A distant view of the monastery of Debra Damo.

as Muslims and Falashas became subjects of the Ethiopian crown.[25] Yet although Christian settlements were made in those areas and churches built there, the priests appointed to minister to the settlers were not for the most part sufficiently well educated to evangelize the pagans. This work was undertaken by monks.

In 1248 Iyasus-Moa, a monk in the ancient community of Debra Damo, founded the monastery of St Stephen on Lake Hayq. His disciples subsequently founded monasteries in the recently conquered provinces, the most notable of such founders being St Tecla Haymanot, born in *c.* 1215. The son of Christian Ethiopians who had settled in Shoa before it came under Ethiopian rule, he became a monk at St Stephens and then went to study in the old monastic centres of Tigré province, where he gathered disciples, some of whom accompanied him on his return to Shoa in *c.* 1270. There he founded the monastery of Debra Libanos, named after the ancient house in Tigré, and it became a centre for the evangelization of the pagan peoples of southern Ethiopia, a work which was continued by his disciples after he died in 1313.

In the early fourteenth century the monk Basalota Mikael led a reform movement which aimed to suppress simony (the sale of church offices) among the clergy and concubinage and polygamy among the laity. This brought him into conflict with the rulers of church and state, for he accused the Abuna John of simony and King Amda-Sion of polygamy and concubinage. The king was willing to support him in his attempts to reform the clergy, but strongly objected to the saint's suggestion that he should become monogamous. After Basalota died, the new abuna Yacob, who was himself a reformer, used the Mikaelite monks as well as those of Debra Libanos to forward the work of evangelization in pagan areas. In this he had the full support of King Amda-Sion, who also assisted monastic missions in the west of his empire among the pagans of the newly conquered lands around Lake Tana. The new monasteries were reasonably successful in their work of evanglization, but in the later Middle Ages a number of religions still co-existed in the Ethiopian Kingdom; there were Falashas to the north of Lake Tana, Muslims in the eastern provinces and in parts of Eritrea, and large pagan enclaves in the south.

The Abuna Yacob was exiled when he reproached the new king, Newaya Maryam, about his concubinage, and that battle was never won by the reformers. The Ethiopian Church finally adopted what was arguably a more realistic policy in regard to lay sexual morality than that of any other branch of the medieval Church. Religious marriages were made obligatory for priests and deacons who wished to marry. Such marriages were indissoluble, and clergy were not free to marry a second time if their wives died. But lay people were not obliged by Church law to have religious marriages, and the civil marriages which most of them contracted were not subject to Church rules. It was therefore possible to dissolve such marriages, and the partners were not required to be monogamous. Nevertheless, the Church would not allow those who failed to observe its teachings about sexual morality to receive Holy Communion. The consequence of this was that although a high proportion of lay people regularly attended church, except for children and old people, lay communicants were rare.

The importance of the monastic clergy in the Ethiopian Church was given formal recognition in the thirteenth century when the office of Ecage, senior monastic leader, was created. This post was initially held by the abbots of St Stephens on Lake Hayq, but after 1445 was transferred to the abbots of St Tekla Haymanot's foundation of Debra Libanos. The Ecage ranked second in the hierarchy, and when there was no abuna he was the senior churchman in the kingdom. He was always an Ethiopian and had considerable power because he was one of the king's chief advisers as well as having oversight of all the Ethiopian monasteries.

It is paradoxical that some of the monks who withdrew from the world also proved to be great travellers. After *c.* 1250 Ethiopian monks begin to be recorded among the pilgrims visiting Jerusalem, where they later established a monastery. From Jerusalem they spread westwards, making foundations in Cyprus, Rhodes, Venice, Florence and Rome. These monastic groups made the West aware of Ethiopia and its Church.

Western rulers wanted to establish contact with Prester John, that great Christian potentate in the Horn of Africa. From the Ethiopian monks who settled in the West they learnt how to get to his kingdom, but it proved very difficult to use these

The monastery of Debra Damo, built on the edge of a sheer cliff.

itineraries because the Mamluk Sultans barred the way. A few intrepid travellers seem to have reached Ethiopia from the West in the fifteenth century, including the Venetian painter Niccolò Brancaleone, whose presence there is attested from *c.* 1480–1526, but their success was largely a matter of chance. When Pope Eugenius IV wished to discuss union with the Ethiopian Church at the Council of Florence he had to do so through Peter, a monk from the Ethiopian monastery in Jerusalem, who offered to act as an intermediary. The outcome of these negotiations was unknown to Eugenius, but almost a century later King Lebna Dengel assured Pope Clement VII that Eugenius's letter about unity had been welcomed by King Zara Jacob (1434–68) and was still preserved in the royal archive.

The first official western embassy to Ethiopia to reach its destination and report back was led by Dom Rodrigo de Lima, Portuguese ambassador to King Lebna Dengel in 1520. The embassy stayed in Ethiopia for six years and Dom Rodrigo's chaplain,

An Ethiopian processional cross and liturgical umbrella carried in procession.

14 *A fresco showing angels, from the monastery of Dionysiou, Mount Athos.*

15 *The Harrowing of Hell, Christ frees Adam and Eve. A fresco from the church of St Saviour in Chora, Constantinople.*

16 *A fresco in the church of Betania, Georgia, showing George III (1156–84), his daughter Queen Tamar (1184–1212) and her son George IV (1212–33).*

17 A thirteenth-century Armenian miniature.

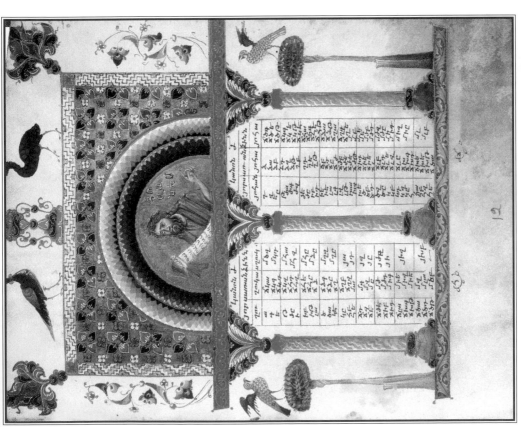

18 Canon Tables from an Armenian Gospel Book illuminated by Toros Rosline at Hromgla in 1269.

19 *John son of Ammonius at prayer, a mosaic in the church of St George at Khirbet-at-Mukhayyah, Jordan (AD 536).*

20 *The Virgin Queen of Heaven, Chartres Cathedral, France.*

Francesco Alvarez, wrote a very full account of the kingdom, and gave a picture of the Ethiopian Church as it was at the very end of the Middle Ages. He reported that the north and centre of the country contained many monasteries, although there were rather fewer in the south. A very intensive programme of church building had been undertaken and almost every village had its own church. The parish clergy were mostly married men and normally trained their sons to succeed them. They learnt the Divine Office and the Mass by heart and sang them from memory, and so the only liturgical books they needed were lectionaries.

The Ethiopians held their churches in great reverence: clergy and laity took off their shoes before entering and were scandalized by the Portuguese habit of spitting in church. Like most later western visitors Alvarez was astonished by the way in which the Feast of the Epiphany was kept. This day was also *timqat*, the commemoration of the Baptism of Christ, an occasion when the entire adult population renewed their baptismal vows by stripping off all their clothes and immersing themselves in great liturgical water-tanks. In Alvarez's day the court was itinerant and he was particularly struck by the imperial cavalcade. The thirteen *tabots* of the court chapels were reverentially carried, each suspended on a stretcher between four priests. The *tabots* were 'covered with brocades and silks. In front of each . . . walk two deacons with thurible and cross, and another with a bell ringing.' In addition, the emperor was always accompanied by four lions, held on leashes made of strong iron chains. On feast days there were processions in which the *tabots* were carried under colourful liturgical umbrellas and accompanied by musicians banging drums and rattling sistra and by the lesser clergy performing spirited liturgical dances.[26] Certainly by the end of the Middle Ages the Ethiopians had found effective ways of expressing their Christian faith in terms which reflected their own unique culture.

The Churches of Nubia

The Roman province of Egypt ended at the first cataract of the Nile and to the south lay Nubia. In the fourth century the Romans settled the Nobatae from the western desert as auxiliaries to hold the west bank of the Nile beyond the frontier and protect Egypt from attack by the warlike Blemmyes, who lived in the eastern desert and had recently also settled along the eastern bank of the Nile in Nubia. In 452 the Roman general Florus negotiated a 100 years' peace with both these peoples, and among other conditions it was agreed that every year their representatives might take the statue of Isis from her temple at Philae to their own country, where it would be consulted as an oracle and later returned to Philae.

By the beginning of Justinian's reign in 527 three independent kingdoms had grown up in Nubia. Nobatia extended roughly from the first to the third cataracts and was ruled by King Silko, who had finally driven the Blemmyes back into the eastern desert. The kingdom of Makuria extended from the third to the sixth cataracts and had its capital at Dongola. The kingdom of Alodia or Alwa lay to the south of the sixth cataract. All three kingdoms remained pagan. In *c.* 536 Justinian closed the temple of Isis at Philae, the last pagan temple to remain officially open in the Roman Empire, and Bishop Theodore of Philae consecrated that temple as the church of St Stephen. Bishop

Theodore acknowledged Theodosius, the anti-Chalcedonian prelate whom Justinian had deposed, as lawful Patriarch of Alexandria, which may help to explain why Theodosius, who was living in exile at Constantinople, was able, with the help of the Empress Theodora, to send a mission to Nobatia led by the priest Julian. It met with success, the king was baptized, and Julian placed Nobatia under the ecclesiastical authority of Bishop Theodore. Before 566 Theodosius consecrated the priest Longinus to be Bishop of the Nubians. Longinus organized the church in Nobatia and spent much time instructing the new converts. In c. 580 the King of Alwa invited him to his court, and evading the King of Makuria, who tried to arrest him, Longinus reached Alwa where he converted the king and organized a church. His rapid success was partly due to the fact that the people of Alwa already had some knowledge of Christianity through their contracts with Aksum.

John of Biclar, a Spanish monk who lived in Constantinople from 567–76, reports how in the reign of Justin II (565–78) 'the people of the Makuritae received the faith of Christ', and how they sent an embassy to the emperor, bringing among other gifts, elephant ivory and a live giraffe.[27] This account implies that Makuria became Melkite, and that is confirmed by the Melkite Patriarch of Alexandria, the annalist Eutychius (933–40), who records that Makuria had originally been subject to his predecessors. If Makuria had recently become Melkite in 580, this would explain why its king tried to prevent the Copt Longinus from reaching Alwa.

Christianity even spread among some of the Blemmyes. The twelfth-century Arab geographer al-Idrisi wrote that the Balliyin, who lived in the eastern desert near the Egptian frontier, 'have followed the Christian religion since the time of the Copts, before the rise of Islam, except that they are heterodox and follow the Jacobite [i.e. Coptic] sect.'[28]

After the Arabs conquered Egypt they twice attacked Nubia, in 641 and again in 651/2. Although they penetrated as far as Dongola, they met with stiff resistance from Nubian archers manning the fortresses along the Nile, and in 652 made a treaty (the *Baqt*, or Pact) with the Christian kings, which originally may have involved simply an annual exchange of gifts between the rulers. The Egyptian antiquarian, al-Makrizi, has preserved what is probably a later text of the treaty, stipulating that the Arabs would not attack Nubia and would recognize the free practice of the Christian religion there, provided that the Nubians paid an annual tribute of 360 slaves and allowed a mosque to be built at Dongola. William Adams has pointed out how unique this treaty was: 'Alone among the world's peoples, the Nubians were excluded from the Dar al'Islam [house of Islam] and the Dar al-Harb (figuratively 'house of the enemy'), the two categories into which the rest of the world was divided.'[29]

At some time before 697, Makuria annexed Nobatia, which had probably been weakened by the Arab invaders. While the Melkite Patriarchate was vacant, between 651 and 731, the Makurian Church came to accept the authority of the Coptic Patriarchs, because they needed bishops. This would also have strengthened the united kingdom of Makuria-Nobatia by ending religious divisions between the two halves.

In 835 King Zacharias of Makuria sent his son, the co-king George, to the court of the Caliph al-Mutasim at Baghdad to renegotiate the Pact. This led to the rare spectacle of a Christian king making a state visit to the Commander of the Faithful. Dionysius, the Syrian Orthodox Patriarch of Antioch (d. 845), has left this description:

[King George] rode a camel . . . An umbrella was held over him, shaped like a dome, covered with ornaments of coral and surmounted by a golden cross. In one hand he held a sceptre and in the other he carried a cross; an escort of young Nubians marched on either side of him carrying crosses in their hands. In front of him rode a bishop, who also held a cross in his hands. All the crosses were made of gold. The other warriors and slaves who formed his entourage were all black.[30]

The Pact was renewed in terms which were favourable to Nubia and remained in force for another 400 years.

During those centuries the Makurian Church flourished. The Coptic Patriarch appointed the metropolitan of Dongola, who consecrated bishops for the rest of the kingdom. Large cathedrals were built, like that of Faras, a five-aisled basilica erected in the abandoned palace of the kings of Nobatia by Bishop Paul in *c.* 700. Excavations conducted during the construction of the Aswan high dam revealed a huge number of other churches and monasteries in Nobatia.

Although the Nubians had a written language at the time of their conversion, they did not adopt a vernacular liturgy, but worshipped in Greek throughout the Middle

The Archangel Michael protecting the three boys in the burning fiery furnace, a fresco from the Nubian cathedral at Faras.

Ages. The iconography of some of the frescoes found in their churches is Byzantine in character, like the Virgin Eleousa at Faras cathedral, executed in the reign of Bishop John (997/8–1005), and the Virgin Galaktrophusa, dating from the reign of his successor, Marianus.[31] There is evidence, if slight, that there were still some Melkites living in Makuria in the central Middle Ages. Moreover, when the Fourth Crusade first reached Constantinople in 1203, Robert de Clari reported that they found a king of Nubia, who had come there as a pilgrim by way of Jerusalem and who was intending to go on to Rome and Compostella. The Emperor Alexius III clearly supposed he was a Melkite and had given him a monastery in the city as his residence for as long as he chose to stay there.[32] Yet although this anecdote suggests that Makuria may have retained an awareness of its links with Orthodox Byzantium, there is no doubt that the Makurian Church recognized the authority of the Coptic Patriarch after c. 700.

The kings of Makuria were on particularly good terms with the Fatimid Caliphs who conquered Egypt in 969 and who, being at war with the Abbasid Caliphs of Baghdad, needed peace on their southern frontier. Large numbers of Nubians were recruited to serve in the Fatimid armies and when Saladin abolished the Fatimid Caliphate in 1171 the Nubians invaded Upper Egypt and seized Aswan. Saladin's brother, Turan-Shah, campaigned against them and advanced as far as Ibrim, where he placed a garrison and turned the cathedral into a mosque. Then in 1175 the Pact was renewed and Egyptian troops withdrew once more to Aswan, for Saladin, threatened by a joint invasion of Egypt by the King of Sicily and the Franks in the Crusader States, could not afford to conduct a war in Upper Egypt as well. This peace lasted as long as Saladin's family ruled in Egypt.

Abu Salih, writing in c. 1200, gave a vivid account of the flourishing state of Makuria and of its churches, from Dongola, 'a large city on the banks of the blessed Nile [which] contains many churches and large houses and wide streets' northwards to 'the church of the glorious Archangel Michael, which overlooks the river, and is situated between the land of the Muslims and the land of Nubia; but it belongs to Nubia'.[33]

Soon after this was written Makuria was attacked by the Damadin, a pagan and warlike people from southern Sudan. This led to a change of settlement patterns: villages were fortified and great castles built in the Dongola reach. Despite this, the Nubian kingdom remained an important military power. In 1272 King David of Makuria sacked the Egyptian port of Aidabh on the Red Sea and in 1275 attacked Aswan. No doubt, as Vantini suggests, these attacks were reprisals for attacks on Makuria, unrecorded in the Muslim sources, by the Mamluk Sultans who had recently come to power in Egypt. In 1276 Sultan Baibars retaliated by invading Makuria and placing King David's cousin Shekenda on the throne as a Mamluk vassal. This marked the end of Makurian independence: its largely Christian population was required for the first time to pay the religious poll tax and the sultan annexed the province of Nobatia outright.

Egyptian control was maintained by exploiting divisions among the Nubians in such a way as to place the sultans' preferred candidates on the throne. There does not seem to have been a policy of deliberate Islamicization, but Muslim influence had been at work in Nubia since the Fatimid era when Nubian troops serving in the caliph's armies had normally been converted to Islam and had taken their new faith back to their homeland when they retired. Once Mamluk overlordship had been established, this process was accelerated and the proportion of Muslims among the ruling class of Makuria increased. The last Christian king died in 1323 and the new king, Kanz ad-Duala, was a Muslim, as were all his successors.

However, the sub-kingdom of Datowa, roughly comprising the area from Qasr Ibrim to a point just above the second cataract, continued to have Christian rulers while acknowledging Muslim overlordship. A letter dated 1464 mentioning Bishop Mark of Ibrim and King Joel of Datowa has been discovered in excavations at Gebel Adda, and King Joel is mentioned in another source of 1484. He is the last Christian ruler and Bishop Mark the last member of the Makurian hierarchy of whom any record has been found. Yet although organized Christianity seems to have collapsed there by *c.* 1500, reports by western travellers in the early modern age bear witness to the continuance of some degree of Christian ritual and devotional practice in the former Nubian kingdom.

The frontier between Alwa and Makuria ran to the south of the sixth cataract. Alwa had its capital at Soba on the Blue Nile, though it is not known how far its authority extended to the south. It had developed rather differently from Makuria because it was too remote to be affected by events in Egypt. One consequence of this was that few medieval Arabic or Christian writers have anything to say about it and, as its medieval sites have not yet been extensively excavated, comparatively little is known about its history. The head of its church was the Bishop of Soba, appointed by the Coptic Patriarch, but it is not known whether he had any suffragans.

One of the earliest descriptions of Alwa was given by al-Yakubi in 872:

> The first [Nubian kingdom] is that of Makurra . . . The second is the Nubian kingdom of Alwa. It is the more formidable of the two. Its capital is Soba. It takes about three months to travel through this kingdom. It is there that the Nile divides into numerous branches.[34]

Ibn Hawqal, who went there in 945–50, reports that it was ruled by King Eusebius, and that the crown normally descended from uncle to nephew. A generation later al-Aswani, the Fatimid ambassador to Dongola, was told that Soba had 'fine buildings and large monasteries, churches rich with gold, and gardens. There is also a great suburb where many Muslims live.'[35] The prosperity of Alwa was also remarked on by Abu Salih in *c.* 1200:

> Here there [is] . . . a large kingdom with wide districts in which there are four hundred churches. The town lies to the east of a large 'island' between the two rivers, the White Nile and the Green [i.e. Blue] Nile. All its inhabitants are Jacobite [i.e. Coptic] Christians. Around it there are monasteries, some at a distance from the stream, and some upon its banks. In the town there is a very large and spacious church, skilfully planned and constructed, and larger than all the other churches in the country . . .[36]

Alwa collapsed in the late Middle Ages. From later reports it would appear that Arab nomads from the eastern desert encroached on its grazing lands and at some unknown date conquered Soba, while at the beginning of the sixteenth century the Funj attacked from the south, captured the remaining Alwan strongholds, and established a new principality with its capital at Sennar.

The overthrow of a Christian government in Alwa led to the end of an organized Church there. Fr. Francisco Alvarez during his stay in Ethiopia (1520–6) met a Syrian Christian, John of Tripoli, who had travelled in 'Nubia', which would seem to have been Alwa rather than distant Makuria. John told him that:

> there are in it 150 churches which still contain crucifixes and figures of Our Lady and other figures painted on the walls, and all old; and the people of the country are neither Christians, Moors nor Jews, *and they live in the desire of being Christians.* These churches are all in ancient castles which they have throughout the country.[37]

While Alvarez was in Ethiopia an embassy from the Christians of Alwa came to the Emperor Lebna Dengel 'begging him to send them priests and monks to teach them'. He declined to do this, pointing out that he owed religious obedience to the Coptic Patriarch and implying that they should appeal directly to him. The absence of a Christian ruler in Alwa would have made the accreditation of any such mission very difficult, and, as had already happened in Makuria, Christianity gradually faded away in Alwa also.

There was nothing ephemeral about Nubian Christianity. It lasted for almost a thousand years and covered an immense stretch of the Nile Valley, from Philae to beyond the junction with the Blue Nile. This whole area contained churches and cathedrals in which the liturgy was sung in Greek and which were decorated with frescoes in the Byzantine style.

The North African Church

Christians in the Roman coastal provinces of Africa to the west of Cyrenaica belonged to the Western Church and worshipped in Latin. The Church was established there by 180 and in the third century produced two important theologians, Tertullian (d. *c.* 225) and St Cyprian, Bishop of Carthage, martyred in 258.

The north African Church suffered quite severely during the persecutions, and in Constantine the Great's reign, when it was granted toleration, was bitterly divided by the Donatist schism. The Donatists, who called themselves the Church of the Martyrs, refused to remain in communion with those who had collaborated with the imperial authorities during the persecution of Diocletian. Caecilian, who was recognized by the rest of the Catholic world as lawful Bishop of Carthage (*c.* 311–*c.* 343), was unacceptable to the Donatists because he had been consecrated by a collaborator. Attempts by the emperor to heal this division proved unsuccessful, and a hundred years later, although the greater part of the population there had become Christian, the African Church remained more or less evenly divided between Donatists and Catholics.

The most distinguished member of the north African Church was St Augustine, born at Thagaste in Algeria in 354. Although his mother Monica was a Christian, he had a pagan father and was not received into the Catholic Church until he was thirty-three years old. At that time he was teaching rhetoric in the imperial schools of Milan, where he was instructed by the learned bishop, St Ambrose. In 388 he returned to Africa and in 395 became co-adjutor to the Bishop of Hippo, whom he soon succeeded, and he remained there until his death in 431. Augustine wrote and preached extensively on the Scriptures and on Christian doctrine and in *The City of God* defended the Church against pagan criticisms that the adoption of Christianity by the empire had led to the collapse of Roman power. His writings had a profound influence on the development of Western Christian thought in the Middle Ages (see p. 22).

As Bishop of Hippo Augustine had to come to terms with the Donatists, with whom he had little natural sympathy, for his own Christian vision had been shaped in the cosmopolitan atmosphere of Milan; the Donatists represented narrow and provincial Christian values, and their self-justification seemed increasingly irrelevant as the age of persecutions receded beyond the memory of living men. Augustine used his considerable influence to urge the imperial authorities to coerce the Donatists into conformity. In 411 a council was held at Carthage, attended by 286 Catholic and 284 Donatist bishops, at which the Donatists were offered the choice of submission or expulsion from their sees. Given the almost equal numbers of the two groups it is clear that such a policy had little hope of success. The use of religious coercion of this kind was not in itself new: the emperors had been attempting to enforce religious uniformity on their Christian subjects by such means throughout the fourth century. Yet Augustine's contribution to this controversy was malign, because it gave the stamp of Catholic episcopal approval to the coercion of religious dissenters and although it had no immediate effect, it was to prove influential in the formulation of Western canon law. (see p. 50). The Donatists did not themselves discourage violence. Among their supporters were the Circumcellions, so called because they lived around the shrines, or *cellae*, of the martyrs. The movement had probably begun as a peasant protest against social injustice, but the Circumcellions came to identify themselves with the Donatist Church of the Martyrs and beat up their Catholic opponents shouting *Iaudes Deo* ('God be praised').

Between 429 and 439 much of Roman north Africa was conquered by the Vandals, one of the Germanic peoples who had settled in the Western provinces in the early fifth century (see p. 19). They had been converted to Arianism by imperial missionaries in the fourth century and were fiercely anti-Catholic. They established an Arian Church in their kingdom, confiscated the lands of the Catholic Church, exiled some Catholic bishops, and under King Huneric (477–84) harshly punished the Catholic laity as well. The Vandals found difficulty in maintaining control over some of the provinces they had conquered. Desert nomads, who were pagans, attacked the settled lands of what is now southern Tunisia, while in much of what is now western Algeria and Morocco, Berber kings, who were Christian, asserted their independence.

In 533–4 Belisarius recovered north Africa for the Emperor Justinian. The Vandals were decisively defeated, Roman government was restored, Arianism was proscribed and the Catholic Church was re-established there. This caused few problems, for Arianism had remained the religion of the Vandal court and had not put down any

The monastery of St Symeon at Aswan in Egypt.

popular roots. Donatism persisted, but was far less powerful than it had been in the pre-Vandal era. Justinian undertook an extensive building programme to demonstrate that Catholic imperial power had indeed been restored; but it did not prove possible to restore the frontier to where it had been before the Vandal invasion. The native kings in the highland regions of the western provinces remained fiercely independent and imperial authority was restricted to the coastal areas. The restored Catholic Church, however, was vigorous. In the reign of Justin II (565–78) it sent missionaries who converted some of the Garamantes, a nomadic people who lived in the Sahara to the south of Tripolitania and whose power extended to the Nile Valley.

The Arabs who had conquered Egypt advanced westwards and captured Tripoli in 647–8; but although they made frequent raids much further to the west, they made no permanent conquests beyond Tripolitania until the 690s. This was due chiefly to the fierce resistance of independent Berber tribes in southern Tunisia. The Byzantine cities of Africa meanwhile offered asylum to Melkites from Egypt and Syria, who sought refuge from the Arabs, among whom was St Maximus the Confessor (d. 662), one of the greatest masters of the mystical life in the Byzantine Church. He was also one of the most vocal critics of the Monothelete compromise which Heraclius and his successors were trying to impose in the empire (see p. 118). Until the end of Byzantine rule African Christianity retained the intellectual vigour which had characterized it since the time of Tertullian.

When the Arabs finally overcame Berber resistance they were able to advance quite rapidly. Carthage fell to them in 698 and Ceuta, the last Byzantine garrison in north Africa, capitulated in 709. The eighth century was a crucial time for Christianity in north Africa, but there are no histories written by north African Christians after 700 and no surviving Arab accounts of the area date from before *c.* 800. The provinces which the Arabs conquered had a population which was almost completely Latin Catholic, belonging to a well organized church which had existed for five hundred years, yet it did not prove resilient under Islamic rule. Although the reasons for this may only be conjectured, the process of Christian decline may be charted with reasonable accuracy.

Some of the ruling families and church leaders fled to Western Europe to escape from the Arabs, but this was a universal phenomenon in all the Roman provinces conquered by the Arabs and does not in itself account for the collapse of the north African Church. Some Berber tribes allied with the Arab invaders, which almost certainly involved their becoming Muslim, but this was by no means true of all the Berbers. In the Ibadite principality founded in western Algeria in 761, Christians had a church in the newly founded capital of Tahert and enjoyed social and legal parity with the Muslims. When the Shi'ite Fatimids conquered Tahert in 908 the Christian inhabitants felt a sense of solidarity with the Ibadite leaders and chose to accompany them into exile at the distant oasis of Wargla. It is true that the Ibadites were members of a radical Muslim sect, but Christians were also well treated at Kairouan, the centre of orthodox Muslim power in north Africa, where in 793 their leader Constantine obtained permission from the governor al-Fadl to build a new church.

Later Arab writers were not very interested in recording Christian survival, which makes the information they do give about it more credible. Ibn Said (fl. 1286) says of the people called the Barkanu who lived to the north of the Air Mountains in the central Sahara, 'those who live near Kanem are Muslims, those who border on the land of Nubia are Christians, those who live at Zaghawa are pagans'. Cuoq speculates that it is possible that the Christian Barkanu were part of the tribe of the Garamantes, converted to Christianity under Justin II.[38] The strangest report is that of al-Zuhri (d. between 1154 and 1161) who affirmed that a people named Barbara, who lived to the south of the Sahara near the city of Ghana, were Christians. Cuoq suggests that, if this report is true, this people may have been descended from Christian Berbers driven from Morocco by the Muslim invaders.[39]

Christianity in the former Roman cities seems to have remained quite vigorous in the early centuries of Arab rule. Pope Formosus (891–6) received a delegation of African bishops seeking advice about a schism which had developed in their provinces. Two generations later, however, a decline had set in. Pope Benedict VII (974–83) received envoys from Carthage asking him to consecrate the priest James as their bishop: 'We ask your holiness to assist our wretched and afflicted city of Africa, which is so destitute, that whereas it was once a metropolitan see, now there are hardly any priests there.'[40] Some eighty years later Pope Leo IX was asked to adjudicate a dispute about precedence between Thomas, Bishop of Carthage, and the Bishop of Mahdia in Tripolitania, and lamented that there were scarcely five bishops left in the whole African Church. In Gregory VII's reign (1073–85), Cyriacus of Carthage was the only bishop remaining in that Church, and being unable to muster the three bishops required by canon law to consecrate a new bishop of Tunis, was told by the pope to send the candidate to Rome for consecration. Gregory VII also entered into correspondence with an-Nasir, the emir of Bugia, about the appointment of a new bishop named Servandus for that see. an-Nasir was extremely cooperative, and this led Gregory to express a degree of warmth towards Islam which was so unusual in its day that it deserves to be cited:

> God the creator of all things, without whom we are unable to do or even to think anything that is good, inspired you to do this good work . . . For there is nothing which Almighty God, who wishes all men to be saved and no-one to perish, more greatly approves in us than that a man love his fellow men as he does himself . . . We and you owe this love to one another more particularly than we [either of us] do to other peoples, because we believe in and profess One God, albeit in a different way, whom we praise and reverence daily as the Creator of all ages and the governor of this world.[41]

Between 1134 and 1148 Roger II of Sicily captured the coastal cities of north Africa from Tripoli as far west as, but excluding, Tunis. He found Christians living in some of them and at Mahdia a bishop named Cosmas, who was confirmed in office by Pope Eugenius III. Between 1154 and 1160, after Roger II's death, the Almohad Caliphs of Morocco annexed the whole area and evicted the Norman garrisons. The local Christians may have suffered because of their identification with the Norman cause. Certainly Bishop Cosmas left with the Normans and sought refuge at Palermo.

Thereafter references to native north African Christianity become very rare. At Qal'a in central Algeria there was still in 1200 a Christian community with a church dedicated to Our Lady. In the fourteenth century the poll tax was still paid by Christians at Nefzawa in southern Tunisia, and Talbi has shown from a legal text of al-Burzuli (d. 1438) that in c. 1400 there were still African Christians in Tunis, who had a church of their own which had recently been rebuilt.[42] This is the last reference so far discovered to the remnants of the church of SS. Cyprian and Augustine. It is noteworthy that Leo the African makes no mention of surviving Christian communities in the Mahgrib in his *History and Description of Africa* written for a Catholic audience in 1526. Leo was a Muslim, born in Fez, who travelled widely through Africa before he was captured by Christian corsairs. He was subsequently freed by Pope Leo X who personally received him into the Catholic Church and it is therefore unlikely that Leo the African would have omitted any information from his account about indigenous Christian communities in Africa known to him, because news of that kind would have been very pleasing to his patrons.

New Western Initiatives

While old African Christianity withered away in the later Middle Ages, new Latin Christian influences began to make themselves felt there in the early thirteenth century. In 1226 when the Almohad Caliph, whose power had grown weak, wished to hire a company of Christian mercenaries, Ferdinand III of Castile agreed to this provided that the sultan allowed a church to be built for their use at Marrakesh. The newly founded Orders of Dominican and Franciscan friars were very anxious to undertake missionary work among the north African Muslims, and some of their brethren learnt Arabic. Theirs was a difficult vocation, because Islamic law forbade, on pain of death, members of other religions to convert Muslims to their own faith. In the 1220s seven Franciscans were put to death at Ceuta for breaking that law. Nevertheless, the mendicants were allowed to establish a few small houses in north African cities. Yet although their members sometimes became involved in religious debates with Muslim theologians, for most of the time they were confined to ministering to Catholic expatriate merchants, who had colonies in many of the north African ports, and to western soldiers of fortune in the service of Islamic rulers.

The capture of Ceuta by the Portuguese in 1415 marked the beginning of a new kind of Christian presence in Africa. This was an extension to North Africa of the wars of the *reconquista* by the rulers of Spain and Portugal. A number of cities and fortresses along the Mediterranean and Atlantic coasts were taken from the Muslims in the next hundred years, extending from Tripoli (1510) to Bugia (1510), Oran (1510), Mellila (1497), Tangier (1471), Agadir (1505) and to Sta Cruz de Mar Paquenda in southern Morocco (1478). These were European military enclaves on north African soil which had little influence over their hinterlands, although the Catholic Church was established in those places and Christianity could be preached freely to all their inhabitants.

During the fifteenth century the Portuguese began to explore the sea route to the Indies by way of the west coast of Africa. In the process they found and colonized Madeira, the Canaries and the Cape Verde Islands. They also established fortresses and settlements on the coast of the African mainland. They were very disappointed not to find evidence of Prester John's overlordship among the native peoples of West Africa, for they had a vastly exaggerated idea of the greatness of the Emperor of Ethiopia and the extent of his dominions. In 1482 the Portuguese reached the estuary of the Congo. King Nzinga a Knuwu later expressed a desire to become a Christian, and in 1491 was baptized as King John I. His new faith proved fragile because he refused to accept the Church's condemnation of polygamy, and he rejected Catholicism formally in 1495. But his son

San Salvador, capital of the Catholic Kingdom of Congo, in 1686.

Mpanza continued to adhere to the new faith and on the death of his father in *c.* 1506 became King Alfonso I. He proved very devout and during his long reign (1506–43) his capital, Mbanza, became known as San Salvador, and three churches were built there. Alfonso's young kinsman, Dom Henrique, was sent to Portugal to be trained as a priest, and in 1518 was consecrated bishop of the titular see of Utica by Pope Leo X. Three years later he returned to Congo, where he stayed until his death. The Catholic Church had received its first bishop from southern Africa, and the new faith quickly spread among King Alfonso's subjects. Unlike the areas settled by the Portuguese, the kingdom of Congo became an independent Christian state. As Charles Boxer has rightly said:

> The Portuguese kings of the house of Avis from 1483 onwards did not attempt to secure political control of the Kingdom of Congo, nor did they try to conquer it by force of arms. They were content to recognize the Kings of Congo as their brothers-in-arms; to treat them as allies and not as vassals; and to try to convert them and their subjects to Christianity by the dispatch of missionaries to the Congo, and by educating selected Congolese youths at Lisbon.[43]

In this way a new prospect for the future of Christianity in Africa seemed to be opening up in the early sixteenth century.

CHAPTER FIVE

THE CHURCH IN MEDIEVAL ASIA

hristianity possibly reached the Persian Empire in the second century and was certainly firmly established there by the third. Although the state religion of the Sassanian rulers was Zoroastrianism, Christians were not persecuted at that time. This changed in the fourth century when Christianity became the favoured religion of the Roman emperors. Sporadic persecutions of the Church in Persia took place from the reign of Shapur I (309–79), because it was seen as a pro-Roman element in the state, and with some reason, since the bishops of Persia were subject to the Patriarch of Antioch, who was a Roman subject.

In the fifth century the Church in Persia began to assert its independence. A synod in 410 recognized the bishop of Seleucia-Ctesiphon, the imperial capital, as Catholicus, that is, primate of all Christians in the Persian Empire, and in 424 the Catholicus Dadhiso declared himself independent of any higher ecclesiastical authority and his successors later became Patriarchs of the East. These changes occurred at a time when divisions were beginning to appear in the Great Church because of disagreements about the relation between the divine and human natures in Christ. The Persian Church had accepted the first two General Councils of Nicaea I (325) and Constantinople I (381). In 431 the Council of Ephesus condemned Nestorius, Patriarch of Constantinople, for holding unorthodox views about Christology which led him to refuse the title of *Theotokos*, the God-bearer, to the Blessed Virgin Mary (see p. 103). Nestorius had been trained in the theological schools of Antioch by Theodore of Mopsuestia (d. 428), whose understanding of the Christian faith was influential also in the schools of Edessa where most of the higher clergy of the Persian provinces received their training. The Church in the Persian Empire did not therefore accept the authority of the Council of Ephesus, and it later also rejected the Christological definitions formulated by the fourth Oecumenical Council of Chalcedon in 451 (see p. 103). Yet there was no formal breach between the Great Church in the Roman Empire and the Church in Persia until after the Emperor Zeno had published his *Henoticon*, or instrument of unity, in 482, and tried to force the members of the theological schools of Edessa to subscribe to it. This document upheld the rulings of the Council of Ephesus against Nestorius, and a large number of Edessan clergy refused to endorse this and migrated to the Persian city of Nisibis where they set up a new academy. The Catholicus Acacius of Seleucia-Ctesiphon (*c.* 486–96) formally severed relations with the Catholic Church at this time.

Thereafter the Persian Church formed a separate communion. It is often called the Nestorian Church, but as Aubrey Vine pointed out, 'Nestorius . . . has provided a name for a heresy which he did not originate, possibly did not hold, and for a Church which he did not found'.[1] Although the Persian Church would not condemn Nestorius, it regarded itself as the true heir not of him but of Theodore of Mopsuestia, whom it called 'Theodore the Interpreter'. Like other Eastern Christians, those of Persia distrusted the word *hypostasis* used in the Christological definition of Chalcedon accepted by the Catholic Church, expressing their belief in the Incarnation of Christ in the phrase, 'two natures, two persons and one presence'. Because it rejected the Council of Ephesus, the Persian Church refused the title of *Theotokos* to the Virgin Mary, which that Council had given her, referring to her instead as *Christotokos*, the Christ-bearer. Despite severing relations with the Church of the Roman Empire, the Church in Persia retained a high regard for St Peter's see of Rome, which was to prove important in later centuries when Western Catholics were able to reach Persia. The Persian Christians called themselves the Church of the East, a title which their later missionary endeavours amply justified and which will be used to describe their Church in this book; but because that is a name which has no adjectival form, the members of that Church will be described as Chaldean Christians, a name which was used of them by western writers in the Middle Ages.

Despite continued sporadic persecution by the Persian emperors, the Church of the East flourished in the sixth and early seventh centuries, and by 650 it consisted of ninety-six dioceses owing obedience to the Patriarch of Seleucia-Ctesiphon. Monasticism held a central place in its life, as it did in that of all Christian Churches at that time. It had been introduced by Mar Awgin (i.e. Eugenius) (d. 370), who according to later tradition had been a pearl fisher in the Red Sea before training as a monk under St Pachomius in Egypt. That link is uncertain, but St Awgin certainly founded a monastery on Mount Itzla outside Nisibis, and from there, after his death, the ascetic movement spread through northern Iraq. Good discipline seems to have collapsed in many of these houses in the following century, particularly because the rule of celibacy was abandoned by some of the brethren. A reform was undertaken by Abraham of Kashkar (d. 580), who had certainly visited Egypt and Sinai, and his restoration of the ascetic tradition gained wide acceptance in the monasteries of Persia.

Not all Christians in the Persian Empire belonged to the Church of the East. There was a strong Jacobite (Syrian Orthodox) presence just across the frontier, particularly in the monasteries of Tur Abdin, and there were bishops of that church in Persia who looked to the Jacobite Patriarch of Antioch as their canonical superior. In 629, after the Byzantine Emperor Heraclius had decisively defeated the Persians, the Jacobite Patriarch, Athanasius Gammala, established the office of Maphrian, or metropolitan of all the Jacobite bishops living in the Persian provinces, a position which was vested in the Bishops of Takrit.

Christianity in Arabia

The Arabian peninsula did not form part of the empires of either Persia or Rome, but Christianity spread from the towns in the frontier provinces to the nomad peoples there. The Arabs were particularly impressed by the witness of Christian hermits who had

The Byzantine basilica at Rusafa in Syria, consecrated in 559.

come to live in the Syrian desert. In 378 Queen Muwaiyya, ruler of the Tanukh federation which dominated the Roman frontier in Syria and Palestine, asked that the recluse, Moses of Raithu in the Sinai, should be consecrated bishop for her people. Christianity took root among the beduin and in 427 a group of nomads living to the east of the Dead Sea received as their bishop their former chieftain Botros, who had abdicated and become a solitary. Three bishops of the nomadic Arabs attended the Council of Chalcedon in 451.

Near the Persian frontier with Arabia the bishoprics of Kufa and al-Hira were founded in *c.* 380; they became centres for the evangelization of the Arabs of the Lakhmid confederacy, and met with considerable success, although it was not until the late sixth century that a Lakhmid ruler, Numan ibn Mundhir (583–*c.* 602), was baptized. In the early fifth century missions from the Church in eastern Persia began to work in the area of Bahrain (which then designated not just the island of that name, but also much of the coast of Arabia bordering the Persian Gulf), and several bishoprics were established there. Some Persian Christians, fleeing from persecution, settled in Oman, and a bishopric is first attested there in 424.

The Emperor Constantius (337–61) sent a diplomatic mission to the Himyarite kingdom in south-western Arabia. It was led by Theophilus, a Christian from Socotra or the Maldive Islands. He is said to have founded churches in the four main Himyarite

The fourth-century basilica at Kharrab Shams, province of Aleppo, in Syria.

cities, including Sana, the capital, and Aden. These churches were almost certainly for the use of visiting Christian traders. Christianity never became dominant in the Yemen, but during the fifth century it took firm root in the small principality of Najran immediately to the north, although the circumstances in which this happened are not known.

By the early sixth century the Ghassanids had become the dominant Arab power along the Roman frontier in Syria. They were Christians and the Emperor Justinian subsidized them to patrol the desert frontier and keep out raiders. By that time the fairly successful attempts which had been made by the imperial authorities to keep the supporters and opponents of the Council of Chalcedon in a single Church had been abandoned. Almost all the Christian nomads living along the Roman frontier in Syria and Mesopotamia became members of the new independent Jacobite (Syrian Orthodox) Church which was organised after 543 by Jacob Baradeus, Bishop of Syria and Mesopotamia, and his companion Theodore, Bishop of Palestine and Arabia (see p. 104). The Arabs who had been converted from Persia, the Lakhmids and the Christians of Bahrain and Oman, became members of the Church of the East in the late fifth century.

The Christian communities of the Yemen, under the influence of the Christian Kingdom of Aksum across the Red Sea, also rejected Chalcedon and the Byzantine Orthodox Church. In 523 the King of Himyar conquered the Christian principality of

Najran and massacred those who protested against his rule. This led King Kaleb of Aksum to annex Himyar and Kaleb's son, Gabra Masqal, built an impressive cathedral in the Yemenite capital Sana, but in 577, before any widespread evangelization had taken place, the province was annexed by the Persians (see p. 154). It seems clear from later evidence that thereafter the Church in the Yemen came under the authority of the Patriarch of the Church of the East.

Thus by the late sixth century Christianity was quite well established in the frontier regions of Arabia, although it had made little impact on the peoples of the interior. There is no evidence of an indigenous Christian presence in the Hijaz, the coastal area of the Red Sea north of Yemen, although Christian merchants traded there. It was there, at Mecca, in c. 570 that the Prophet Muhammad was born.

The Impact of Islam on the Churches of Arabia

Mecca was a place of pilgrimage in pre-Islamic times: this centred on the Ka'ba, a shrine built around a sacred stone. When Muhammad gained control of Mecca in 628 he dedicated this shrine to the worship of the One God. It was decorated inside with pictures of prophets and angels, and al-Azraqi, the historian of Mecca, reports:

> The day of the conquest of Mekka, the Prophet entered the Ka'ba and sent for al-Fadil ibn Abbas, who brought water from Zemzem, and ordered him to bring a rag soaked in water and efface the pictures, which he did. They say that the Prophet put his two hands on the picture of Isa ibn Maryam [Jesus son of Mary] and His Mother and said: 'Efface all these pictures except those under my hands'.[2]

As this anecdote implies, Muhammad was on good terms with Arab Christians. In 631 he is said to have sent envoys to Najran, ordering the people to submit to Islam or to be attacked, but making this provision: 'A Jew or a Christian [who] . . . holds fast to his religion is not to be turned from it.'[3]

It was claimed that as the Prophet was dying he counselled those present that the whole of Arabia should hold a single faith. The second Caliph, Omar (634–44), began to implement this policy by deporting some of the Christians of Yemen to the Mesopotamian frontier, yet although Arabian Christianity did subsequently decline, that was a slow process. Indeed, the Caliph Muawiya (661–80) was friendly with Arab Christians: he married a princess of the Christian Kalbite tribe, who was the mother of his successor, Yezid I. In Muawiya's reign the Patriarch of the Church of the East, George I, held a synod at Qatar in 676, attended by bishops from Bahrain and Oman. Muawiya's son, the short-lived Yezid I (680–3), was a close friend of the Christian Arab poet al-Akhtal. After that time such tolerant attitudes towards Arabian Christians became rarer. Under the Caliph Abd al-Malik (685–705), Moad, the sheikh of the Christian Taghlabites, was killed because he refused to apostatize. His people, nevertheless, were not intimidated by this and remained Christian. The Caliph al-Mahdi (775–85) is said to have coerced members of the Abu Tanukh who lived near Aleppo to become Muslims and to have executed those who refused to do so.

Such persecutions were erratic, perhaps partly because after the capital was moved from Damascus to Baghdad in 762 the centre of Islamic power was remote from Arabia. Certainly, Christian communities continued to exist there. Dionysius II, Jacobite Patriarch (818–45), consecrated bishops for the Taghlabites of northern Arabia, and Timothy I, Patriarch of the Church of the East (778–820), appointed Bishop Peter to Sana, the capital of Yemen, in 800. As late as 901 Timothy's successor, John V, received questions from a priest, Hasan, working in Yemen. The Christian Arab nomads living to the west of the lower Euphrates continued to be served by the Bishops of Hira until the early eleventh century.

There is little evidence of organized Christianity in Arabia after that time, but one outpost remained entirely Christian throughout the Middle Ages, the island of Socotra off the south Arabian coast. Cosmas Indicopleustes, who sailed on the Indian Ocean in the reign of Justinian, reports:

> In the . . . island of Dioscorides [Socotra], which is situated in the same Indian Sea, and where the inhabitants speak Greek, having been originally colonists sent thither by the Ptolemies who succeeded Alexander the Macedonian, there are clergy who receive their ordination in Persia and are sent on to the island, and there is also a multitude of Christians. I sailed along the coast of this island but did not land upon it. I met, however, with some of its Greek-speaking people who had come over into Ethiopia.[4]

Almost a thousand years later the island was still Christian and still part of the Church of the East, when the Portuguese annexed it in 1507.

The Impact of Islam on the Church of the East

The Arabs conquered the Persian Empire between 637 and 651. They treated the 'peoples of the book' whom they found there, Jews, Christians and Zoroastrians, in the same way as they did those in the lands which they conquered from Rome, granting them religious toleration but treating them as second-class citizens. Unlike the Christians of Syria and Egypt, who had been members of the established Church, Persian Christians had always been a tolerated minority in a state whose established religion was Zoroastrianism. The introduction of a new state religion, Islam, therefore made little difference to them. The Islamic authorities treated all Christian Churches in terms of parity. The Church of the East lost the favoured position which it had enjoyed under the Sassanians, while the Jacobites became able to compete with the Chaldeans on equal terms. Moreover, there were so many Byzantine Orthodox prisoners of war and traders in the Persian provinces that the caliphs allowed an Orthodox hierarchy to be established there with its own Catholicus. Because the Islamic conquest removed the frontier which had existed between Roman and Persian territory, the Church of the East was able to found churches in Jerusalem and Egypt. These were important as potential links with Western Christendom.

Although there was some intermittent persecution and although some caliphs enforced discriminatory laws harshly, the Christians of Persia were, on the whole, reasonably well treated. In 775 the Chaldean Patriarch moved his see from Seleucia-Ctesiphon to the new Abbasid capital of Baghdad, which does not suggest that his Church wished to keep a low profile. Indeed, Christians, many of whom had administrative skills, were employed in government, while a high proportion of physicians were Christians, including many of those attached to the caliph's court. The theological schools of Nisibis remained a centre of intellectual excellence, and Christian scholars, bilingual in Greek and Arabic, took a leading part in translating the corpus of classical Greek philosophical and scientific writings into Arabic. In the mid-ninth century a Christian, Husain ibn Ishaq (d. 873), was head of the House of Knowledge, the University of Baghdad.

Until the end of the eighth century the rate of conversion of Christians to Islam was low. The strength of the Church of the East at that time is shown by the fact that in *c.* 780 the Patriarch Timothy I erected a new province, that of Daylam, within the Islamic state. This area, immediately to the south-west of the Caspian Sea, had a pagan population and had not yet been garrisoned by the Muslims. Thomas Bishop of Marga (fl. 832–52) records how when Mar Elijah first went to Mokta to take up his post as metropolitan of the province, he found that local people revered a great oak tree called Yazd:

> And he asked for an axe . . . and rolled up the sleeves of his tunic, and he took the axe like a warrior and went to the tree, more especially . . . against the devil which dwelt therein . . . saying: 'The voice of the Lord moveth the hinds to calve and uprooteth the trees of the forest.' (Ps. 29, v. 9) . . . and he hewed down all its ancient strength and thickness with three strokes of the axe . . . and . . . he made signs to those people to come down to him . . . and they gathered together reeds and pieces of bramble and pieces of dry wood, and laid them upon the tree and upon its branches, and burnt them up, and thus the error of the devil ceased.[5]

Although few new monasteries were founded after the Islamic conquest, monasticism remained a very important part of the life of the Church of the East, not least because all parish clergy were required to marry, whereas bishops had to be celibate, so that the hierarchy was recruited from monks. The Church worshipped in Syriac, a learned language, like Latin in the Western Church. The eucharistic liturgy around which Chaldean piety was centred was attributed to St Addai, said to have been one of the seventy disciples of Christ, and his pupil St Mari, though it was in fact derived from the rite of Antioch. It was revised by the Patriarch Isoyahb III (*c.* 647–58). The Church of the East is unique in providing for the bread of the sacrament to be liturgically prepared in an oven in the church sacristy, and the eucharistic rite begins with prayers to be said while the bread is made and baked, and these include a substantial part of the Psalter. Like all eastern liturgies, that of SS. Addai and Mari emphasizes the transcendental nature of the eucharist and the way in which the hosts of Heaven and the Church on earth are drawn together to worship the Lamb that was slain. The deacons, for example, prepare the congregation for Holy Communion by singing:

The monastery of St Symeon, Qalaat Seman, Syria.

I am the bread which came down from on high said our Saviour in the mysteries to his disciples. Whoso hath love approacheth and receiveth it and liveth for ever in me and inheriteth the kingdom. . . . The cherubim and seraphim and archangels in fear and trembling stand before the altar and gaze at the priest breaking and dividing the body of Christ for the pardon of trespasses . . . O thou who in mercy dost open the door to the penitent and callest sinners to come to thee, open to us, O my Lord, the door of thy mercies and let us enter by it and sing praise to thee by night and by day.[6]

The Church of the East shared with the rest of medieval Christendom the belief that holy men and women who sought to lead the life of perfection could exercise authority in the natural world, just as Adam had done before the Fall. Thomas of Marga tells how Rabban Gabriel, abbot of the monastery of Birta, was given some fish by a villager whose son had been cured of a painful skin infection by the prayers of the brethren:

And while the fish, which they were about to fry on the fire in Rabban's chamber, were lying in the pan, Rabban's cat came and took one of them. And Rabban . . . laughing, said to him: ' . . . he that brought the fish did not receive healing from thee, but through the prayers [of the brethren]; let it go, wretched creature, that chastisement may not fall upon thee'. [Whereupon] a strong eagle seized the cat and bore him up into the air. And Rabban said: 'Let him go and [let him] offend not a second time.' And the eagle let him down and laid him upon the ground uninjured.[7]

Although the Church of the East remained separate from the rest of Christendom, the doctrinal differences which set it apart became less significant as the centuries passed. The Patriarch Timothy I, while calling Mary the Mother of Christ rather than the Mother of God, glossed this term: 'Mary is the Mother of Christ Our Lord who is above everything: that is [she is] both the mother of God and of man.'[8]

About a century later, another member of the same Church, Elijah Jauhan, wrote with a degree of candour unusual among Christian apologists in any age:

So whereas [the Chaldeans, Jacobites and Byzantine Orthodox] differ in word, they agree in meaning; and although they contradict one another outwardly, they agree inwardly. And all of them follow one faith and believe in one Lord and serve one Lord. There is no difference between them in that, nor any distinction, except from the point of view of party feelings and strife.[9]

By the year 1000 the Church of the East still had fifteen provinces in the Islamic lands ruled from Baghdad and over seventy bishops, but the Christian population was being eroded by conversions to Islam. These losses were in large measure offset by the Church's expansion into parts of Asia beyond the Islamic frontiers. This was a process which pre-dated the coming of Islamic rule, for even in the sixth century the Patriarch of Seleucia-Ctesiphon had been regarded as their canonical head by the Christians of South India.

The St Thomas's Christians

The Christians of South India claimed that their church had been founded by the Apostle Thomas. His apocryphal acts, which were widely known in the Middle Ages, told how Thomas had been given a large amount of money by the king of India, Gundophorus, to build him a palace, but had given it all away to the poor. The king intended to have Thomas executed for embezzlement until his dead brother appeared to him in a dream and complained that whereas he had no palace in heaven a splendid one was awaiting Gundophorus there. Thereupon the king believed the apostolic preaching and was baptized with all his family. Gundophorus, or Gundophernes, was an Indian king of the first century AD whose coinage is known, but he ruled in north-western India. If there is any truth in this legend it would not preclude the possibility that St Thomas might also have preached in South India. It would certainly have been possible for an Apostle to reach India in the first Christian century for Roman ships regularly sailed there by way of the Red Sea, but there is no proof except in South Indian oral tradition that St Thomas went there.

Christianity had probably reached South India by the fourth century when the Emperor Constantius (337–61) sent Theophilus as his ambassador to the Christians of the Yemen, the Maldive Islands and India, in order to persuade them to adhere to the moderate Arianism of the imperial court. Theophilus claimed to have reformed some of the customs of these churches. He was particularly scandalized by the way in which Indian congregations sat through the reading of the Gospel at Mass, whereas everywhere else in the world Christians stood to hear the Gospel. There is no doubt that his mission took place, but the term 'India' is a vague one and does not necessarily refer to South India, although it probably did so since that is the part of India nearest to the Maldive Islands.

Cosmas Indicopleustes, a retired sea captain who became a monk at Alexandria and in *c.* 550 wrote *The Christian Topography* in order to prove, contrary to the opinion of all educated Christians, that the earth was flat, had travelled in the Indian Ocean, and his information about places there is generally considered accurate. He reports the presence of a Christian community in Ceylon, who had a church served by a priest and deacon sent from Persia. Nothing else is known about Christianity in Ceylon during the Middle Ages and it seems likely that this church had been built for the use of Christian merchants trading there, rather than for an indigenous Christian community.

Cosmas also reports that, 'In the country called Male, where the pepper grows, there is also a church and at another place called Calliana there is moreover a bishop, who is appointed from Persia.'[10] It is generally agreed that Male refers to the Malabar coast of India, that Calliana is Quilon and that, when Cosmas wrote, the Church in South India formed part of the Church of the East under the jurisdiction of the Patriarch of Seleucia-Ctesiphon. This situation had not changed when the Portuguese reached South India almost a thousand years later.

The history of that thousand years is not easy to reconstruct because when, at the Synod of Diamper in 1599, the Portuguese authorities sought to make the St Thomas's Christians conform to the rulings of the Council of Trent, books written in Syriac and considered heretical were ordered to be burnt and as a result most of the medieval evidence about the Church of the Malabar was destroyed. There is, however, some other fragmentary evidence which survives from the medieval centuries. The British resident in Travancore in 1806 recovered from the Dutch archive there two copper plates dating from *c.* 880, which record grants made by King Ayyan of Venad to the Christian Church in Quilon. These include the right to administer customs duties and weights and measures in the port of Quilon and the plates also record that the king took the Church and its lands under royal protection and assigned to the Church peasants to work those lands.

There is also the report made by Abbot Odo of St Rémi at Rheims, corroborated by an anonymous independent writer, of the visit to the court of Pope Calixtus II in 1122 of an Indian archbishop called John. Odo was present at the papal audience when the archbishop, speaking through an interpreter, painted a glowing picture of the number and wealth of the Indian Christians. The River Pison, one of the four rivers of Eden, flowed through their capital city, he claimed, bringing down gold and jewels from the earthly Paradise, and the body of St Thomas was preserved incorrupt in the cathedral. On his patronal feast the body of the Apostle was placed on a throne in the choir to preside at the liturgy, and during the Mass he opened his hand to receive the offerings of the faithful, but closed it if a heretic approached him. At this point Pope Calixtus intervened and ordered John not to tell such lies in his court, but the archbishop swore solemnly that everything he had said was true. It is possible that, as some scholars have argued, Archbishop John was an impostor, but he may equally well have been, as he claimed, an Indian prelate who had gone on pilgrimage to Jerusalem (then ruled by the crusaders) and had come on to visit Rome, where he had given an exaggerated account of the strength and riches of Indian Christians because he thought that this was what western people wanted to hear.

In the following century western visitors were able to go to India and judge for themselves. Marco Polo, who visited south India on his way back from China in c. 1293, saw the tomb of St Thomas at Mylapore near Madras. His is the earliest account of the site:

> The body of Messer St Thomas the Apostle lies in this province of Maabar at a certain little town having no great population. It is a place where few traders go, because there is very little merchandise to be got there, and it is . . . not very accessible. Both Christians and Saracens [Muslims] . . . frequent it in pilgrimage. For the Saracens also do hold the saint in great reverence and say that he was one of their own Saracens.[11]

When the Portuguese reached India the church at Mylapore was in ruins, although a Muslim guardian kept a light burning there claiming that the shrine was the tomb of a Muslim holy man. In 1523 the Portuguese excavated the site and found human bones at a deep level beneath the tomb, but there was no indication of their provenance. Then in 1547, when they dug the foundations for an oratory on a nearby hill, which was the alleged site of St Thomas's martyrdom, they found a granite cross with an inscription which they could not read. It is now dated by archaeologists to the eighth century and in 1925 the script was identified as Pehlevi and was translated, 'My Lord Christ, have mercy on Afras, son of Chaharbukht the Syrian, who cut this [stone].'[12] This shows that the site of the martyrdom was venerated by South Indian Christians in the early Middle Ages, but proves nothing more than that.

In the early fourteenth century the Dominican Order sent a mission to India. Despite the martyrdom of four of the brethren at Tana near Bombay, the friars met with some success. The Dominicans had no very high opinion of the clergy of the St Thomas's Church, and in addition to their other shortcomings considered them heretics. This mission was still in existence in 1350 when John of Marignolli, the pope's legate to China, visited Quilon on his way back to Europe (see p. 205), for he found a Catholic church there dedicated to St George. The political situation in the Middle East made it almost impossible for western Europeans to travel on the Indian Ocean in the later fourteenth century and when the Portuguese arrived in south India in 1498 by way of the Cape of Good Hope they found no trace of the Dominican mission.

On his second voyage to India in 1502 Vasco da Gama went to Cochin where he was met by a delegation of St Thomas's Christians who handed him a red staff decorated with three silver bells on the top, and asked him to represent their interests with the Indian rulers. In 1510, when the Portuguese captured Goa and established a viceroyalty of the Indies, they began to number St Thomas's Christians among their subjects. The Portuguese established a Catholic hierarchy in their Indian dominions but at first the relations between the Catholic clergy and the St Thomas's Christians were very good, and in 1517 they made a joint pilgrimage to the shrine of St Thomas at Mylapore, for example.

The St Thomas's Christians worshipped in Syriac. Copies of their liturgical books were taken to Rome and presented to the pope by one of their bishops, Mar Joseph, in 1556 and are still in the Vatican Library. From these it is clear that the St Thomas's Christians used the rite of the Church of the East in a form which dated from about the seventh century. The patriarch of that Church consecrated a metropolitan archbishop and three suffragans for the Malabar Church; they were always Persians, but the priests and deacons were Indians. In 1590 the Portuguese estimated that there were some 70,000 St Thomas's Christians in South India. It was a substantial community, with no known history of persecution: the Hindu rulers seem to have tolerated the Christians because they did not attempt to make converts. Yet although the Christians of the Malabar were members of the Church of the East in the forms of worship they used and in their understanding of the faith, many of their social attitudes had inevitably been shaped by the Hindu society in which they lived.

The Church of the Malabar, like all churches, had some idiosyncrasies. Thus its members accepted trial by ordeal (just as the Western Church had done until it was abolished by the Fourth Lateran Council in 1215) and suspects were sometimes required to prove their innocence by swimming across crocodile-infested rivers. The most controversial aspect of South Indian Christian practice was their acceptance of the caste system. Those who could claim descent from the thirty-two brahmin families said to have been converted by St Thomas took precedence in the community. Moreover, although the Church would baptize untouchables, it continued to observe Hindu rituals of cleansing in its relations with them, and they therefore could not worship with the rest of the community. The St Thomas's Christians could have had no social dealings with the dominant Hindu society unless they had acted in this way, but the Papacy was later to forbid Jesuit missionaries to adopt such practices because they are contrary to the belief that all Christians are spiritually equal. That is a controversy which falls outside the scope of this book.

The Spread of Christianity in Central Asia and China

A remarkable expansion of Christianity took place in Asia in the early Middle Ages for which the Church of the East was mainly responsible. As early as 424 a bishopric was established at Merv, an important stage on the Silk Road which led from the Persian Empire through Central Asia to China. A century later Merv was given metropolitan status and became the centre of a church province. Then in 549 the Patriarch Mar Aba I sent a bishop to the White Huns (the Hephthalites), who were the dominant power in the lands beyond the River Oxus. Any progress made there was shortlived because Hephthalite power collapsed within a decade, but a precedent had been established for sending missions to the peoples beyond the Persian frontiers.

One of the earliest and most successful of such missions was sent along the Silk Road to the Chinese Empire. This is known from the stele discovered at Sianfu [Xian] in 1625. It had been erected in 781 and recorded the arrival in 635 of a delegation of clergy from the West led by Alopen, who had brought the Christian Scriptures with him. The Emperor T'ai-tsung (626–49), the second emperor and real founder of the Tang dynasty, had those writings translated into Chinese and studied them carefully. In 638 he licensed the practice of the Christian faith in his Empire in a decree which was copied on the Sianfu stele:

Alopen, a Persian monk, bringing the religion of the Scriptures from far, has come to offer it at the chief metropolis [Xian]. The meaning of his religion has been carefully examined. It is mysterious, wonderful, calm. It fixes the essentials of life and perfection. It is right that it should spread through the Empire. Therefore let the ministers build a monastery in the Ining-fang [a city square in Sianfu] and let twenty-one men be admitted as monks.[13]

Among the writings found by Sir Aurel Stein when he excavated the library of Tunhuang were Chinese translations of works ascribed to Alopen which seek to explain Christian beliefs using terminology drawn from Taoist and Buddhist texts with which educated Chinese people would have been familiar. The new religion proved popular, and the next emperor, Kao-tsung (649–83), gave Alopen permission to found a monastery in every prefecture.

Although in the last years of the century there was an anti-Christian reaction at court and members of the Church were persecuted, this hostility was temporary. The Patriarch of Baghdad sent a new group of clergy to lead the Chinese Church in 732 and the Emperor Hsuan-tsung (712–54) restored to that Church all its former privileges. The stele was erected at Sianfu in 781 by Bishop Adam and the chief Christian leaders in China, and in 789 the Patriarch Timothy I appointed the monk David from Beth Abe as new metropolitan of the Church in China.

The continuing success of Christianity was halted by the Emperor Wu-tsung, who favoured Taoism, and in 845 forbade the practice of foreign religions and ordered the closure of monasteries. These measures took some time to implement, but Abu-l-Faraj, a scribe in the service of the Church of the East, reported in 987 that there were no Christians left in China. This statement should not, perhaps, be taken literally, and may simply mean that there was no longer a hierarchy appointed by the Patriarch of Baghdad. There were certainly Christians in Canton a century later, though they may have been traders rather than an indigenous community.

The Church of the East evangelized other peoples living along the Silk Road. A new church province, with its capital at Samarkand, had been established in the most easterly region of the Abbasid Empire by the last quarter of the eighth century. Using this as a base, the Patriarch Timothy I was able to undertake various initiatives, such as appointing a metropolitan for the nomad Turks of western Turkestan in 782–3. The spread of Christianity among the peoples of what later became the province of Sinkiang is not well documented, but undoubtedly occurred. By the ninth century there was a

Niccolò Polo, his brother Maffeo and his son Marco present the pope's letter to Kubilai Khan, from an English manuscript, c. 1400.

church in Khotan, while a Chaldean monastery has been excavated at Turfan and a cemetery found at Serenice to the south of Lake Balkash containing Christian burials dating from 825–1367/8. The inscriptions show that there were Christian monasteries in that area also.

In 795–8 Timothy I consecrated a metropolitan for Tibet. At that time Buddhism was still struggling to establish itself there and was meeting with strong opposition from the indigenous religion of the *Bon-po* shamanists. There seems no doubt that the Church of the East had a presence there; three large Chaldean crosses have been found inscribed in the rocks at Dran-tse in Ladakh, for example. David Snellgrove and Hugh Richardson comment on the fact that:

Both *rNying-ma* [the oldest form of Tibetan Buddhism] and *Bon-po* possess a special kind of ritual, known as the 'Consecration for Life' (*Tshe-dbang*), the main part of which is the distribution to all present of little pellets of barley-flour and sips of consecrated ale (*chang*). The receiving of these sacred items of food serves to strengthen the 'life-force' or 'soul' (*bla*) of the faithful. One may wonder whether such a ritual was copied from the Nestorians [the Church of the East] . . . But to prove this beyond doubt would be difficult.[14]

In the event Christianity did not take root in Tibet, but it is important to remember that in the late eighth century this was not a foregone conclusion because Buddhism did not become firmly established there until the tenth or early eleventh centuries.

The greatest success of the Church of the East was to convert some of the Mongol-Turkic peoples. A letter written in 1009 by the Metropolitan of Merv to the Patriarch of Baghdad, John VI, relates how the Khan of the Keraits had been drawn to Christianity because he had successfully invoked the help of St Sergius to guide him when he was lost on the steppes and how he had requested baptism for himself and his people. The metropolitan reports that the entire people had been baptized.[15] By the twelfth century the new faith had spread from the Keraits to their neighbours, the Naimans and the Merkits.

By the twelfth century some Christian communities were to be found almost everywhere along the main trade routes of Central Asia between Samarkand and China. Christianity also took root at that time among the Onguts, a Turkic people living in the Ordos region of Inner Mongolia immediately north of the Great Wall. Christians were to be found among the Kara-Khitai, or Black Cathayans, a Mongol people from north-western China, who moved westwards in the first half of the twelfth century and by attacking the easternmost lands of Islam activated the legend of Prester John in Western Europe.

The Kingdom of Prester John[16]

The first report of Prester John reached Western Europe in 1145. Bishop Otto of Freising, who was visiting the papal court, met there Bishop Hugh of Jabala from the Crusader States, who told him how, a few years before, 'a certain John, King and Priest, who lived in the extreme East beyond Armenia and Persia', had launched an attack on the lands of eastern Islam. Prester John (in Latin *presbyter Iohannes*) was immensely rich and was reputed to be of the race of the Magi who had come to worship the infant Christ. Otto of Freising was writing a history of the world and included this story in it. As Otto was a learned churchman and uncle of the Emperor Frederick Barbarossa, Prester John entered the western consciousness with impeccable credentials. The story which Bishop Hugh had told was not entirely unfounded: the Kara-Khitai, or Black Cathayans, had attacked eastern Islam in 1141 and defeated the armies of Sultan Sinjar, and there had been Christian troops among them.

If he had been mentioned only in the work of Otto of Freising, Prester John would probably have remained a scholarly curiosity known only to a few people, but this changed when in *c.* 1165 a letter written in Latin, which purported to be from Prester John himself, began to circulate in Western Europe.[17] In it the Priest King gave more information about the extent of his dominions:

Ho Preste Joam das indias.

Verdadera informaçam das terras do Preste

Joam, segundo vio z escreueo ho padre Francisco Aluarez capellã del Rey nosso senhor. Agora nouaméte impresso por mandado do dito senhor em casa de Luis Rodriguez liureíro de sua alteza.

'Prester John of the Indies', the title page of Francesco Alvarez' account of the kingdom of Ethiopia, published 1540.

Our Magnificence rules in the Three Indies, and our land extends from the furthest India, in which the body of St Thomas the Apostle is laid to rest, and stretches through the desert towards the sunrise, and returns westwards to the deserted [city of] Babylon beside the tower of Babel.

In its earliest form the letter tells how seventy-two kings are subject to Prester John, and how when he goes to war 10,000 cavalry and 100,000 infantry march behind each of his twelve banners. In his palace 30,000 guests dine each day at a table made of emerald; among his subjects are the Pygmies, the Amazons and the Ten Lost Tribes, and through his kingdom flows one of the rivers of Paradise which carries gold and gems; among the fauna of his realm are elephants, camels, gryphons and the phoenix.

This letter aroused great interest; it circulated widely and was translated into most western languages. It assured the Priest King a place in the western imagination. Although many of the elements which go to make up the account of Prester John's Kingdom can be traced to sources available in Western Europe in the twelfth century, this is not true of all of them and the name Prester John is not found in any source earlier than Otto of Freising. Although it is often thought that the name was suggested by the visit to Rome in 1122 of Archbishop John from India (see pp. 186–7), this explanation is not entirely satisfactory because the archbishop did not claim to be a king. Vasiliev has argued persuasively that the name related to St John the Evangelist, who was reputed to be deathless and who styled himself presbyter in the Greek text of his Epistles.[18] David Wasserstein has recently pointed out the similarities between some of the material in the Prester John letter and the account sent in 883 by the Jews of Kairouan to the head of the rabbinic academy of Babylon in Iraq of the report given to them about his homeland by a certain Eldad ha-Dani, who claimed to have been a member of the Ten Lost Tribes. Since this Hebrew source was 300 years older than the Prester John letter and was not accessible to Christian writers at the time that letter was drawn up, the possibility exists that there may have been some oral tradition circulating in the Near East in the early Middle Ages from which the Prester John legend was in part derived.[19]

It is not known who wrote the Prester John Letter or what his motives were. It may have been intended as a literary fantasy, describing the wonders of the East, or it may have been a product of the quarrel between Pope Alexander III and the Emperor Frederick Barbarossa, since it describes a Christian utopia in which the Church is firmly subordinated to the Empire. Certainly the pope seems to have believed that the letter was a piece of anti-papal propaganda, for as soon as he had emerged the victor in his quarrel with the emperor in 1177 he devised some counter-propaganda by writing to Prester John, upbraiding him for his pride and telling him that he was sending his physician Philip to put him right about those matters of doctrine in which he erred. This is a sure sign that the letter was an exercise in public relations, not, as it is often claimed, evidence that the pope also believed in Prester John and wished to contact him. No pope has ever entrusted a religious mission to a layman and Alexander had no shortage of cardinals to represent him. The general public was less critical of the Prester John Letter than the pope. It appeared when the crusade movement was vigorous and the crusader kingdom was threatened by the growth of Muslim power in the Near East under Nur ad-Din of Damascus. People in the West wanted to believe that beyond the vast empire of Islam there was a great Christian ruler with whom it might be possible to make common cause.

Western people in the Middle Ages were not particularly gullible; the problem was that their knowledge of Asia was very patchy. The rise of the Arab Empire in the seventh century had cut the West off from all direct means of communication with lands further to the east, so Westerners had to rely for information on the reports of classical writers. These were a strange mixture: on the one hand there were the factual accounts of travellers who had visited India, Ceylon, and perhaps more distant regions, voyaging from Roman Egypt by way of the Red Sea and the Indian Ocean; while on the other hand there were mythical accounts of the marvels of the East – the monstrous races and strange animals that were to be found there, described by Solinus in his uncritical account of world geography and also by the medieval *Alexander Romance*. Since western people were unable to visit those regions they had no means of empirically testing the reliability of these sources. Moreover, no adequate means of recording geographical information had yet been devised; there were no scientifically designed maps. The Three Indias over which Prester John claimed to rule were part of that world picture. The areas were not precisely defined, but in general terms the First India designated the lands which we now think of as Afghanistan and northern India and perhaps Tibet; the Second India meant the southern part of the Indian subcontinent; while the Third India referred to the Horn of Africa, the area from which, in antiquity, men had sailed to the other two Indias.

People in the Medieval West thought that there might be Christian communities in all these unknown lands. Most educated opinion held that the Apostles had literally carried out the Lord's command and preached the Gospel to all nations (Mk. 16:15), and it was known that there were Christians in Asia because pilgrims from those regions came to Jerusalem while it was ruled by the crusaders. All these factors combined to make the alleged kingdom of Prester John seem more credible. The Prester John was even translated into most western languages, and also into Hebrew, because the Jews were interested in the information it gave of the Ten Lost Tribes who lived beyond the stony River Sambatyon. Naturally the marvels of Prester John's kingdom grew as scribes added new information to the copies they made of it.

However, when Prester John made no attempt to come to the help of his fellow Christians after Saladin had captured Jerusalem in 1187, it seemed likely that he would become simply part of western lore about the marvels of the East, like the Fountain of Perpetual Youth in the *Alexander Romance*, and cease to be thought of as a potential ally. This did not happen because of events which took place during the Fifth Crusade. Having attacked Egypt in 1219 and captured Damietta on the Nile delta, the crusade came to a standstill while waiting for reinforcements from the West with which to attempt the conquest of the rest of Egypt. The papal legate, Cardinal Pelagius, presided over the war council and exercised great moral authority although he lacked military experience. In 1221 the Eastern Christians in Damietta presented him with a prophecy in Arabic called *The Book of Clement* which purported to have been written by St Clement of Rome (*c.* AD 100) and to record prophecies made by St Peter himself. It was in fact based on an *Apocalypse of Peter*, an ancient apocryphal book, which had been updated to include topical allusions.

The legate was impressed by this work, which had apparently been written in the apostolic age. He had a translation made and found that it foretold how the fall of Damietta would mark the beginning of the total collapse of Islam, which would be completed by the arrival of two kings, one from the East and the other from the West, who would meet in Jerusalem in a year when Easter fell on 3 April. The legate was expecting a king to come from the West: the Emperor Frederick II had written to announce his arrival at Damietta later in 1221. Moreover, startling news had been received about an unknown king from the East. One of the senior Catholic clergy on

The battle between Genghis Khan and Prester John from a miniature in a manuscript of Marco Polo's Travels.

the Crusade, James of Vitry, Bishop of Acre, received a message from Prince Bohemond IV of Antioch in the early months of 1221. The prince reported how spice merchants coming from the East had brought him a written account of the deeds of David, King of the Indies, who was commonly called Prester John, but who in fact was the Priest King's great-grandson. Bohemond sent a copy of the Arabic text to James, who had a Latin translation made. It told how David had attacked the Great King of Persia and captured Bokhara, Samarkand, Ghazna and Khorasan.

At the same time, James received what seemed to be objective evidence corroborating this account. In 1219, when the Caliph of Baghdad asked the Sultan of Egypt for military support against a powerful new threat from the East, the sultan sent a group of crusader prisoners of war to Baghdad as evidence that he had a serious campaign on his own hands and could not second troops to defend Iraq. The caliph presented those prisoners to the leader of the invading forces, hoping perhaps to impress on him that his vassals were powerful enough to defeat great western armies. However, if that was his intention his ploy was used against him, for the enemy commander, realizing that the crusaders were fighting the Muslims just as he was, sent the prisoners under safe-conduct to Antioch, so that they might rejoin the crusade at Damietta. Since, because of language problems, they can only have had a very imperfect idea of who their benefactor had been, it seemed reasonable to the crusader leadership to assume that he had indeed been King David, commonly called Prester John, as the account sent by Prince Bohemond claimed.

In the legate's view therefore the prophecy of the *Book of Clement* was about to be fulfilled: Damietta had fallen, the King from the West was clearly the Emperor Frederick II, while the King from the East was equally clearly King David about whom James of Vitry had just received such encouraging news. The prophecy claimed that the two kings would meet in Jerusalem when Easter fell on 3 April and that would happen in 1222. The logic of this seemed inescapable to the cardinal: Jerusalem belonged to the Sultan of Egypt, if it was to be restored to Christian rule by Easter 1222, then the crusade must capture Cairo, the headquarters of Egyptian power, as soon as possible. He persuaded the lay commanders to set out for the south on 17 July 1221, ignoring the annual flooding of the Nile delta. The consequence was inevitable; a few weeks later the crusading army became immobilized by the floodwaters and had to surrender to the Sultan.

The *Book of Clement* had proved a false guide. Neither Frederick II nor King David came to Jerusalem in 1222. Indeed in that year the armies which had threatened the lands of the caliph from the East withdrew to inner Asia. As Jean Richard has shown, the account of King David given to Prince Bohemond was in fact an account of the rise of the Mongol Empire in western Asia, ending with the campaign of Genghis Khan and the Mongol horde against the lands of eastern Islam in the years 1219–21.[20]

The Impact of the Mongol Empire on Christianity in Asia

Genghis Khan, whom Cardinal Pelagius supposed was Prester John, was hereditary Khan of the Mongols. His personal name was Temujin, and he was a fine general who by 1206, having united all the tribes of Mongolia under his rule, was elected as the Great Khan. Among his subjects were the Keraits, the Naimans and the Merkits all of whom were wholly or in part Chaldean Christians (see p. 191), and members of his family married princesses from those peoples. Although this led to recurrent rumours that the Great Khans had themselves become Christian, Genghis and his own Mongol tribe remained shamanists, who believed in the one God of the heavens and in a multitude of spirits inhabiting the natural world with whom their shamans were able to communicate. The Mongols had a merited reputation for ruthlessness; at first they regarded the settled agrarian way of life of the surrounding nations with whom they went to war with total contempt. They slaughtered large numbers of people, sacked cities and destroyed irrigation systems; but they were always tolerant of all forms of religion because of the variety of faiths which existed in their own confederation. There are no statistics about the size of a Mongol horde, but the most conservative estimate places it at 125,000 armed cavalrymen. It was their speed and skill in manoeuvring that gave the Mongols their capacity to overcome enemies who were far better armed and equipped than themselves.

21 *Mosaic of a gazelle from the Theotokos chapel of the church on Mount Nebo, Jordan, early seventh century.*

22 *Mosaics from the baptistery of the church on Mount Nebo, Jordan (AD 531).*

23 Monastery of St Antony the Great in the eastern desert of Egypt.

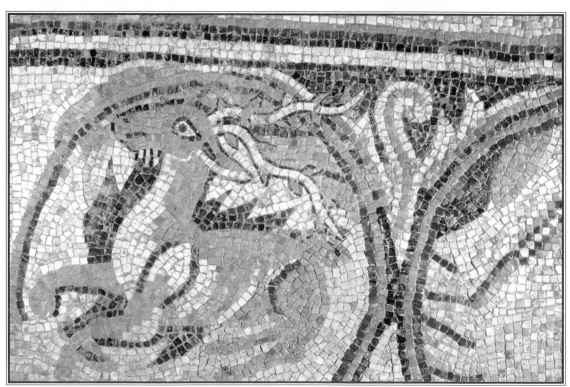

24 Byzantine mosaic of a deer, from Jerash, Jordan, fifth to sixth centuries.

25 *The exterior of the rock-hewn church of Abba Libanos at Lalibela in Ethiopia, thirteenth century.*

26 *The reliquary of St Francis Xavier in the basilica of Bon Jesus, Goa, India.*

27 *The late seventh-century Muslim shrine of the Dome of the Rock, on the Temple Mount in Jerusalem.*

Under Genghis Khan's leadership the Mongols expanded eastwards into the Chin Empire of north China, where, by 1215, they had made substantial conquests, and westwards through the central Asian lands until in 1218 they reached the borders of the Empire of Khwarazm, the most easterly of the Islamic states. Merchants from northern China, who were now Genghis's subjects, travelled along the Silk Road to Persia, but in 1218 the Shah of Khwarazm executed 450 of them, alleging that they were spies, and maltreated the Mongol ambassadors who came to lodge a protest. This led Genghis Khan to bring the Mongol army west in 1219. In the next three years the Khwarazmian Empire was totally devastated: ancient cities like Bokhara and Samarkand were sacked and large numbers of their inhabitants slaughtered. Their corpses were decapitated and the skulls piled in pyramids outside the walls where they could still be seen a generation

Genghis Khan with his horse, from a Persian miniature.

later. One part of Ghengis's army conducted a raid through the Caucasus in 1222, ravaging Georgia and defeating an army of Russian princes which came against them near the Crimea, but this was the only attack on Christians during the campaign and did not receive much publicity in western sources. In 1223 Genghis withdrew his armies to Mongolia, leaving viceroys and small garrisons in Khwarazm. He died in 1227 and the assembly of Mongol chieftains elected his son Ogedai as his successor.

In 1231 the Mongols conquered part of Persia and in 1243 subdued the Seljuk Turks in Asia Minor (see p. 130). They also moved against the West, overrunning the principalities of Russia between 1237–40 and in 1241–2 invading Catholic Europe. One army invaded southern Poland, sacked Cracow and defeated the combined forces of Poland and the Holy Roman Empire at Liegnitz in Silesia; the other army invaded Hungary, defeated the royal army at Mohacs and advanced to join up with the first Mongol army near Vienna. The Great Khan Ogedai died in 1241 and when news of this reached the West the Mongol generals withdrew their forces to the banks of the lower Volga in 1242 to prepare to attend the assembly which would choose a successor. They never returned to the West, but fixed their capital at Sarai and became known as the Khanate of the Golden Horde (see pp. 83–4). The West had been terrified by the attack and was in complete ignorance about who the invaders were, except that they were clearly not the long awaited armies of Prester John. There was some speculation that they might be the peoples of Gog and Magog, who it was believed would appear to make war on Christians when the end of the world was approaching (Rev. 20:8).

Pope Innocent IV (1243–54) decided to send a mission to gather accurate information about the new barbarian invaders. The man he chose to lead it was a Franciscan friar, John of Piano Carpini, who since 1239 had been attached to the curia. He was not a very obvious choice in other ways, since he was about sixty years old and, as he tells us, quite fat and had taken to riding everywhere on a donkey. The party left Lyons, where the pope was then living, on Easter Day 1245 and travelled to Kiev, where there was a Mongol garrison. The commander provided them with an escort, and they rode 3,000 miles across the steppes to the Mongol capital of Karakoram, a great city of felt tents, where the Mongol leaders had finally assembled to elect a new Great Khan, a ceremony at which John and his party were present. The new Khan Guyuk received John, who presented the pope's letter protesting about the attack on Hungary and

Kubilai Khan gives Niccolò and Maffeo Polo a golden tablet to guarantee their safe conduct.

urging the Great Khan to become a Christian. Guyuk sent back a reply, written in Persian, claiming that he had a mandate from God to rule the world and bidding the pope to lead the kings of the West to make their submission to him. It bore Guyuk's seal, inscribed 'the seal of the Lord of all men'. John returned to the papal court in November 1247, a thinner man, so he says, and wrote a detailed report about the Mongols and their government, society, religion and military strength. Diplomatic relations had been established with the Mongol court, even though John had not been given a very cordial reception.

The first western religious mission to Mongolia was undertaken by a French Franciscan, William of Rubruck, trained in theology in the schools of Paris, who accompanied St Louis on his crusade to Egypt in 1248. When a rumour reached the crusader camp that Sartach, a Mongol prince in southern Russia, had become a Christian, William persuaded the king to allow him to visit the Golden Horde. Louis would not appoint William as his ambassador in case the Mongols should misrepresent this as an act of homage, but undertook to finance him in a religious mission and to provide him with letters of introduction. William was accompanied by another Franciscan, Brother Bartholomew, and they hired an interpreter who spoke Mongolian. William wrote an account of his journey for the king, which has a claim to be the first great travel book produced in Western Europe.[21]

The group went by way of Constantinople to the Crimea and then to the court of prince Sartach. William was unable to discover whether the rumours about his conversion were true, for the prince sent him on immediately to his father, the commander of the Golden Horde, who sent him to the Great Khan in Karakorum. William was interested in all he saw on his journey. About the Mongols, moving with their herds across the steppe lands of southern Russia, with their felt tents loaded on to huge ox-drawn carts, he wrote, 'When I found myself among them it seemed to me that I had been transported to another century.' The Mongols were equally interested in this visitor from the unknown lands of the West. They asked him whether it was true that the pope was five hundred years old, and they were unable to grasp the concept of the Western ocean which was not landlocked.

William and his party reached Karakorum on 27 December 1253 and were given an audience by the Great Khan Möngke, Guyuk's cousin and successor. When they entered his huge tent made of white velvet, William and Bartholomew stood and sang the office hymn for Christmas:

> A solis ortus cardine
> Et usque terre limitem
> Christum canamus principem
> Natum Maria Virgine.
>
> (From the rising of the sun
> To the ends of the earth
> We sing the praises of Christ the King
> Born of the Virgin Mary.)

Möngke, whose mother was a devout Chaldean Christian, thought it quite natural that two friars should make the long journey from the extreme West to pray for his well-being and he gave them leave to stay at his court as his guests through the winter.

William was thus able to meet the people of many races who came to pay their respects to the Great Khan, Armenians from Cilicia, envoys from the tribes of Siberia and Buddhist lamas from China, which William called Cathay. He also had a surprise encounter with a fellow-countrywoman called Paquette, who came from Metz in Lorraine. She had been living in Budapest when the Mongols attacked Hungary in 1241 and, together with the other captives (skilled craftsmen, young women and able-bodied men) whom the Mongols had taken, had been made to walk to Karakorum. Though legally a slave, she was in the service of a Mongol Christian princess and had been able to rebuild her life. She had married a young Russian joiner, like her a prisoner of war, and they had three sons. This is unique evidence of what happened to the victims of the Mongol raids on Europe. Paquette also introduced Brother William to William Bouchier, a master goldsmith from Paris who had been in Hungary at the time of the Mongol attack. He was making a centre-piece for the great assembly tent where the Mongol generals would meet in 1254 to plan their next campaign. This was a silver tree with golden leaves and jewelled fruit, among whose branches were twined four metal serpents (probably Chinese dragons) whose mouths were conduits for different kinds of wine, while at the foot of the tree were sculpted four tigers from whose mouths flowed the favourite drink of the Mongols, *koumiss*, fermented mares' milk. The tree was surmounted by an angel holding a trumpet. Bouchier made a gridiron for the friars on which they could bake unleavened bread for Mass and a silver pyx in which to reserve consecrated hosts. Astonishingly the gridiron survived until *c.* 1900 in a Buddhist monastery.[22]

On the eve of Pentecost 1254 Mönke staged a debate between representatives of the four main religions present at his court, Mahayana Buddhists, Muslims, Chaldean Christians and Latin Catholics. This is the first inter-faith debate ever reported. William was the Catholic spokesman and claims that he won the argument. His is the only account of the proceedings and no doubt judged by his own standards his claim was true, since he used the scholastic method of debate. His opponents, trained in other traditions, might have judged the outcome rather differently.

Soon after this William returned to the West, leaving behind Friar Bartholomew as chaplain for the Catholic community. William travelled by way of the Caucasus, passing through Armenia and speculating whether the remains of Noah's Ark might still be visible on top of Mount Ararat.

In 1256 the Mongols, led by Möngke's brother Hulegu, attacked the Islamic heartlands. In 1258 they sacked Baghdad, killed the Abbasid Caliph and slaughtered the entire population except for the Chaldean Patriarch Makika II and his flock who stayed in their cathedral and were unharmed. They almost certainly owed their protection to the intervention of Hulegu's chief wife, Dokuz Khatun, who was a devout Chaldean Christian. In 1260, when the Mongol armies advanced into Syria and Palestine, they were decisively defeated by the Egyptian Mamluks at the Battle of Ain Jalut in Galilee. Thereafter the Euphrates became the frontier between Mamluk

Egypt and the Mongol llkhanate of Persia ruled by Hulegu and his descendants. This marked the end of Mongol expansion in western Asia, but in the east Hulegu's younger brother Kubilai, who had succeeded Möngke as Great Khan in 1261, completed the conquest of South China by 1279 and moved his capital from Karakorum to Khan-baliq (Beijing).

The Church of the East benefited greatly from Mongol rule. The Mongols tolerated all the religions of their subjects and treated their adherents even-handedly. In China Chaldean Christians were able to live wherever they wished and to practise their faith openly for the first time in centuries, though their most numerous communities were to be found in the north, the area most heavily settled by the Mongols, many of whom were Christians. There is also some evidence for the presence of Chaldeans in Tibet at this time. Mongol overlordship had been acknowledged there in 1244, and Kubilai Khan was very well disposed towards the lamas of the Sakya Order, so that there was no impediment to Mongols visiting, or settling in Tibet during his reign, and there were some Chaldean Christians among them.[23]

One unexpected long-term benefit of the Mongol conquests was the establishment of peace throughout Central Asia, which had come to form part of a single empire. This undoubtedly strengthened the Chaldean communities in those provinces because regular communications with Baghdad became much easier. This would have helped to solve the problem which scandalized William of Rubruck, who reports about the Mongol Christian peoples that, 'The bishop takes his time about visiting those parts [doing so] perhaps hardly once in fifty years. On that occasion they have all the male children, even those in the cradle, ordained as priests.'[24] No doubt there is a strong element of exaggeration in this avowedly polemical passage, but it is also quite accurately reflects the problems which the Chaldean Church had faced in administering its distant provinces in pre-Mongol times.

In the lands of the Mongol Ilkhanate of Persia, which had formerly been under Muslim rule, Christians benefited considerably from the change of government. They were no longer required to pay a religious tax, all the discriminatory laws against them were rescinded, they were free to build new churches and monasteries as they wished, to practise their religion in public, to voice their criticisms of Islam openly and to convert Muslims to their faith. The Ilkhans relied on their Christian subjects to assist them in the work of government; indeed Abagha (1265–82) excluded Muslim clerks from his administration and employed only Christians and Jews. Although the Ilkhans remained pagan, many Christian Mongols were placed in positions of power, while members of the ruling house had Christian wives and mothers. Sorghatani Beki, the mother of Möngke, Hulegu and Kubilai, was a Kerait princess and a Chaldean Christian and exercised considerable political power, as did Dokuz Khatun, Hulegu's Christian wife, who is said to have ordered the destruction of some mosques in Persia. Such actions were exceptional, and the Muslim subjects of the Ilkhans were granted full religious toleration. Yet nothing in their history had prepared them for living on terms of parity with members of other religions and losing their own privileged status. Some Christians, suddenly finding that they were no longer second-class citizens, indulged in provocative triumphalism. The Muslim antiquary al-Makrizi reports:

[The Christians] produced a diploma of Hulegu guaranteeing them express protection and the free exercise of their religion. They drank wine freely in the month of Ramadan, and spilt it in the open streets . . . When they traversed the streets bearing the cross they compelled the merchants to rise and ill-treated those who refused. . . . When the Muslims complained, they were treated with indignity by the governor appointed by Hulegu, and several of them were by his orders bastinadoed.[25]

Hulegu's favourable treatment of Christians was continued by his son, Abagha (1265–82) and, no doubt because of this, when the Patriarch Denha I died in 1281 the electoral college chose a Mongol to succeed him. He was an Ongut from north China named Mark, born in 1245, the son of a Chaldean archdeacon. When he was fifteen he became the disciple of a Chaldean hermit, Rabban Sauma, who lived in the Fang Mountains near Khan-baliq. In 1275 the two monks set out on a pilgrimage to Jerusalem, but, because of the state of war between the Mongols and the Mamluks of Egypt, who ruled Palestine, they were unable to achieve their goal. They therefore returned to Baghdad, where the Patriarch Denha consecrated Mark metropolitan of China in 1280. Before Mark had set out Denha died, so Mark was present in Baghdad when the new patriarchal election was held and was himself chosen to succeed him. He took the name of Yaballaha ('the gift of God') III. He was only thirty-six and was the first patriarch of the Church of the East ever to be chosen from the 'exterior' provinces beyond the Persian frontier. Obviously this choice was made to please the Ilkhan and it achieved its purpose. When Mark visited Abagha to receive confirmation of this election, his biographer tells us that the Ilkhan placed the cloak which he was wearing round Mark's shoulders, gave him his own chair of state, conferred on him the privilege of using a ceremonial parasol and funded the expenses for his enthronement ceremonies. Abagha died in 1282 and was succeeded by his brother Tegedur, who became a Muslim and took the name of Ahmad, but he was dethroned two years later by Abagha's son Arghun, who, though a pagan, reverted to his father's policy of favouring Christians.

The Mongols and the Papacy

Arghun was concerned to establish good relations with the West. Their defeat at Ain Jalut had been a great psychological blow to the Mongols who had never previously been worsted in battle, and in 1263 Hulegu had sent an embassy to Pope Urban IV suggesting an alliance against the Mamluks of Egypt. His son, Abagha (1265–82), continued this policy and in 1274 a Mongol delegation was present at the second Council of Lyons at which plans were discussed for a new crusade. One consequence of this *volte-face* in Mongol policy was that western merchants were able to travel freely throughout the Mongol Empire. They could either use the land route through Central Asia, as the first papal envoys had done, or they could travel through Mongol-controlled Asia Minor to the Persian Gulf where they could take ship for India and China. Nicolo, Maffeo and Marco Polo are the best known group of such merchants and they used both routes on their two journeys.

A miniature showing merchants at the court of Kubilai Khan.

The Mongol rulers also allowed Catholic missionaries to work in their countries. These were almost all members of the Dominican and Franciscan Orders who thus had a unique opportunity to preach the Christian faith to Muslims without fear of reprisals. The friars founded communities in Asia Minor, Persia and southern Russia, and the benevolence with which they were treated by most of the Mongol rulers led the Papacy to hope that those princes themselves might be converted to Catholicism.

In their dealings with the West the Ilkhans sometimes used Chaldean clergy as their envoys, a tradition continued by Arghun when in 1286 he chose Rabban Barsauma to head a new delegation to Western Europe. Barsauma was the Mongol hermit from Khan-baliq, who had been the spiritual director of the new Patriarch, Yaballaha III, and the patriarch had appointed him his vicar-general. The account which Barsauma wrote of his mission to Europe is the first description of the West to have been made by a visitor from China. He went first to Constantinople and then by sea to Italy, but when he reached Rome in 1287 he found the cardinals in conclave because the pope had just died. He therefore went to France, where he stayed at Paris as the guest of Philip IV, and admired the newly built Sainte Chapelle, returning to Italy by way of Bordeaux in

English Gascony, where he met King Edward I. When he reached Rome in Lent 1288 a new pope had been elected, Nicholas IV, the first Franciscan to occupy the Holy See. He gave Barsauma a cordial welcome and the envoy celebrated Mass in the Chaldean rite before the papal court. Nicholas IV was clearly satisfied that Barsauma and his Church held the same faith as the Catholic Church of the West. On Palm Sunday the pope himself gave Holy Communion to the Mongol ambassador, and Barsauma relates how, at his final audience:

> [Pope Nicholas] sent to Mar Yaballaha a crown for his head which was of fine gold and was inlaid with precious stones; and sacred vestments made of red cloth through which ran threads of gold; and socks and sandals on which real pearls were sewn; and the ring from his finger; and a *pethikha*, or bull, which authorized him to exercise patriarchal dominion over all the children of the East. And he gave to Rabban Sauma a *pethikha* which authorized him to act as Visitor-General over all Christians.

This claim is supported by a papal letter of 7 April 1288; it is clear that at this time union was achieved between the Catholic Church of the West and the Chaldean Church of the East.[26]

The Catholic Archbishop of Khan-baliq

It was perhaps as a result of this meeting with a Christian from China that the pope decided to send a mission to the court of the Great Khan Kubilai, led by John of Monte Corvino, a Franciscan from south Italy who already had experience of working in Mongol Persia. John set out in 1291 and travelled to China by sea, taking ship from the Persian Gulf. He stayed for some months on the Malabar coast of India and wrote to his brethren describing the society and beliefs of the peoples he met there. There was then silence for fifteen years, until in 1306 the Franciscan convent at Tabriz in Persia received a letter from John telling them of his progress. He does not say whether he had reached Khan-baliq in the lifetime of Kubilai, who died in 1294, but he was on good terms with Kubilai's grandson and successor, Temur Oljeitu (1294–1307). John reports that he had been joined by another Franciscan, Arnold of Cologne, and that they had been greatly helped by the financial support of Pietro da Lucalongo, an Italian merchant living in China. John claimed to have baptized some 5,000 Mongols, to have translated the New Testament and the Book of Psalms into Mongolian, and to have built two churches in Khan-baliq. He relates how he had ransomed a group of slave boys, baptized them, and taught them Latin and plainsong, so that the full Catholic liturgy could be performed in his churches. The letter was forwarded to Pope Clement V (1305–14) who consecrated seven Franciscans as bishops and sent them to work under John in China. Only three of them survived the long and hazardous journey, but they consecrated John as Archbishop of Khan-baliq and in *c*. 1313 set up a second diocese in the port of Zayton where there was a substantial colony of European merchants.

When John of Monte Corvino died in Khan-baliq in 1328 at the age of eighty-one the Mongol Empire was beginning to break up. This meant that the Mongol peace was at an end and that travel in Asia was more difficult. Thus, the new archbishop sent by Pope John XXII to replace John was unable to reach China. Sometimes conditions were more favourable and the journey could be made. In 1338 a delegation of Chinese Catholics sent by the Great Khan came to the papal court at Avignon to ask Pope Benedict XII to send them a new archbishop. The pope sent a mission consisting of some fifty Franciscans led by the Florentine friar John of Marignolli. They returned with the Mongol delegation, taking the land route through Central Asia, and reached Khan-baliq in 1342. Among the gifts which the pope had sent to the Great Khan were some European war-horses, one at least of which survived the journey and made such a favourable impression on the horse-loving Mongols that its portrait was painted and survived to be admired by a western visitor in 1815. Most of the friars probably stayed in China but John of Marignolli returned to the West by the sea route to Persia and reached Avignon again in 1353.

John's embassy was the last certain contact to have been made between the West and the Catholic mission in China during the Middle Ages. Popes continued to nominate Archbishops of Khan-baliq, and some of them may have reached their see, but this is not known. There is no evidence that organized Catholicism survived in China after *c.* 1400. In 1368 a revolution had broken out there; Mongol rule came to an end and the new Ming dynasty was not well disposed towards Western clergy, who had enjoyed the support of the Mongol Emperors. In any case, the Catholic mission in China was dependent on Western Europe for a supply of clergy and the distances involved were too great for this relationship to be successfully sustained after the Mongol peace had ended.

The Search for Prester John

John of Piano Carpini and many of the envoys and missionaries who followed him had been concerned to find Prester John. They noted that there were large numbers of Chaldeans in the Mongol confederacy, and they established that there had once been independent Christian states in Central Asia, which Genghis Khan had absorbed. William of Rubruck rightly concluded that there had been two independent Christian peoples in Central Asia before Genghis Khan's day, the Naimans and the Keraits. He inferred that Prester John had been the Khan of the Naimans and that his brother, Unc Khan, had been ruler of the Keraits, and that Genghis Khan, having initially been subject to Unc Khan, had subsequently annexed all the lands of the two brothers. William has this to say of the Prester John of Asia:

[he was] a mighty herdsman and the ruler over a people called the Naiman, who were Nestorian [i.e. Chaldean] Christians . . . The Nestorians called him King John, and only a tenth of what they said about him was true. For this is the way with the Nestorians who come from these parts: they create big rumours out of nothing.[27]

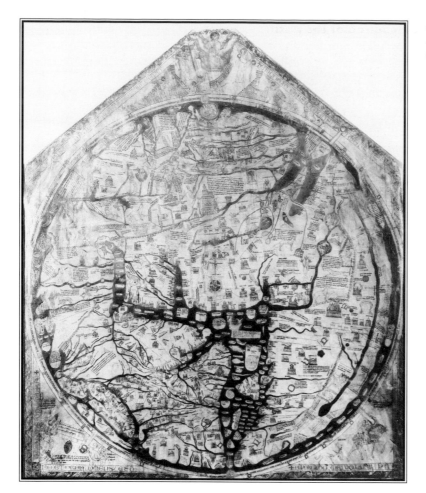

Mappa mundi of the Hereford Cathedral, c. 1300.

Many later western travellers shared this view in a simplified form; the Khan of the Naimans was forgotten, and Prester John was identified exclusively with Unc Khan, ruler of the Keraits. His descendants could still be traced in the early fourteenth century, and in one of his letters John of Monte Corvino described how:

> A certain King George . . . of the sect of the Nestorians [Chaldeans], who was of the family of the great king who was called Prester John of India, attached himself to me in the first year that I came here, and was converted by me to . . . the Catholic faith. And he took minor orders and served my Mass wearing the sacred vestments . . .[28]

Thus the vast dominions of John King and Priest had by the end of the thirteenth century been reduced to the small nomadic realm of George King and Acolyte. Indeed, the general consensus among educated people at the time was that Prester John had long been dead. His return to life in the Third India during the fourteenth century has been discussed in Chapter Four.

The Decline of the Church of the East

The Ilkhan Arghun died in 1291 and was succeeded by his brother Geikhatu, who had a reputation for drunkenness but was also very generous, which benefited the Church of the East. When he died in 1295 Arghun's son Ghazan, who was a Buddhist, became a Muslim in order to claim the throne: his advisers believed that the Muslims, who formed the majority of the population of Persia, would never accept a Buddhist ruler. Many pagan Mongols followed his example and accepted the Islamic faith, and in his reign Muslims were once again admitted to positions of authority in the Ilkhanate. Ghazan himself was not particularly hostile to the Church of the East, but it lost the privileged position it had held under his predecessors. Moreover, because the Muslim community in general felt considerable resentment towards the Christians who had been favoured more than they had for a generation, there were local riots in which churches and monasteries were sacked and Christians attacked and sometimes killed. Although such incidents were illegal, it proved very difficult for Christians to obtain redress from the provincial authorities, who were now mainly Muslims.

Mar Yaballaha III lived to see the beginnings of this change of fortune. He died in 1317 after a reign of thirty-six years, as head of a Church with more than thirty provinces which stretched from the Mediterranean to the Pacific and included South India, and which was in full communion with the pope and the Catholic Church of the West. Thereafter the Church of the East entered upon a period of steady decline, but because its history in the late Middle Ages is very poorly documented, the reasons for that decline may only be conjectured. The religious tax on Christians had been imposed once more in 1304 and the discriminatory laws against Christians, which had been in force before the Mongol invasions, were re-introduced. After the death of Abu-Said (1316–35) central government collapsed in the Ilkhanate, which meant that the Church was completely at the mercy of local war-lords. These factors led some Christians to become Muslims, and also brought about a decline in the economic prosperity of the Church and therefore of its political influence.

In China, Chaldean Christians, like Catholic Christians, were identified with Mongol rule by the Ming Emperors who came to power in 1368, and were therefore viewed with disfavour by them. Although Chaldean lay people in China may have kept their faith, they became priestless, because the emperors would not allow new bishops appointed by the patriarchs in Persia to take up their positions.

In Central Asia, where the Church of the East had flourished for centuries, parallel evidence of decline is apparent. It is generally, and probably correctly, assumed that the last remnants of organized Chaldean Christianity died out there as a result of the campaigns of Tamerlane.

He was a minor Mongol prince, born in *c.* 1336, who in his youth carved out a dominion for himself in the lands to the east of the River Oxus and in 1370 was proclaimed Lord of the Fortunate Conjunction – an allusion to his horoscope – at Samarkand, which he made his capital.[29] He fought a series of highly successful campaigns in western Central Asia, northern India, Persia, Mesopotamia, Turkey, the Caucasus and the Russian steppes and died while setting out to recover China for the

Mongols in 1405. He was then aged about seventy and had never suffered a serious defeat. Tamerlane was a dedicated Muslim. He despised Christians and destroyed many churches and monasteries in the course of his campaigns. He was also ruthless, slaughtering the entire populations of cities which resisted him. By the time of this death there was no longer any evidence of organized Chaldean Christianity among the peoples of Central Asia to the west of Kashgar. No evidence has come to light either about Chaldean survival in the lands of Sinkiang and Mongolia after that time, although it was not until the sixteenth century that the peoples of Mongolia were converted to Tibetan Buddhism.

The chief reason for the collapse of the Chaldean Church perhaps lies in its over-centralization. Like all branches of the medieval Church it was hierarchical – only bishops could ordain priests and only priests could celebrate the eucharist – but the Patriarchs of Baghdad never delegated the appointment of bishops to provincial churches, retaining the right to appoint all bishops themselves. As a result, the entire Chaldean episcopate throughout Asia (with the exception of the Patriarch Yaballaha III), had been trained in the monasteries of Persia. The wars which accompanied the break-up of the Mongol Empire in the fourteenth century made communications between Baghdad and the outlying provinces difficult, and consequently no new bishops were sent there. There came a time when there were no ordained clergy left in the eastern provinces to celebrate the Chaldean liturgy, though it is possible that communities of lay people continued to remain loyal members of the Church of the East.

Catholic Missions in Western Asia

Although the Muslim Ilkhans no longer showed favour to the Chaldean Church, they continued to allow Catholic clergy to work in their dominions, initially because they wanted western aid against the Mamluk Sultans of Egypt. As a result, some western rulers found it difficult to grasp that the Ilkhans had become Muslims. Edward II of England, for example, in his reply to a letter from the Muslim Ilkhan Oljeitu in 1307, urged him to extirpate 'the abominable sect of Mohammed'.[30] Yet even after Abu Said (1316–35) had made a secure peace with Egypt in 1328, the Ilkhans remained tolerant of Western clergy, because they wanted to promote trade with the Christian powers.

Although Dominican and Franciscan friars had been working in Persia, in the lands of the Golden Horde and in the Mongol lands of western Central Asia since the last quarter of the thirteenth century, it was not until 1318 that a Catholic hierarchy was set up in those territories. This would have been difficult during the reign of Yaballaha III because Pope Nicholas IV had recognized him as canonical head of the Church of the East, thereby implying that the Chaldean bishops represented the Catholic Church in Asia. No similar recognition was extended by the Holy See to the new Chaldean Patriarch, Timothy II (1318–32), nor was it sought by him. In 1318 Pope John XXII appointed the Dominican, Franco of Perugia, to be Archbishop of Sultaniya, the new capital of the Ilkhans. Latin dioceses were later set up in various cities of this province, including Tabriz, Maragha and Samarkand. In 1318 Pope John also appointed a Bishop of Caffa, a port in the Crimea which formed part of the maritime empire of Genoa. This was a

A western portrait of Tamerlane, who tried to restore the Mongol Empire.

good point of entry to the Mongol lands of southern Russia and Central Asia, and Catholic bishoprics were founded later in the century at Sarai on the Volga, the capital of the Golden Horde, at Tana, and at Almaligh, far to the east beyond Lake Balkash.

The friars who held those sees were responsible for the spiritual oversight of western merchants living there, but they also tried to convert those Mongols who were still shamanists. In territories which had Islamic rulers, like Persia, the Catholic clergy could not proselytize Muslims, and in such places they tended to work among the indigenous Christian communities, seeking to bring them into communion with the Papacy. This proved divisive, because eastern churches were split into two groups, those who adhered to the union with Rome and those who did not.

The position of these fourteenth-century Catholic missions was always precarious. In 1339 Muslim rioters wrecked the Catholic cathedral of Almaligh and killed Bishop Richard of Burgundy and six of his flock; although John of Marignolli, the pope's legate, when he passed through Almaligh on his way to China in 1341 (see p. 205), supervised the restoration of the cathedral, the mission there had effectively come to an end. The Catholic diocese of Samarkand had an equally ephemeral life: founded in *c.* 1329, its bishop had returned to the papal court by 1342 and nothing more is known about his see.

The *coup de grâce* to the Catholic hierarchy in Asia was administered by Tamerlane. Cities such as Tana and Sarai, both of which were the sees of Catholic bishops, were destroyed by him in his campaign of 1395–6 and the hierarchy was not restored there. Yet like the Ilkhans a century before, Tamerlane did not wish to frighten away western traders from his dominions. He therefore sent an embassy in 1398 to Genoa and Venice, led by John, the Catholic Bishop of Nakhidjevan in Armenia. While he was in Italy John had an audience with Pope Boniface IX, who appointed him to the vacant Archbishopric of Sultaniya, but when John returned to Persia in 1403 he could not take up his duties because Tamerlane immediately sent him back to Europe on a mission to the King of France.

Although Tamerlane died in 1405 and his empire soon collapsed, John never did go to Sultaniya, but retired to Caffa in the Crimea, where he wrote a description of the state of Catholicism in the East, the *Libellus de notitia orbis* (*A Short Description of the World*). He reported that there were still many Latin Catholics in China, but that they lacked priests to administer the sacraments, and he blamed the Papacy for failing to address this problem. He related that in Persia there were still still Catholic congregations in Baghdad and in Kurdistan to whom Dominican priests were ministering. Catholic bishops continued to be appointed to Sultaniya until 1425 and to Tabriz until 1450, but there is no certainty that they ever occupied their sees. Indeed, in 1431 the Republic of Genoa asked the pope to transfer the Archbishopric of Sultaniya to Caffa, claiming that it had become impossible for Catholic clergy to travel in Persia. There may have been some element of exaggeration in this report, and in any case the pope did not take any notice of the request; nevertheless, by the early fifteenth century any realistic hope of setting up a Latin hierarchy in Asia had disappeared. The Catholic diocese of Caffa remained the chief relic of this earlier papal initiative, until the city was captured by the Ottoman Turks in 1475 and the bishopric came to an end.[31]

The Church of the East in the Fifteenth Century

When the Council of Florence wished to discuss Church unity with the Chaldeans, the Fathers contacted Timothy, nominally Metropolitan of Tarsus in Cilicia, who was living in Cyprus as the head of a small Chaldean congregation. He came to Rome, where on 7 August 1445 he made a detailed profession of faith, in Syriac, which was completely in accordance with the teachings of the Holy See, and Pope Eugenius IV issued the bull *Benedictus sit Deus (Blessed be God)*, announcing that Timothy of Tarsus and his flock had been brought into full communion with the Western Church. Timothy, unlike the other representatives of Eastern Churches who attended this Council, did not act on behalf of his Church as a whole, but simply on behalf of his own province. The Chaldean Patriarch at that time was the long-reigning Simon IV Basidi (1437–97), who is said to have made the office of patriarch hereditary in his own family, just as, in earlier centuries, the headship of the Armenian Church had been hereditary in the family of St Gregory the Illuminator (see p. 125). Chaldean bishops and patriarchs were monks, vowed to the celibate life, and the office therefore passed to brothers or nephews of the previous incumbent.

By 1500 the Church of Asia was still dominant in the area to the east of the Tigris between Lake Van and Lake Urmia, where most of its monasteries were situated; and it also had churches in Baghdad, Tabriz, Nisibis, Irbil and Gezira. In the western Islamic lands there were Chaldean churches at Edessa, Damascus and Jerusalem. The St Thomas's Christians of South India and the people of Socotra still looked to the Chaldean Patriarch as their head and received their bishops from him. Yet compared to the thirty provinces scattered throughout all Asia over which Yaballaha III had presided 200 years before, the Chaldean Church of the early sixteenth century was indeed diminished. It may be mistaken to try to gauge the extent of Chaldean Christianity at that time solely in terms of its hierarchy. Jean Dauvillier drew attention to a passage in the memoirs of the Italian traveller, Ludovico di Varthema, who visited India in 1506:

> In Bengal he met Chaldean merchants who had come there from Ayudya, the capital of Thailand. He accompanied them to Pegu, where the king had 1,000 Christians in his service, then to Borneo, to Java and to the Moluccas. But he does not mention any Christian establishment in any of those countries.[32]

Clearly there were many Chaldean Christians living in regions where there was no church organization. Varthema's travels were a manifestation of the new western European presence in Asia made possible by the Portuguese circumnavigation of Africa in 1498. This was to lead to a fresh period of Christian evangelization which effectively began in 1542 when St Francis Xavier arrived in Goa; but his achievements lie beyond the time-limits of this book.

EPILOGUE

JERUSALEM, THE CENTRE OF THE CHRISTIAN WORLD

In 325 Bishop Macarius of Jerusalem attended the Council of Nicaea and asked the Emperor Constantine for permission to demolish the temple of Aphrodite in his city and to search for the Sepulchre of Christ. Constantine not merely agreed to this, but also ordered that three great basilicas should be built, at imperial expense, in the Jerusalem diocese: one at Bethlehem, in honour of Christ's birth, one on the Mount of Olives, the church of the Eleona, in honour of His teaching, and the third on the site of Calvary.

Fourth-century Jerusalem bore little resemblance to the city of the early first century where Jesus had been crucified and where his followers believed that he had risen from the dead and ascended into Heaven. That city had been destroyed when Titus suppressed the great Jewish revolt in AD 70, and it remained a ruin until 135 when the Emperor Hadrian ordered it to be rebuilt as the Roman city of Aelia Capitolina. A temple to Jupiter was erected on the Temple Mount, and a temple of Aphrodite on the sites associated with the crucifixion and resurrection of Christ. Jews were excluded from the Holy City, but Christians were not specifically forbidden to live there, although, like Christians throughout the empire, they were members of an illegal cult and liable to arbitrary persecution. The centre of Christian worship for the next 200 years was Mount Sion, just outside the walls of Aelia, which was said to be the site of the house of John Mark in whose upper room Christ had celebrated the Last Supper and where the Holy Spirit had descended on the Apostles at Pentecost. The church built there in the fourth century claimed to have the chair used by the first bishop of Jerusalem, St James, 'the brother of the Lord' (Acts 15:13; Gal. 1:19).

Throughout the age of persecution the bishops of Jerusalem and their flock preserved the memory of the sacred geography of the city as it had been in Jesus's day. The position of Calvary was known because the pinnacle of the rock could be seen in the court of the temple of Aphrodite. When Bishop Macarius cleared the site, a rock-cut tomb was also found in a nearby mound and was identified as the burial place of Christ. Constantine's architects linked these two sites in a single complex. A large basilica, called the Martyrion, or church of Witness, was built to the east of Calvary; doors at the west end of the side aisles opened on to a courtyard, the south-east corner of which was occupied by the rock of Calvary, on which in 420 the Emperor Theodosius II commissioned a large gold cross to be set up. On the west side of the courtyard was the tomb of Christ; the masons cut away the burial chamber from the mound and it became a free-standing rock-chapel, which was incorporated in a rotunda entered from the courtyard. Modern archaeological excavations, while they cannot determine whether Constantine's great shrine-church really did mark the site of Christ's crucifixion and burial, have shown that the early fourth-century tradition is not incompatible with the facts related in the Gospels. The evangelists record that the crucifixion took place when Pontius Pilate was governor of Judaea (AD 26–36) and that Mount Calvary (or Golgotha) was outside the city walls. In Constantine's day the temple of Aphrodite was inside the walls of Aelia Capitolina; but as Kathleen Kenyon has shown, the north-west quarter of the city, in which that temple stood, was not enclosed until the reign of Herod Agrippa (AD 40–44). Martin Biddle, in his recent work on the Edicule, the shrine of the Holy Sepulchre, has argued that the evidence relating to the excavations of 325/6 shows that what was found then was a tomb of the Second Temple period (and therefore one appropriate in date), and one which was consistent with the description contained in the Gospels.[1]

Constantine did not visit Jerusalem himself, but in *c.* 327 his mother, the Augusta Helena, came there from Rome. She was a baptized Christian, and Constantine's biographer Eusebius emphasizes that her visit was inspired by religious motives, that she wished to pray at the places where Christ's feet had touched the ground. She also had official duties to perform: while in Jerusalem she oversaw her son's building programme and arranged suitable endowments for the new churches. Helena was almost eighty years old and the long journey must have strained her health; she died at Trier soon after her return to the West.

Throughout the rest of the fourth century pilgrims came to Jerusalem from all over the Christian world. Among those from the West was a devout lady called Egeria who travelled there in 381–4 leaving a very detailed narrative of what she saw. By that time an impressive public liturgy had been developed to re-enact events in Christ's life in the places where they had happened, and this was particularly effective in Holy Week. Egeria reports that the liturgy was normally celebrated in Greek and translated into Aramaic for the local population, while informal Latin translations were made for the benefit of western visitors such as herself.

Jerusalem was full of sacred sites and during the period of Christian Roman rule, 324–614, many churches and chapels were founded in and around the city. A church was built on top of the Mount of Olives to commemorate Christ's Ascension into Heaven. A basilica dedicated to St Stephen was built at the supposed site of his stoning just outside the walls, and a great church was built at the pool of Siloam, scene of Christ's healing of the paralytic. The pool of Bethesda, to the north of the Temple, was incorporated in the church of St Mary, while the Emperor Justinian (527–65) endowed the New Church in honour of Our Lady in the south of the city. The smaller sanctuaries included the church built where St Peter had wept when the cock crew, the chapel which marked the spot where Christ prayed in Gethsemane, and the church built at the place where the body of the Blessed Virgin had rested between her death and her Assumption into Heaven. In addition, there were some important shrines in the country round Jerusalem, such as the churches of St Lazarus at Bethany, and St John the Baptist at Ain Karim, while the basilica of the Holy Nativity at Bethlehem was within walking distance of the city.

The Golden Gate of Jerusalem, now walled up, through which Heraclius carried the Holy Cross in triumph in 630.

In 451 the Council of Chalcedon made Jerusalem the fifth patriarchate. During the Christological controversies of the fifth and sixth centuries the patriarchs remained Orthodox and retained control of the chief churches and shrines in the city and its environs. The Western Church was at that time in full communion with the Orthodox Churches so this created no problem for western visitors, but in *c.* 600 Pope Gregory I founded a hospice in Jerusalem for western pilgrims, thus establishing a distinctively Latin presence in the city. Some of the non-Chalcedonian churches may have had monasteries and chapels in and about Jerusalem, like the Armenians who before 614 had a church near what is now the Damascus Gate as well as a monastery on the Mount of Olives. Members of these separated Churches certainly went on pilgrimage to Jerusalem throughout the late Roman period, but before 638 the only bishop in the city was the Orthodox Patriarch, and all the major shrines were served by clergy in communion with him.

In 614 Jerusalem was captured by the Persians. The initial occupation was peaceful, but a revolt in the city shortly afterwards led to savage reprisals. Churches and monasteries were sacked and severely damaged and the great reliquary of the Holy Cross was carried off to Ctesiphon. The only major church to escape unharmed was the basilica of the Nativity at Bethlehem. In 630 Heraclius, having defeated the Persians, brought the Holy Cross back to Jerusalem in triumph carrying it on his shoulders through the Golden Gate (which seems to have been specially pierced in the eastern wall for this occasion). This event has been commemorated ever since by the Churches of East and West on 14 September, the feast of the Holy Cross.

The Patriarch Modestus (632–4) began an intensive rebuilding programme, which was continued under his successor, Sophronius (634–8), but this had not been completed when the city was besieged by the Islamic army led by the Caliph Omar. Sophronius, taking charge of the defences, capitulated early in 638 when it was evident that no Christian relief force could be expected. Jerusalem became a holy city for Muslims because of the account which the Prophet gives in the Koran of his mystical Night Journey:

Entrance to the Armenian monastery and cathedral of St James, Jerusalem. The cathedral was built by the crusaders in c. 1160.

Glory be to Him who carried His servant by night from the Sacred Temple [of Mecca] to the Temple that is more remote [al-aqsa], whose precinct we have blessed, that we might show him of our signs. He is the Hearer, the Seer. (Sura XVII)

Tradition asserted that on his night journey Muhammad had met there with the prophets who had gone before him, and then had been carried on high before the throne of God. Muslim commentators identified the Further Sanctuary with the Noble Sanctuary of Jerusalem, the site of the Jewish Temple. In 638 the great platform built by Herod the Great was mainly occupied by the ruins of the temple of Jupiter erected by Hadrian. These were gradually cleared and the shrine of the Dome of the Rock was completed under the Caliph Abd al-Malik in 691. It was so called because it was built over the outcrop of living rock thought to mark the point of the Prophet's ascent to Heaven. The Caliph al-Walid I (705–35) built the mosque of al-Aqsa at the south end of the platform.[2] The Temple area had not formed part of the Christian topography of Jerusalem so there was no competition between Muslims and Christians about its use. Moreover, because of this, the Muslims did not need to sequestrate any of the Christian churches of Jerusalem for use as mosques.

Under Arab rule Jerusalem ceased to be an exclusively Christian city. Not only did Muslims settle there, but the Jews were also readmitted and given their own quarter by the western wall. In Jerusalem, as in all Islamic lands, Christians were tolerated but became second-class citizens. The Patriarch Sophronius died a few weeks after the Arab occupation, and a new patriarch was not appointed for almost seventy years, until John V was enthroned in 705. This was almost certainly a consequence of the ongoing war between the Arabs and the Byzantine Empire, and a similar break occurred at this time in the appointment of Orthodox Patriarchs to the see of Alexandria (see p. 147). Nevertheless, relations were sustained between the Churches of Jerusalem and Constantinople and a representative of the Orthodox Church of Jerusalem attended the council in Trullo in 692. The Byzantine Emperors were the natural protectors of the Orthodox in Jerusalem and therefore of the Holy Places which they administered,[3] but living under Islamic rule enabled the Orthodox to maintain some measure of independence from the imperial Church. In the eighth and early ninth centuries the Patriarchate of Jerusalem, like the Catholic Church of the West, consistently opposed the Iconoclast policies of the Byzantine Emperors: St John of Damascus, writing at the Orthodox monastery of St Sabas in Judaea, was the most coherent and incisive critic of Iconoclasm, and the Church of Jerusalem refused to send a representative to the Iconoclast Council of 754 (see p. 67). When the emperors once again implemented an iconoclastic policy in the ninth century, the Patriarch Basil convoked a synod at Jerusalem, attended by representatives of the Orthodox Patriarch of Alexandria, which condemned this teaching.

One consequence of the Arab conquest was that the non-Chalcedonian Churches were able to establish themselves in Jerusalem on terms of parity with the Orthodox. The Armenians appointed a bishop there in c. 650; the presence of a Jacobite (Syrian Orthodox) bishop is attested from 793, although the office may well have existed for

The exterior of the al-Aqsa mosque, Jerusalem.

longer; and Timothy I, Patriarch of the Church of the East (780–823), appointed a Chaldean Bishop of Jerusalem. The Latin Church accepted the legitimacy of the Orthodox Patriarchs and saw no need to have a bishop of its own rite, but a new Latin monastery and hospice for western pilgrims was founded in *c.* 800 by Charlemagne, in place of that endowed by Gregory I, which seems to have been destroyed in the Persian Wars. This hospice fulfilled a function analogous to that of a modern embassy by protecting and representing the interests of western pilgrims.

The most important shrines in Jerusalem continued to function under Muslim rule, but those churches damaged by the Persians, which had not been rebuilt at the time of the Arab conquest, remained in ruins. The Christians of Jerusalem enjoyed a considerable degree of religious freedom; until the eleventh century, for example, they were allowed to hold public processions on great feast days. Nevertheless, the extent of Muslim tolerance should not be exaggerated. The Christian communities in Jerusalem were subjected to sporadic outbursts of violence, particularly if the Christian powers had inflicted a major defeat on Islamic forces in the eastern Mediterranean. Thus, in 966 mobs broke into the Martyrion and also into the church of Mount Sion, causing considerable damage, in reaction to the news of Nicephorus II's victorious campaigns in Cyprus and Cilicia.

A much more severe threat was posed by the Caliph al-Hakim who in 1009 ordered the destruction of all churches and monasteries in his empire (see p. 108). Many churches in and around Jerusalem were destroyed, though once again the Holy Nativity at Bethlehem was left unscathed. The caliph specifically ordered the governor of Palestine 'to demolish the church of the Resurrection . . . and to get rid of all traces and remembrance of it'. The Byzantines called the shrine of the Holy Sepulchre the *Anastasis*, the church of the Resurrection. The contemporary chronicler, Yahya of Antioch, reports that al-Husayn ibn Zahir al-Wazzan, who was the overseer of this task, 'worked hard to destroy the tomb and to remove every trace of it, and did in actual fact hew and root up the greater part of it'.[4] Yet the destruction was less complete than al-Hakim would have wished. The entire Constantinian complex was wrecked, but the outer wall of the rotunda still survives today to a height of thirty feet. Moreover, Martin Biddle has recently examined all the literary evidence relating to the reconstruction since 1009 of the Edicule, the chapel which houses the Holy Sepulchre, and has also made a detailed survey of this shrine, which in its present form dates from 1809. He has concluded:

This consideration of the evidence for the survival of the original rock-cut tomb-chamber found in 325–6 suggests that much of it still survives inside the Edicule. In part it may even stand to more than the height of a man.

The Church of the Holy Sepulchre seen from the air. The large dome is that of the Byzantine rotunda; the small dome that of the crusaders' cathedral.

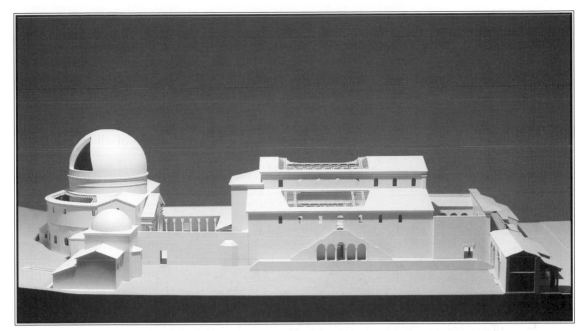

H.R. Allen's model of the Constantinian basilica linked to the rotunda of the Holy Sepulchre.

Using photogrammetric techniques Biddle has shown that there is certainly space inside the walls of the modern structure for the presence of a rock formation of that kind, although the detailed evidence of this will only become available when the Edicule is restored.[5]

In 1037–8 the Byzantine Emperor Michael IV obtained the agreement of the Caliph of Egypt, al-Mustansir (1036–94), that the church of the Resurrection should be rebuilt at the emperor's expense. The Byzantine historian John Scylitzes, writing soon after 1057, says that the building was completed before Michael's death in 1041, whereas William of Tyre (d. *c*. 1186), the historian of the Crusader States, says it was not finished until 1048, in the reign of Constantine IX. The new building was less ambitious than the one it replaced. No attempt was made to restore the Constantinian Martyrion. The Byzantine craftsmen concentrated on the shrine of the Holy Sepulchre. The remains of Constantine's outer wall were incorporated in a great rotunda, which had a pillared gallery and a wooden dome with a circular opening at the centre to symbolize the Resurrection. Below this stood the rebuilt shrine of the tomb of Christ, which was clad in marble and had a silver-gilt dome. At the east end of the rotunda was an apse which formed the sanctuary of the new cathedral. The former courtyard, which had linked the Holy Sepulchre to the Martyrion, was restored. In the south-east corner was the rock of Calvary where a new chapel was built, and a range of two-storey buildings was erected round the courtyard, some of which contained chapels dedicated to the events of Christ's Passion.

Some other new church building was carried out at this time, notably the Georgian monastery of the Cross, to the west of the city, completed in 1038, but the majority of

Crosses carved by western pilgrims at the time of the crusades in the crypt of St Helena at the church of the Holy Sepulchre.

the churches destroyed on Hakim's orders were not rebuilt. This was probably not because the Egyptian government tried to obstruct such work, but because the Christian community did not have enough money to undertake it. This was the situation which the First Crusaders found when they captured Jerusalem in 1099. The Egyptian governor had expelled the Christians from the city before the crusading armies began to besiege it, because he considered them a security risk. The crusaders therefore had no compunction about massacring the entire population when they forced an entry on 15 July. For the next eighty-eight years Jerusalem was an almost entirely Christian city: no Muslims were allowed to live there and the size of the Jewish community was very restricted; but as there were not enough Frankish settlers, a large part of the population of crusader Jerusalem was made up of eastern Christians.

One of the first acts of the crusader leaders was to appoint a Latin Patriarch with authority over the Byzantine Orthodox as well as the western Catholics in the city, since the crusaders considered that they were all members of a single Church (see pp. 110–11). Although the Orthodox were allowed to keep their churches and monasteries, they were at first expelled from the Holy Sepulchre and those other main shrine churches which were still in operation in and around the city, which were handed over to Latin clergy. It soon became necessary to modify this policy, because at Eastertide 1101 the New Fire failed to ignite. Throughout much of the Christian world it was customary from at least the eighth century to begin the liturgical commemoration of Christ's Resurrection on the night of Easter Eve by kindling fire and lighting the Paschal candle. In Jerusalem the fire was not kindled with tinder and flint, but appeared, it was popularly supposed through Divine intervention, in one of the lamps in the Edicule. This was known as the 'miracle of the New Fire' and was the highlight of their pilgrimage for the huge number of eastern Christians who came to keep Holy Week in the city. In 1101 the Latins were forced to ask the intercession of the main eastern communities to produce the miracle which they themselves had failed to do and thereafter the Orthodox clergy were always invited by the Latins to participate in the Easter liturgy. They were later allowed to have altars in the chief shrine churches and to celebrate the liturgy there daily in their own rite, and by the reign of King Amalric (1163–74) a chapter of Greek canons had been instituted to serve the Holy Sepulchre alongside the Latin clergy.

Non-Chalcedonian Christians enjoyed more autonomy. Their bishops remained independent of the Latin hierarchy and they were allowed to keep their own churches and monasteries. King Baldwin II (1118–31) had an Armenian wife and the royal family therefore had strong Armenian sympathies, and it was no doubt as a result of this that the great Armenian cathedral of St James was built in Jerusalem by western masons working in accordance with Armenian liturgical tradition. It stood near the royal palace and was completed by *c.* 1170. The Franks were also anxious to conciliate the Jacobites, who were powerful in Muslim territory, and whose Church was in full communion with the Coptic Church of Egypt (see pp. 114–15). The Kings of Jerusalem allowed the Syrian Orthodox bishop, Ignatius Hesnun (d. 1124/5), to build a new monastery and cathedral there dedicated to St Mary Magdalene, and a large pilgrim hostel was attached to it. Andrew Palmer writes of it:

> The ruins of [St Mary Magdalen] survived into the mid-nineteenth century and were planned and drawn then. The reconstruction of the church . . . by de Vogüé is impressive. One can well believe that it was accounted fourth in importance among the churches of Jerusalem.[6]

Yet although they were well disposed to the non-Chalcedonian churches, the Frankish rulers turned Jerusalem into a Catholic city. This did not, for the most part, involve the sequestration of property belonging to eastern Christians, because by the early twelfth century the city and its environs had not recovered from the vandalism of al-Hakim. The pilgrim Saewulf who visited the Holy Land in 1101–3, reported:

> The city of Bethlehem . . . is six miles away from Jerusalem to the south. Nothing habitable is left there by the Saracens, but it is all ruined, exactly as it is in all the other places outside the walls of Jerusalem, except for [the church and monastery of the Holy Nativity].[7]

The Franks set about restoring these shrines. The church of Our Lady of Josaphat in the Kidron Valley, the site, it was believed, of Mary's Assumption into Heaven, was

The crusader church of St Anne's, Jerusalem.

entrusted to a community of Benedictine monks, who rebuilt and embellished it, and also built chapels, such as the oratory of the Sleep of the Apostles, nearby in the garden of Gethsemane to commemorate the events of Christ's vigil there before his arrest. On the Mount of Olives the Franks restored the shrine of the Ascension of Christ, which was administered by Austin Canons. Nearby a memorial church was erected in 1152 to two noble Danish pilgrims and was dedicated to the *Pater Noster* (the Our Father) of which it claimed to possess the autograph text. The Muslim shrine of the Dome of the Rock was converted into a Christian church, the Temple of the Lord, and was served by a group of Austin Canons who covered the rock outcrop with a marble floor and placed an altar and a choir in the centre, enclosed by an ironwork screen. The Knights Templar set up their headquarters in the mosque of al-Aqsa, to which they made some important additions. To the north of the Temple area was the site alleged to have been the home of SS. Joachim and Anne, the parents of the Virgin. The Franks built the church of St Anne there which was administered by a community of Benedictine nuns. The ruined church of Mount Sion, the original cathedral of the city, was rebuilt and served by a group of Austin Canons. The Latin hospital, dating from before the First Crusade, evolved into three independent institutions, the Benedictine monastery of St Mary of the Latins, the Benedictine convent of St Mary's the Great and the headquarters of the Order of St John of Jerusalem (the Hospitallers). The hospital they ran in twelfth-century Jerusalem was one of the largest and best equipped in the Christian world. The Franks also built many other churches in and around the Holy City.

Their greatest architectural achievement was to rebuild the Church of the Holy Sepulchre. This was the Latin Patriarch's see, from 1114 administered by a chapter of Austin Canons. The Franks enlarged the existing Byzantine church in an innovative way. The chapels around the courtyard were demolished and a new romanesque cathedral was built there. The apse was flanked by a number of chapels. The Calvary chapel was rebuilt and incorporated into the east end of the south aisle, and the rotunda was left untouched except that its apse was demolished and a triumphal arch inserted, so that looking west from the sanctuary of the new cathedral one could see the entrance to the Edicule of Christ's Tomb. The site of the old Constantinian basilica was occupied by the buildings of the new Latin canons, but St Helena's crypt beneath that church, where tradition held that the relic of the True Cross had been found, was kept open and was entered by a staircase from the ambulatory in the new cathedral apse. The popularity of the crypt chapel among crusaders may be gauged from the large number of crosses which they carved on its walls. The main entrance to the new cathedral was a door in the south aisle, outside which was a large courtyard, flanked on the west side by a row of chapels and a tall campanile. The Armenians and the Jacobites, who were highly favoured by the Franks, each had one of these chapels, although they were not allowed to officiate inside the cathedral. The new cathedral was consecrated in 1149 on the fiftieth anniversary of the crusader conquest of the city, but the building work was not completed for almost another twenty years.

The new churches and monasteries were built and endowed partly through the liberality of the Franks who settled in the East, but partly through the generosity of western pilgrims and people in Western Europe, many of whom gave estates to the Holy Places of Jerusalem. Western pilgrims came there in huge numbers during the century of crusader rule. They found it a congenial place, since most of the settlers spoke some kind of French, the major churches were administered by Catholic clergy who conducted worship in the Latin rite, the pilgrim roads were patrolled by the Knights Templar, and excellent hospital facilities were provided by the Order of St John, which cared for the sick, the destitute and the old. Pilgrims particularly wished to keep Easter in Jerusalem. The liturgies of Holy Week in all the churches of East and West were designed to re-enact the events of Christ's Passion, from his triumphal entry into Jerusalem on Palm Sunday to his Resurrection on Easter Day. In Jerusalem the liturgy

The Edicule of the Holy Sepulchre, Jerusalem, within which is the shrine of Christ's tomb.

was performed in the places where events had occurred and provided a unique stimulus among pilgrims to a devotion to the humanity of Christ.

Large numbers of eastern pilgrims also continued to come to crusader Jerusalem. John of Würzburg, who visited the city in *c.* 1170, concludes his account in this way:

> I omitted [giving an account of] many chapels and churches of minor interest, which hold people of every race and tongue. For there are Greeks, Bulgars, Latins, Germans, Hungarians, Scots, people of Navarre, Britons, Angles, Franks, Ruthenians, Bohemians, Georgians, Armenians, Jacobites, Syrians, Nestorians, Indians, Egyptians, Copts, Capheturici, Maronites and many others which it would be a long task to list.[8]

Nevertheless, despite the presence of Christians from all over the known world, Jerusalem in the twelfth century was predominantly a Western Catholic city. It was the capital of the Crusader Kingdom and the see of the Latin Patriarch. The many new churches it contained were decorated with romanesque sculptures and their interiors were embellished with frescoes and mosaics. The spiritual centre of this city was the tomb of Christ in the church of the Holy Sepulchre. The Edicule which was built over the shrine was marble-clad and the Franks had inscribed in letters of gold round the cornice, 'Christ being raised from the dead dieth no more; death hath no more dominion over him. In that he liveth he liveth unto God' (Rom. 6:9–10). The pilgrim Theodoric, who visited it in *c.* 1170, says of this shrine:

> The mouth of the Cave cannot be entered by anyone without bending his knees. But arriving there he finds the treasure for which he has longed, the Sepulchre in which our most benevolent Lord Jesus Christ rested for three days. It is wonderfully decorated with Parian marble, gold and precious stones.

A few years later Manuel I Comnenus paid for the tomb to be covered with sheets of pure gold, and the holes made by the nails with which they were held down may still be seen in the marble slab covering the tomb.[9]

In 1187 Jerusalem surrendered to Saladin and Frankish rule came to an end. The crusaders had taken over a neglected city with many derelict buildings, but had undertaken a building programme worthy of the first city in the Christian world. Saladin's secretary, al-Fadil, described his impressions when he entered Jerusalem in the Sultan's suite:

> Islam received back a place which it had left almost uninhabited, but which the care of the unbelievers had transformed into a paradise garden . . . those accursed ones defended with the lance and sword this city, which they had rebuilt with columns and slabs of marble, where they had founded churches and the palaces of the Templars and the Hospitallers . . . One sees on every side houses as pleasant as their gardens and bright with white marble and decorated with leaves, which make them look like living trees.[10]

The Latin Catholics were all expelled from the city, though eastern Christians were allowed to remain there. Saladin also allowed the Jews to live there once more and for that reason was hailed by them as a new Cyrus. He was concerned to make Jerusalem a Muslim holy city again and one of his first acts was to restore the Temple Mount to Islamic worship. The great golden cross was pulled down from the top of the Dome of the Rock and it and the al-Aqsa mosque were cleansed with rose water and restored to Muslim worship. The church of the Holy Sepulchre was handed over to local Orthodox clergy, who celebrated the liturgy there in Syriac, and after Saladin's death the Greek Orthodox Patriarch Euthymius came to Jerusalem from Constantinople. The other eastern Christian communities were confirmed in their possessions, except for the Jacobites, whose cathedral of St Mary Magdalen was turned by Saladin into a *madrasa,*

The Psalter world map of c. 1250, showing Jerusalem in the centre.

an Islamic religious school. In return the Jacobites received a small disused Frankish church near the citadel. This harsh treatment was almost certainly caused by the pro-Frankish policies of the Jacobite Patriarch, Michael III, whose brother, equally Francophile, was bishop of Jerusalem.

The former Benedictine convent of St Anne's was made into a Muslim law school, and a Sufi college was established in the palace of the Latin Patriarch. In 1192, at the end of the Third Crusade, when Richard I of England made a treaty with Saladin by which the Franks regained control of the coastal region centred on Acre, Saladin allowed crusaders to go on pilgrimage to Jerusalem (see p. 115). Among them was Hubert Walter, Bishop of Salisbury, who persuaded the Sultan to allow four Catholic priests to be attached to the church of the Holy Sepulchre to administer the sacraments to western pilgrims. This is evidence that although there may not yet have been a formal schism between the Orthodox Church and the Western Church, in practice the members of the two bodies no longer considered themselves to be in communion with each other. The Latin Patriarch of Jerusalem set up his court in the new crusader capital of Acre and the Catholic clergy of the shrine churches of the Holy City all established priories there, so that Acre became a kind of crusader Jerusalem in exile.

The Western world was not resigned to the loss of Jerusalem, and in the thirteenth century several crusades were launched to recover it. When the Fifth Crusade achieved some success in its campaign against Egypt in 1219, Saladin's nephew, al-Muazzam, who was ruling Jerusalem, demolished the walls of the city so that it would not prove possible for the Franks to hold it even if they did succeed in recovering it. The Fifth Crusade ended in failure, but in 1229 the Emperor Frederick II succeeded in negotiating a treaty with the Sultan al-Kamil by the terms of which the crusaders regained Jerusalem but the Temple Mount remained in Muslim hands. Frederick disconcerted his contemporaries, both Muslims and Christians, by being prepared to make jokes about religion. The historian Ibn Wasil recounts that when the Emperor made a state visit to Jerusalem in 1229, the *cadi* Shams ad-Din called on him as representative of the Muslim community and the following conversation took place:

> [Frederick] said: 'O cadi, why did the muezzins not give the call to prayer last night in the usual way?' 'This humble slave', I replied, 'prevented them out of respect and regard for your majesty.' 'You did wrong to do that', he said. 'My chief aim in passing the night in Jerusalem was to hear the call to prayer given by the muezzins, and their cries of praise to God during the night.' Then he left and returned to Acre.[11]

Because the walls had not been rebuilt and the city was not secure, most of the Frankish religious communities continued to live at Acre, although a group of Catholic clergy did return to take charge of the Holy Sepulchre. In 1244 Jerusalem was sacked by an army of Khwarazmian mercenaries who were riding from north Syria to take service with the Sultan of Egypt. They caused considerable damage to the fabric of the church of the Holy Sepulchre and killed the Latin priests whom they found there. Jerusalem did not return to Christian rule during the Middle Ages.

After 1260, when the Mamluk Sultans of Egypt defeated the Mongol armies at Ain Jalut (see p. 150), the city became part of the Mamluk Empire. Although the Mamluks were willing to allow western pilgrims to visit Jerusalem, few such pilgrims did so, because after 1187 they had to obtain a papal dispensation on pain of excommunication in order to go there. The Holy See wanted to prevent the infidel from reaping any economic benefit from the pilgrim trade and this restriction was imposed again after 1244, remaining in force throughout the rest of the Middle Ages.[12] Many pilgrims therefore contented themselves with visiting those shrines like Nazareth and Mount Carmel which remained in crusader hands. Moreover, the popes granted spiritual privileges to pilgrims who visited the chapels belonging to the communities from the shrine churches of Jerusalem who were living in exile in Acre. This made it possible to have 'the Jerusalem experience' without visiting Jerusalem at all. But among those who did obtain a dispensation to visit Jerusalem were the Venetian brothers, Niccolò and Maffeo Polo, together with Niccolò's son Marco, in 1271. They were on their way to the court of Kubilai Khan in Cathay, who had commissioned the two elder Polos on their previous visit to his court to obtain oil from the lamps in the Holy Sepulchre, presumably for his mother, who was a devout Chaldean Christian.

In 1291 the Mamluks captured the last crusading strongholds in Syria and Palestine, but this did not lead to any break in pilgrimage to Jerusalem, even though there was no longer any permanent western presence in the Holy Land. In 1332/3 King Robert II of Naples bought the shrine church of Mount Sion, site of the *Cenaculum*, the Upper Room, from the Sultan of Egypt, who allowed it to be administered by the Franciscans. They were made responsible by the Mamluk authorities for Catholic pilgrims visiting the Holy Land. Such pilgrims normally came by sea, usually from Venice, to the port of Jaffa, and on arrival were placed in the charge of the Franciscans. They lived in their guest house on Mount Sion and were escorted by them in their visits to the Holy Places.

The church of the Holy Sepulchre remained the focus for all pilgrims from East and West, and although the Byzantine Orthodox always had charge of the sanctuary and choir of the cathedral, other churches came to acquire important rights inside the basilica. This happened in response to diplomatic pressures on the Mamluk government, sometimes supported by substantial gifts. When the German Dominican, Felix Fabri, went to Jerusalem in 1480 he reported that three Franciscan priests lived in the church of the Holy Sepulchre to minister to Latin visitors. They had the chapel of St Mary and also controlled the Edicule, which contained Christ's tomb. The Georgians, with whose kings the Mamluks wished to remain on good terms because they obtained their supply of military slaves from the Caucasus area, had been granted control of the Calvary chapel and the crypt chapel of St Helena. The Jacobites had a chapel in the rotunda, behind the Holy Sepulchre; a group of Ethiopian monks had a chapel, dedicated to the Crown of Thorns, situated at the entrance to the rotunda; while the Armenians had a chapel and cells for their monks in the gallery of the rotunda. The Ethiopians had established a community in the church for the first time in the Mamluk period, as had the Egyptian Copts.[13] Mamluk officials charged entrance fees to pilgrims who wished to

The courtyard of the church of the Holy Sepulchre.

see the church and locked them in during their visit. Friar Felix complained about this system:

> Until a few years ago it was the custom for the Saracens to open the church at sunrise, to keep the pilgrims locked up therein until vespers, and to turn them out at sunset; and this was bearable; but now they manage it the contrary way, for they open the doors for us late, and turn us out in the morning, which is very troublesome and uncomfortable, because we get little or no sleep on those nights which we pass in the church, because of the frequent visits which are made to the holy places in procession, the long continuance of Divine service, the yells and strange outcries of the Eastern Christians, who fill the church all night long with their discordant clamour . . .[14]

Eastern Christians continued to live in Jerusalem where, in addition to their chapels in the Holy Sepulchre, they had churches and monasteries and also ran hostels for the use of the many members of their churches who came there on pilgrimage. The Armenians still kept the monastic compound around the cathedral of St James which they had held since the days of the Crusader Kings. The Jacobites established their cathedral in St Mark's Church, which they bought from the Copts in 1470 and which remains their headquarters. The Chaldeans continued to have a church in Jerusalem throughout the Middle Ages, together with a bishop, but they were few in number.

Most of the many churches which had been built by the crusaders in the twelfth century were either taken over by Muslims for other purposes, or were allowed to fall into ruins. The exception to this was the shrine of the burial and Assumption of the Blessed Virgin Mary in the valley of Kidron. The Latin monastic buildings were destroyed, but although the shrine was owned by a Muslim, Christians were allowed to say Mass there, perhaps because of the reverence in which Islam held Mary, the mother of the prophet Jesus.

In the Mamluk period Jerusalem became predominantly a Muslim holy city. Politically it was a backwater: its walls were not repaired until the sixteenth century. Pious Muslims retired there and a great deal of money was spent on the building and endowment of religious schools, mosques and charitable foundations for the poor and sick.

Yet every year, and particularly at Eastertide, large numbers of pilgrims came there from all over the Christian world; like the Empress Helena at the beginning of the Christian Middle Ages, they came to pray where Christ's feet had touched the ground. Felix Fabri gives the most detailed description of the reactions of a group of pilgrims who came to Jerusalem at the very end of the Middle Ages. His party had ridden on donkeys from Lydda, escorted by a Franciscan friar from Mount Sion. When they reached the outskirts of Jerusalem:

> we dismounted from our asses . . . and taking our scrips, walked two and two towards . . . the Fish Gate, in silent prayer, with our hands clasped before our breasts. Some of the pilgrims out of piety threw away their shoes, and walked

barefoot all the time that we were in the Holy Land, thereby honouring the glorious footsteps of our Lord . . . From the Gate we went through a long street, and came to a great closed church, before which was a fair large courtyard, paved with polished marble, of exceeding whiteness. When we were all standing in the courtyard, one of the brethren of the convent of Mount Sion put himself in a higher place and addressed us saying that this was the holiest of churches, worshipped by the whole world, wherein is laid up the treasure most precious to all Christians, the sepulchre of our Lord. When we heard this, we flung ourselves down in the courtyard before the door of the church, and prayed, and kissed the very earth many times. Of a surety it seemed to the pilgrims as they lay thus on the ground, that virtue breathed forth from the earth itself, whereby their feelings were forcibly driven to prayer. [15]

NOTES

INTRODUCTION

1. W.H.C. Frend, *Martyrdom and Persecution in the Early Church* (Oxford, 1965), pp. 536–7; J.H.W.G. Liebeschuetz, *Continuity and Change in Roman Religion* (Oxford, 1979), pp. 251–2.

2. A.H.M. Jones, *The Later Roman Empire, 284–602*, 2 vols. (Oxford, 1964), I, p. 89.

3. J.C. Toynbee and J.B. Ward-Perkins, *The Shrine of Saint Peter* (London, 1956). There is no certain evidence that Constantine built the basilica of St Paul's: R. Krautheimer, *Rome. Profile of a City, 312–1308* (Princeton, 1980), pp. 3–31.

4. R. Beck, 'The Mysteries of Mithras. A new account of their genesis', *Journal of Roman Studies*, 88 (1998), pp. 115–28; 'Ritual, Myth, Doctrine and Initiation in the Mysteries of Mithras: new evidence from a cult vessel', ibid., 90 (2000), pp. 145–80.

5. St Hippolytus, *Refutatio omnium haeresium*, VI, 37, 7, trans. D. Hill, cited by K. Rudolph, *Gnosis. The Nature and History of Gnosticism*, trans. P.W. Coxon and K.H. Kuhn (San Francisco, 1987), p. 318.

6. G. Widengren, trans. C. Kessler, *Mani and Manichaeism* (London, 1965), p. 97.

7. *The Treatise on the Apostolic Tradition of St Hippolytus of Rome*, ed. and trans. G. Dix, corrected edn, H. Chadwick (London, 1968), pp. 36–7. Children of Christian parents might be baptized in infancy and this usually took place at the Easter Vigil ceremony as well.

8. The Fourth Lateran Council defined that the Devil had been created good by God and had become evil by his own free choice, endorsing a decision made by the Spanish Council of Braga in 581.

9. A list of seven virtues dating from the late fourth century and regularly used in the medieval Church was made up of the three theological virtues of Faith Hope and Love, drawn from St Paul (1 Cor. 13), and the four cardinal virtues of Prudence, Moderation, Courage and Justice, drawn from the Stoic philosophers. The cardinal virtues were considered natural to all men: they are not specifically Christian virtues.

10. The latter source is sometimes called the Gelasian Decree because it was reproduced in a decretal of Pope Gelasius I in 495.

11. In Greek this text is based on a pun, πετροσ (Peter) and πετρα (rock). This is preserved in Latin (*Petrus, petra*) and also in modern French (*Tu es Pierre et sur cette pierre . . .*), but loses its force in English.

12. Such councils are sometimes called Oecumenical Councils, since their members were drawn from the whole known world (*oecumene*).

13. J. Daniélou and H. Marrou, *The Christian Centuries, I. The First Six Hundred Years*, trans. V. Cronin (London, 1964), p. 250.

14. The Council of Chalcedon in 451 attributed this creed to the Council of Constantinople. This view is not universally accepted now. See J.N.D. Kelly, *Early Christian Creeds* (2nd edn, London, 1960), pp. 296–331.

CHAPTER ONE

1. T.D. Barnes has argued that Ulfilas's mission was to Constantine in 336, but the evidence for this is not conclusive. 'The consecration of Ulfila', *Journal of Theological Studies*, n.s. 41 (1990), pp. 541–5.

2. Discussion of the relationship between *The Rule of St Benedict* and *The Rule of the Master* led to strong scholarly disagreements, chiefly between members of the Benedictine Order, described by D. Knowles, 'The *Regula Magistri* and the *Rule of St Benedict*', in *Great Historical Enterprises. Problems in Monastic History* (London, 1963), pp. 139–95.

3. P.R.L. Brown, *The Cult of the Saints* (London, 1981); *Memoirs of a Renaissance Pope. The Commentaries of Pius II. An Abridgement*, trans. A. Cragg, ed. L.C. Gabel (London, 1960), p. 246.

4. K. Hughes, *The Church in Early Irish Society* (London, 1966), p. 31.

5. Cited in the translation of Kathleen Hughes, *ibid.*, p. 58.

6. At that time the Scots, who were Christian, controlled Dalriada, an area round Dumbarton on the Clyde, from which they later expanded to become, in the ninth century, the rulers of the whole kingdom to which they have given their name.

7. Adomnán, *Vita S. Columbae*, Bk. II, ch. 27, ed. J. Fowler (Oxford, 1894), pp. 95–6.

8. The chief though not the sole contentious issue between the Anglo-Saxon clergy trained in the Roman tradition and their Celtic colleagues concerned the different methods they used to calculate the date of Easter. Although this generated much heat at the time, it was not a matter of such great significance as some later writers, influenced by Bede, have made it appear. In the course of the eighth century all the Celtic churches came to adopt the Roman method which was in use throughout the rest of Latin Christendom.

9. There is some evidence that the ceremony of the royal anointing was first revived in seventh-century Visigothic Spain. M. Bloch, *The Royal Touch. Monarchy and Miracles in France and England*, trans. J.E. Anderson (New York, 1989), pp. 262–3.

10. *Orkneyinga Saga. The History of the Earls of Orkney*, *c.* 12, trans. H. Pálsson and P. Edwards (Harmondsworth, 1981), p. 37.

11. O. Vésteinsson, *The Christianization of Iceland. Priests, Power and Serial Change 1000–1300* (Oxford, 2000), pp. 17–24.

12. T.E. Lee, 'The Norse presence in Arctic Ungava', *American-Scandinavian Review*, 61 (1973), pp. 242–57, claims to have found vestiges of a medieval stone church at Payne Lake in the Ungava peninsula, Quebec province. Bishop Eric is mentioned in several Icelandic annals and also by the contentious Vinland Map: R.A. Skelton, T.E. Marston and G.D. Painter, *The Vinland Map and the Tartar Relation*, new edn (New Haven and London, 1995), pp. 130–1, 223–6, 257–62.

13. Cited by E. Wahlgren, *The Vikings in America* (London, 1986), p. 15, who suggests that the date may have been 24 April 1333.

14. Cited by F. Gad, *History of Greenland*, I, *Earliest Times to 1700*, trans. E. Dupont (London, 1970), p. 157.

15. Wenceslas was later canonized. He is known to the English-speaking world as Good King Wenceslas because of the carol translated by J.M. Neale.

16. H. Kennedy, *Muslim Spain and Portugal. A Political History of al-Andalus* (London, 1996), p. 67.

17. In the twelfth century there were six independent Christian states in Spain: Léon, Castile, Navarre, Aragon, Barcelona and (after 1137) Portugal. Barcelona and Aragon were united in 1162 and Léon and Castile in 1230.

18. Ramon Lull, who founded an Order whose members learned Arabic and worked among the Moors of newly conquered Majorca as well as training for missionary work in Morocco, was exceptional.

19. J.S.C. Riley-Smith, *The Crusades. A Short History* (London, 1987), p. 214.

20. Simony took its name from Simon Magus, who tried to buy the power to confer the Holy Spirit from the Apostles (Acts: 8, 5–24).

21. See the unpublished Ph. D. thesis of J.M.B. Porter, '*Compelle Intrare*: Monastic Reform Movements in Twelfth-Century Northwestern Europe' (Nottingham, 1997).

22. *St Francis of Assisi, Writings and Early Biographies. English Omnibus of the Sources for the Life of St Francis*, ed. M.A. Habig (2nd edn, London, 1979), p. 93.

23. In medieval western canon law the age of majority for boys was fifteen and for girls twelve.

24. For a recent discussion see C. Taylor, 'The letter of Héribert of Périgord as a source for dualist heresy in the society of early eleventh-century Aquitaine', *Journal of Medieval History*, 26 (2000), pp. 313–49.

25. Some Cathars also accepted the wisdom and prophetical books of the Old Testament as divinely inspired. No Cathars accepted the historical books of the Old Testament as canonical except for John of Lugio and his followers. Mark Pegg has recently argued that the Cathars were not dualists. M.G. Pegg, 'On Cathars, Albigenses, and the good men of Languedoc', *Journal of Medieval History*, 27 (2001), pp. 181–95.

26. C. Douais, ed., *Documents pour servir à l'histoire de l'Inquisition dans le Languedoc*, 2 vols (Paris, 1900), II, p. 92.

27. The southern French Inquisition records of Cathar trials only report three cases in which torture was used. It is possible that it was used more often and that this was not recorded, but there is no evidence to support that inference.

28. The power of persecution in medieval Western Europe is forcefully argued, in my view too forcefully argued, by R.I. Moore, *The Formation of a Persecuting Society* (Oxford, 1987).

29. Many unscholarly works have been written about the Templars' trial. For a sound assessment see M.C. Barber, *The Trial of the Templars* (Cambridge, 1978).

30. The story told of Bede's completing an Anglo-Saxon translation of St John's Gospel as he was dying probably relates to a gloss of this kind.

31. The Synod of Toulouse of 1229 had banned the possession of Bibles in any language by the laity. This was an enactment by a local council and had no force in the Church at large. It was part of a set of measures to combat Catharism. I know of no evidence that it was enforced except in cases where people were suspected of Cathar sympathies on other grounds.

32. In 1309 Avignon was part of the Holy Roman Empire, not of the Kingdom of France, and was held of the emperor by King Robert of Naples. Pope Clement VI bought the city from Queen Joanna I of Naples in 1348 and the Emperor Charles IV freed it from imperial control.

33. The medieval form of the Hail Mary was 'Hail Mary full of grace the Lord is with thee, blessèd art thou among women and blessèd is the fruit of thy womb, Jesus', which is a composite form of Gabriel's greeting to Mary, Lk. 1:28, and Elizabeth's greeting to her, Lk. 1:42.

34. The consecrated bread at Mass was called the Host, from the Latin *hostia*, meaning victim, because it was believed to be the Body of Christ, offered in sacrifice on Calvary. A monstrance is a liturgical container with a glass window in which the Host may be displayed on the altar.

35. Julian of Norwich, *Revelations of Divine Love*, ch. 5, trans. into modern English by

C. Wolters (Harmondsworth, 1966), p. 68.

36. Complutum was the Latin name for Alcala, the university where the Bible was produced. Polyglot means a version published in several languages.

37. Except for Adrian VI (1522–3), who came from Utrecht, where the Renaissance had developed in rather different ways.

38. P. Portoghesi, *Rome of the Renaissance*, trans. P. Sanders (London, 1972), pp. 11–12.

CHAPTER 2

1. C. Diehl, 'Byzantine Art', in N.H. Baynes and H. St L.B. Moss, eds., *Byzantium. An Introduction to East Roman Civilization* (Oxford, 1948), p. 167.

2. E. Herman, 'The Secular Church', in J.M. Hussey, ed., *Cambridge Medieval History*, IV (II) (Cambridge, 1967), p. 113.

3. The hymn, of uncertain authorship, is older than the siege of 626 when it was adapted for liturgical use. Cited in the translation of V. Limberis, *Divine Heiress. The Virgin Mary and the Creation of Christian Constantinople* (London, 1994), p. 149. I have altered the final invocation, rendered by Limberis as 'Hail, O Bride unwedded', which is a literal translation of Χαιρε, νυμφη ανυμφευτε, as it has a different connotation in English from that intended by the poet, which was to praise Mary as the virgin bride.

4. G. Brett, 'The automata in the Byzantine Throne of Solomon', *Speculum*, 29 (1954), pp. 477–87. The Golden Tree was designed for the Emperor Theophilus (830–43).

5. In fact the Dalmatian cities and Bosnia, which had been part of the old Roman province of Illyricum, were evangelized from Italy, and despite Leo's intervention they remained under the direct ecclesiastical jurisdiction of Rome.

6. II Thess., 2, vv. 7–8. I have departed slightly from the King James' translation here. μυστηριον της ανομιας is better rendered as 'the mystery of lawlessness' than as 'the mystery of iniquity', and 'he who now letteth will let' is obscure to a modern reader, so I have paraphrased it, 'there is at present someone who holds it in check'.

7. Eusebius, *De laudibus Constantini*, II, p. 201, cited in the translation of S. Runciman, *The Byzantine Theocracy* (Cambridge, 1977), p. 22.

8. The Holy Synod was the chief advisory body of the patriarch and took charge when the see was vacant. It consisted of bishops and church officials chosen by the patriarch, members of the patriarch's secretariat and imperial officials chosen by the emperor.

9. Constantine VII Porphyrogenitus, *Le Livre des Cérémonies*, ed. A. Vogt, 2 vols. (Paris, 1935), I, p. 2; A. Cameron, 'The Construction of court ritual: the Byzantine *Book of Ceremonies*', in D. Cannadine and S. Price, eds., *Rituals of Royalty. Power and Ceremonial in Traditional Societies* (Cambridge, 1987), pp. 106–36.

10. E. Wellesz, *A History of Byzantine Music and Hymnography* (2nd edn, Oxford, 1961).

11. G. Mathew, *Byzantine Aesthetics* (London, 1963), p. 29.

12. D.J. Constantelos, *Byzantine Philanthropy and Social Welfare* (New Brunswick, 1968).

13. K. Weitzmann, 'Byzantine Art and Scholarship in America', *American Journal of Archaeology*, 51 (1947), p. 418.

14. S. Runciman, *The Last Byzantine Renaissance* (Cambridge, 1970), p. 78.

15. St Cyril's baptismal name was Constantine and he only took the name Cyril when he was professed as a monk towards the end of his life. He is normally called Cyril because that was the name by which he was canonized and by which he is therefore best known.

16. Peter the Hegoumenos: an abridgement of Peter of Sicily's *History of the Paulicians*, ch. 9, trans. J. and B. Hamilton, *Christian Dualist Heresies in the Byzantine World, c. 650–c. 1450*

(Manchester, 1998), p. 94. N. Garsoian, *The Paulician Heresy* (The Hague, 1967), argues from the Armenian sources that the Armenian Paulicians were not dualists but Adoptionists. I do not find her arguments convincing; see J. and B. Hamilton, *Christian Dualist Heresies*, Appendix 2. 'Armenian Sources and the Paulicians', pp. 292–7.

17. P. Lemerle, 'L'histoire des Pauliciens d'Asie Mineure', *Travaux et Mémoires*, 5 (1973), p. 52.
18. Euthymius of the Periblepton, trans. J. and B. Hamilton, *Christian Dualist Heresies*, p. 158.
19. M. Yovkov, *The Pavlikians and the Pavlikian Towns and Villages in the Bulgarian Lands in the Fifteenth to Eighteenth Centuries* (Sofia, 1991), pp. 190 ff. (in Bulgarian with an English summary).
20. *The Discourse of the Priest Cosmas against the Bogomils*, ch. 1, trans. Y. Stoyanov, in J. and B. Hamilton, *Christian Dualist Heresies*, p. 116.
21. R.C. Zaehner, *Zurvan: a Zoroastrian Dilemma* (Oxford, 1955), Appendix; Y. Stoyanov, *The Other God. Dualist Religion from Antiquity to the Cathar Heresy* (London, 2000), pp. 157–8, 163–4.
22. Anna Comnena, *Alexiad*, Bk. XV, ch. viii, 1, trans. J. and B. Hamilton, *Christian Dualist Heresies*, p. 175.
23. J.V.A. Fine, *The Bosnian Church, a new interpretation: a study of the Bosnian Church and its place in state and society from the thirteenth to the fifteenth centuries* (New York and London, 1975), argues that the Bosnian Church was Catholic but schismatic and that the Bogomils were only a minority group in the country; F. Sanjek, *Les Chrétiens bosniaques et le mouvement Cathare XII–XIVe siècles* (Paris, 1976), argues that Bogomilism became the established church in Bosnia after *c.* 1250.
24. Byzantine theologians considered the term 'and from the Son' inexact because it suggested a dual creative principle in the Godhead. They would have preferred to express the relationship as 'through the Son' (*per Filium*).
25. Michael Cerularius, *Epistola III*, in J.P. Migne, *Patrologia Graeca*, vol. 120 (Paris, 1880), cols. 794–5.
26. Prince Alexius was the son of Isaac II who had been deposed and blinded in 1195. Isaac was still alive in 1203 and the Byzantines insisted on restoring him as *autocrator* with Alexius IV as co-emperor, despite Isaac's mutilation which in the Byzantines tradition would normally have debarred him from office, since only a physically whole man could represent Christ the King. His enthronement is a measure of the Byzantine opposition to Alexius's pro-Western policies.
27. Cited in the translation of E. Barker, *Social and Political Thought in Byzantium from Justinian I to the last Palaeologus* (Oxford, 1957), p. 195.

CHAPTER 3

1. The problems about the evidence are discussed by G. Fowden, *Empire to Commonwealth. Consequences of Monotheism in late Antiquity* (Princeton, NJ, 1993), p. 77, n. 81.
2. S. Brock, *The Luminous Eye. The Spiritual World Vision of Saint Ephrem the Syrian*, Cistercian Studies Series, 124 (Kalamazoo, 1985), p. 62.
3. Theodoret of Cyrrhus, *A History of the Monks of Syria*, c.xxvi, 24, trans. R.M. Price, Cistercian Studies Series, 98 (Kalamazoo, 1985), p. 171.
4. John Moschos, *The Spiritual Meadow*, c. 127, trans. J. Wortley, Cistercian Studies Series, 139 (Kalamazoo, 1992), pp. 104–5.
5. Fowden, *Empire to Commonwealth*, p. 159.
6. P. Brown, *The World of Late Antiquity* (London, 1971), p. 194.

7. Some recent writers, none of them professional historians, have claimed that the Mandylion of Edessa was an early manifestation of the Holy Shroud of Turin. The evidence is reviewed by M. Barber, 'The Templars and the Turin Shroud', *Shroud Spectrum International*, II (1983), pp. 16–24; and A. Cameron, *The Sceptic and the Shroud*, Inaugural Lecture, King's College London, 1980.

8. Michael the Syrian, *Chronicle*, XVI, i, ed. with French trans. J.B. Chabot, 4 vols. (Paris, 1899–1924), III, p. 222.

9. B.Z. Kedar, 'Some new sources on Palestinian Muslims before and during the Crusades', in H-E. Mayer and E. Müller-Luckner eds., *Die Kreuzfahrerstaaten als multikulturelle Gesellschaft* (Munich, 1997), pp. 129–40.

10. Later Maronite historians claimed that the Maronite hierarchy had established contacts with the Papacy earlier in the twelfth century, but there is no contemporary evidence for this.

11. M. Moosa, *The Maronites in History* (Syracuse, NY, 1986), p. 241.

12. H. Skrobucha. *Sinai* (London, 1966), p. 65.

13. Cited by H.F.M. Prescott, *Once to Sinai. The Further Pilgrimage of Friar Felix Fabri* (London, 1957), p. 95.

14. Nerses Šnorhali, *Lament on Edessa*, trans. and annotated by T.M. van Lint, in K. Ciggaar and H. Teule, eds., *East and West in the Crusader States. Context – Contacts – Confrontations, Orientalia Lovaniensia Analecta*, 92 (1999), p. 50.

15. Burchard of Mount Sion, trans. A. Stewart, Palestine Pilgrims' Text Society, XII (London, 1895–6), pp. 107–8.

16. F.C. Conybeare, ed. and trans., *Rituale Armenorum* (Oxford, 1905), pp. 227–8.

17. F. Thelamon, *Païens et chrétiens au iv᷎ siècle. L'apport de l'"Histoire Ecclésiastique" de Rufin d'Aquileé* (Paris, 1981), pp. 85–122.

CHAPTER 4

1. *De Principiis*, IV, 1, 16, trans. F. Crombie, *The Writings of Origen*, 2 vols, Ante-Nicene Christian Library (Edinburgh, 1871), I, pp. 315–6. Some of Origen's teachings, perhaps misrepresented by his opponents, were later condemned by the fifth General Council of Constantinople in 553, but despite this his work remained extremely influential throughout the Middle Ages.

2. *Pistis Sophia*, trans. G.R.S. Mead (London, 1955), p. 1.

3. See the comments of Timothy Aelurus about the Chalcedonian definition, A. Grillmeier in collaboration with T. Hainthaler, trans. O.C. Dean, *Christ in Christian Tradition*, vol. II, pt. IV (London, 1996), p. 33.

4. Translated by H. Waddell, *The Desert Fathers* (London, 1936), pp. 157–8. John Cassian (d. after 430), the founder of the monastery of Lérins in southern France, spent many years among the monks of Egypt (see p. 22). The noonday demon is mentioned in the Septuagint text of Psalm 91:6.

5. Grillemeier, *Christ*, II (IV), p. 186.

6. M. Meyer and R. Smith, eds., *Ancient Christian Magic. Coptic Texts of Ritual Power* (San Francisco, 1994), No. 25, pp. 48–9.

7. G.C. Anawati, 'The Christian communities in Egypt in the Middle Ages', in M. Gervers and R.J. Bikhazi, eds., *Conversion and Continuity. Indigenous Christian Communities in Islamic Lands. Eighth to Eighteenth Centuries* (Toronto, 1990), p. 240.

8. *Ibid.*, p. 243. The *dhimmis* were non-Muslims.

9. J. den Heijer, *Mawhub Ibn Mansur Ibn Mufarrig et l'historiographie Copto-Arabe. Étude sur la*

composition de l'Histoire des Patriarches d'Alexandrie, Corpus Scriptorum Christianorum Orientalium, 513, Subsidia, 83 (Louvain, 1989), pp. 132–3.

10. Through the work of the Conservation of Coptic Icons Project, directed by Zuzana Skalova and financed by the Department for International Relations of the Dutch Ministry of Foreign Affairs.

11. den Heijer, *Mawhub Ibn Mansur*.

12. G.W.B. Huntingford, *The Historical Geography of Ethiopia from the first century A.D. to 1704*, ed. R. Pankhurst (Oxford, 1989), p. 59.

13. D.W. Phillipson, *Ancient Ethiopia*, (London, 1998), pp. 114–6.

14. Abu Salih, *The Churches and Monasteries of Egypt and some neighbouring countries*, ed. and trans. B.T.A. Evetts (Oxford, 1895), pp. 300–1.

15. J.S. Trimingham, *Islam in Ethiopia* (Oxford, 1952), p. 52.

16. T. Tamrat, *Church and State in Ethiopia, 1270–1527* (Oxford, 1972), p. 57.

17. J. Perruchon, 'Notes sur l'histoire d'Éthiopie. Extrait de la vie d'Abba Jean, 74 patriarche d'Alexandrie, relatif à l'Abyssinie (texte arabe et traduction)', *Révue Sémitique*, 7 (1899), pp. 81–2.

18. Cited T. Tamrat, 'The Horn of Africa: the Solomonids in Ethiopia and the states of the Horn of Africa', *UNESCO General History of Africa*, IV (London, 1984), p. 435.

19. Jordan Catalani, *The Wonders of the East*, VI, 3, trans. H. Yule, Hakluyt Society, 1st ser., 31 (London, 1863), p. 42.

20. G. Gerster, ed., *Churches in Rock. Early Christian Art in Ethiopia*, trans. R. Hosking (London, 1970), p. 87.

21. Abu Salih, *Churches*, pp. 287–8.

22. I. Shahid, 'The *Kebra Nagast* in the light of recent research', *Le Muséon*, 89 (1976), pp. 133–78.

23. E. Ullendorff, *The Ethiopians. An Introduction to Country and People,* 3rd edn (Oxford, 1973), pp. 92–110.

24. E. Hammerschmidt, 'The Ethiopian Orthodox Church', in Gerster, *Churches in Rock*, p. 45.

25. Falashas are in religion non-Talmudic Jews. On their origins, which are much disputed, see 'Falashas', *Encyclopaedia Judaica*, VI (Jerusalem, 1971), cols. 1143–54.

26. Francisco Alvarez, *The Prester John of the Indies*, eds. and trans. C.F. Beckingham and G.W.B. Huntingford, Hakluyt Society, 2nd ser., 114, 115 (Cambridge, 1961).

27. John of Biclar, *Chronica*, ed. T. Mommsen, *Monumenta Germaniae Historica, Auctores Antiquissimi*, XI, (Berlin, 1894), pp. 212–13.

28. Cited by G. Vantini, *Christianity in the Sudan* (Bologna, 1981), p. 98.

29. W.Y. Adams, *Nubia, corridor to Africa* (London, 1977), p. 452.

30. Michael the Syrian, *Chronicle*, Bk, XII, ch. xix, ed. with French trans. J.B. Chabot, 4 vols. (Paris, 1899–1924), III, pp. 92–3.

31. Grillemeir, *Christ*, II (IV), pp. 280–4.

32. Robert de Clari, *La conquête de Constantinople*, ch. liv, ed. P. Lauer (Paris, 1924), pp. 54–5.

33. Abu Salih, *Churches*, pp. 261–74 (description of Nubia), citations from pp. 265, 274.

34. J.M. Cuoq, ed. and trans., *Recueil des sources arabes concernant l'Afrique occidentale du VIIIe au XVIe siècle* (Paris, 1985), p. 50.

35. Cited by Vantini, *Christianity*, pp. 5–6.

36. Abu Salih, *Churches*, pp. 253–4.

37. Alvarez, *Prester John, c.* cxxxviii, II, p. 461. Italics mine.

38. Cuoq, *Recueil*, p. 217 and n. 1.

39. *Ibid.*, pp. 120–1 and n. 3.

40. Cited in *Acta Concilii Remensis ad S. Basolum*, in J.P. Migne, *Patrologia Latina*, 139, cols. 342–3.

41. E. Caspar, ed., *Das Register Gregors VII*, Bk. III, no. 21, *Epistolae selectae in usum scholarum ex Monumenta Germaniae Historica separatim editae* (Berlin, 1955), II (i), p. 288.

42. M. Talbi, 'Le Christianisme maghrébin: de la conquête musulmane à sa disparition', in Gervers and Bikhazi, eds., *Conversion and Continuity*, p. 344.

43. C.R. Boxer, *The Portuguese Seaborne Empire 1415–1825* (London, 1969), p. 98.

CHAPTER 5

1. A. Vine, *The Nestorian Churches* (London, 1937), p. 21.

2. Cited in the translation of A.C. Creswell, who comments on al-Azraqi (d. 858): 'I think it advisable to mention that he is the oldest existing historian of Mekka'. A.C. Creswell, 'The Ka'ba in A.D. 608', *Archaeologia*, 94 (1951), pp. 98–9. The painting presumably remained there until the fire of 683 A.D.

3. This citation from Ibn Ishaq comes from H. Goddard, *A History of Christian-Muslim Relations* (Edinburgh, 2000), p. 31.

4. Cosmas Indicopleustes, *The Christian Topography*, ed. and trans., J.W. McCrindle, Hakluyt Society, 1st ser., 98 (London, 1897), p. 119.

5. Thomas of Marga, *The Book of Governors*, trans. E.A. Wallis Budge, 2 vols. (London, 1893), II, pp. 511–2. I am indebted to my friend Peter R.L. Brown for this reference.

6. F.E. Brightman and C.E. Hammond, ed. and trans. *Liturgies Eastern and Western* (Oxford, 1896), I, p. 290.

7. Thomas of Marga, II, pp. 667–8

8. M. Gordillo, *Mariologia Orientalis, Orientalia Christiana Analecta*, 141 (1954), p. 34.

9. Cited in I. Gillman and H.J. Klimkeit, *Christians in Asia before 1500* (Richmond, 1999), p. 127.

10. Cosmas, *Christian Topography*, p. 119.

11. *The Book of Ser Marco Polo the Venetian concerning the Kingdoms and Marvels of the East*, trans. and annotated by H. Yule and H. Cordier, 2 vols. (London, 1903), II, p. 353.

12. Cited in L.W. Brown, *The Indian Christians of St Thomas. An account of the Ancient Syrian Church of Malabar*, 2nd. edn (Cambridge, 1982), p. 80.

13. Cited in Vine, *The Nestorian Churches*, p. 131.

14. D. Snellgrove and H. Richardson, *A Cultural History of Tibet* (Boulder, Colorado, 1968), p. 110.

15. This letter is recorded by the Syrian Orthodox historian, Bar-Hebraeus, *Chronicon Ecclesiasticum*, ed. with Latin translation, J.B. Abeloos and T.J. Lamy (Louvain, 1872–7), vol. III, pp. 280–2. P. Pelliot considered that the word Kerait might have been interpolated in this source, but I do not find his argument convincing. There is certainly abundant independent evidence that the Keraits were converted to the Church of the East in the central Middle Ages.

16. The sources on which this section is based are discussed more fully in *Prester John, the Mongols and the Ten Lost Tribes*, ed. C.F. Beckingham and B. Hamilton (Aldershot, 1996), where the Latin text of the Prester John Letter may also be found.

17. It was addressed to the Byzantine Emperor Manuel I Comnenus, but no Greek text of it has ever been found.

18. A.A. Vasiliev, *Prester John. Legend and History*, p. 114. This is an unpublished manuscript

deposited in the Dumbarton Oaks Library, Washington D.C. My thanks to the Director of Dumbarton Oaks for allowing me to read it.

19. D. Wasserstein, 'Eldad ha-Dani and Prester John', in Beckingham and Hamilton eds., *Prester John*, pp. 213–36.

20. J. Richard, 'The *Relatio de Davide* as a source for Mongol History and the Legend of Prester John', in Beckingham and Hamilton, eds., *Prester John*, pp. 139–58.

21. There is an excellent translation of this text, P. Jackson, ed. and trans. with D. Morgan, *The Mission of Friar William of Rubruck*, Hakluyt Society, 2nd ser., 173 (London, 1990).

22. 'Henry Cordier reports that a French traveller who visited the region at the end of [the nineteenth] century found in the large Buddhist temple at Erdeni Tso an iron, bearing a Latin cross, which certainly is the instrument manufactured by William the Parisian in 1254.' L. Olschki, *Guillaume Boucher. A French Artist at the Court of the Khans* (Baltimore, 1946), p. 38.

23. G. Tucci, *Transhimalaya*, trans. J. Hogarth (London, 1973), p. 39.

24. William of Rubruck, trans. Jackson, p. 163. A similar policy was said to have been adopted in medieval Ethiopia and for the same reasons.

25. al-Makrizi (1364–1442) compiled his history from the works of many earlier Islamic writers who would otherwise be unknown. I cite the translation of Vine, *Nestorian Churches*, pp. 146–7.

26. J. Richard, *La Papauté et les missions d'Orient* (Rome, 1977), p. 109. The quotation is from E.A. Wallis Budge, trans., *The Monks of Kublai Khan Emperor of China* (London, 1928), p. 196.

27. *William of Rubruck*, trans. Jackson, p. 122.

28. John of Monte Corvino, Letter II, trans. by a nun of Stanbrook Abbey, in C. Dawson, ed., *The Mongol Mission* (London, 1955), p. 225.

29. In Mongol law only the descendants of Genghis Khan could hold sovereign power. Tamerlane appointed Kabil-Shah, a prince of that family, as ceremonial head of state and ruled in his name.

30. D. Sinor, 'The Mongols and Western Europe', in his Collected Studies, *Inner Asia and its Contacts with Medieval Europe* (London, 1977), No. IX, p. 538.

31. Papal influence remained strong among some groups of Eastern Christians who had entered into communion with the Roman See; see Chapter Three.

32. J. Dauvillier, 'Les provinces Chaldéennes 'de l'Extérieur' au Moyen Age', in his Collected Studies, *Histoire et Institutions des Églises orientales au Moyen Age* (London, 1983), No. 1, pp. 315–6. The translation is mine.

EPILOGUE

1. K.M. Kenyon, *Digging up Jerusalem* (London, 1974), pp. 236–55; M. Biddle, *The Tomb of Christ* (Stroud, 1999), pp. 109–119.

2. I. Hasson, 'The Muslim view of Jerusalem. The Quran and Hadith', in J. Prawer and H. Ben-Shammai, eds., *The History of Jerusalem. The Early Muslim Period, 638–1099* (New York, 1996), pp. 349–85.

3. The Patriarch George (fl. 807) sent the keys of the Holy Sepulchre to Charlemagne, but Amnon Linder is surely right in saying, 'Historians of a later age erred when they interpreted these relations as acceptance of a Frankish 'protectorate', as an exchange of the relationship with Constantinople for a new one with the West . . . In fact this is no more than part of the continuous efforts by Jerusalem's patriarchs to raise funds throughout the

Christian world.' A. Linder, 'Christian Communities in Jerusalem', in Prawer and Ben-Shammai, eds., *History of Jerusalem*, pp. 133–4.

4. I cite Yahya's work in the translation of M. Biddle, *The Tomb of Christ*, p. 72.

5. M. Biddle, 'The Tomb of Christ: sources, methods and a new approach', in K. Painter, ed., *'Churches Built in Ancient Times'. Recent Studies in Early Christian Archaeology*, vol. 16 of Occasional Papers from the Society of Antiquaries of London (London, 1994), pp. 73–147 (the quotation is p. 120).

6. A. Palmer, 'The History of the Syrian Orthodox in Jerusalem', *Oriens Christianus*, 75 (1991), p. 30.

7. Saewulf, *A reliable account of the situation of Jerusalem*, ed. and trans. J. Wilkinson in *Jerusalem Pilgrimage, 1099–1185*, p. 108.

8. The Capheturici have never been satisfactorily identified. The Scots are almost certainly Gaelic speakers and therefore include the Irish, the Britons are Bretons and perhaps also Welsh: John of Würzburg, ed. and trans. Wilkinson, *Jerusalem Pilgrimage 1099–1185*, p. 273.

9. Theoderic, *On the Holy Places*, ed. and trans. J. Wilkinson, *Jerusalem Pilgrimage 1099–1185*, p. 279. The observation about the marks of the nails in the marble tomb-slab was made by Professor Martin Biddle in a lecture given at the British Museum in October 2001.

10. Cited by Ibn Khallikan, 'Extraits de la vie du Sultan Salah el-Din', in *Recueil des Historiens des Croisades. Historiens Orientaux*, III (Paris, 1884), pp. 421–2 [my translation].

11. Ibn Wasil, in F. Gabrieli, *Arab Historians of the Crusades*, English trans. E.J. Costello (London, 1969), p. 272. I wish to thank Robert Irwin for bringing this passage to my attention and for pointing out that the author clearly failed to realize that Frederick was being flippant.

12. D. Webb, *Pilgrims and Pilgrimage in the Medieval West* (London, 1999), pp. 86–7, 104–5.

13. It is commonly said that Saladin admitted the Ethiopians to the Holy Sepulchre, but there is no good evidence for this: E. van Donzel, 'Were there Ethiopians in Jerusalem at the time of Saladin's conquest in 1187?', in K. Ciggaar and H. Teule, eds., *East and West in the Crusader States. Context – Contacts – Confrontations, Orientalia Lovaniensia Analecta*, 92 (1999), pp. 125–30. Fabri makes no distinction between the Copts and the Jacobites, for although they used different liturgical languages, they were members of sister Churches.

14. *The Book of the Wanderings of Brother Felix Fabri*, trans. A. Stewart, Palestine Pilgrims Text Society, vols, 7–10 (London, 1893–6), vol. 8, p. 428.

15. *Felix Fabri*, vol, 7, pp. 282–3.

BIBLIOGRAPHY

This bibliography is intended for non-specialist readers. I have listed only books, not articles in learned journals, although some of the books are collections of articles. All the works are in English. Even so, the number of works written on this subject is prodigious, and I have only included a selection here. Readers with specialist interests will find some guidance in the footnotes accompanying the text.

The Oxford Dictionary of the Christian Church, ed. F.L. Cross, 3rd edn revised and ed. E.A. Livingstone (Oxford, 1997) is a valuable work of reference for all the topics covered in this book.

THE CHURCH IN THE LATER ROMAN EMPIRE

Brown, P.R.L., *The World of Late Antiquity* (London, 1971)

Brown, P.R.L., *Society and the Holy in Late Antiquity* (London, 1982)

Cameron, A., *The Later Roman Empire* (London, 1993)

Daniélou, J. and Marrou, H., *The First Six Hundred Years, The Christian Centuries*, vol. 1, trans. V. Cronin (London, 1964)

Fowden, G., *Empire to Commonwealth. Consequences of Monotheism in Late Antiquity* (Princeton, 1993)

Herrin, J., *The Formation of Christendom* (Princeton, 1987)

Liebeschuetz, W., *Continuity and Change in Roman Religion* (Oxford, 1979)

Lieu, S.N.C. and Monserrat, D., *Constantine: history, historiography and legend* (London, 1998)

The following works deal with both the Western and Eastern Churches

Brown, P. *The Rise of Western Christendom. Triumph and Diversity A.D. 200–1000* (Oxford, 1996). Despite its title, this study pays a good deal of attention to all the Eastern Churches

Knowles, D. and Obolensky, D., *The Middle Ages, The Christian Centuries*, vol. 2 (London, 1969), deals with the Western Church and the Byzantine Church (including Russia)

McGinn, B., Meyendorff, J. and Leclercq, J., eds, *Christian Spirituality. Origins to the Twelfth Century* (London, 1986)

Raitt, J., McGinn, B. and Meyendorff, J., eds, *Christian Spirituality. High Middle Ages and Reformation* (London, 1988)

Both volumes cover the Orthodox Churches as well as the Western Church

THE WESTERN CHURCH

Brown, P.R.L., *The Cult of the Saints. Its Rise and Function in Latin Christianity* (London, 1981)

Forey, A., *The Military Orders* (London, 1992)

Hamilton, B., *Religion in the Medieval West* (London, 1986)

Hamilton, S. *The Practice of Penance, 900–1050* (Woodbridge, 2001)

Knowles, D., *The Evolution of Medieval Thought* (London, 1962)

Lawrence, C.H., *Medieval Monasticism* (London, 1984)

Lawrence, C.H., *The Friars* (London, 1994)

Leclercq, J., *The Love of Learning and the Desire for God*, trans. C. Misrahi (New York, 1961)

Morris, C., *The Papal Monarchy. The Western Church from 1050 to 1250* (Oxford, 1989)

Reeves, M. *Joachim of Fiore and the Prophetic Future* (London, 1976)

Smalley, B., *The Study of the Bible in the Middle Ages*, 3rd edn, (Oxford, 1983)

Thomson, J.A.F., *The Western Church in the Middle Ages* (London, 1998)

Vauchez, A., *The Laity in the Middle Ages. Religious Beliefs and Devotional Practices*, trans. Schneider, M.J., ed, D.E. Bornstein (Notre Dame and London, 1993)

REGIONAL STUDIES

Gad, F., *History of Greenland*, I, *Earliest Times to 1700* trans. E. Dupont (London, 1970)

Hughes, K., *The Church in Early Irish Society* (London, 1966)

Kennedy, H., *Muslim Spain and Portugal. A Political History of al-Andalus* (London, 1996)

Krautheimer, R., *Rome, Profile of a City, 312–1308* (Princeton, 1980)

MacKay, A., *Spain in the Middle Ages. From Frontier to Empire, 1000–1500* (London, 1977)

Maryr-Harting, H., *The Coming of Christianity to Anglo-Saxon England*, 3rd edn (London, 1991)

Sawyer, B. and P. and Wood, I., eds., *The Christianization of Scandinavia* (Alingas, 1987)

Vésteinsson, O., *The Christianization of Iceland. Priests, Power and Social Change 1000–1300* (Oxford, 2000)

Wahlgren, E., *The Vikings and America* (London, 1986).

Wallace-Hadrill, M., *The Frankish Church* (Oxford, 1983)

GENERAL WORKS ON THE EASTERN CHURCHES

Atiya, A.S., *A History of Eastern Christianity* (London, 1968)

Attwater, D., *The Christian Churches of the East*, 2 vols (Leominster, London, 1961, 1963)

Gill, J., *The Council of Florence* (Cambridge, 1959), deals with the attempt to reunite all the Churches of East and West

Zernov, N., *Eastern Christendom. A Study of the Origins and Development of the Eastern Orthodox Church* (Oxford, 1961)

THE CHURCH IN BYZANTINE LANDS

Angold, M., *Church and Society in Byzantium under the Comneni, 1081–1261* (Cambridge, 1995)

Every, G., *The Byzantine Patriarchate, 451–1204,* 2nd edn (London, 1962)

Fennell, J., *A History of the Russian Church to 1448* (London, 1995)

Franklin, S. and Shepard, J., *The Emergence of Rus, 750–1200* (London, 1996)

Grabar, A., *Byzantium. Byzantine Art in the Middle Ages,* trans. B. Forster (London, 1966)

Hussey, J.M., *The Orthodox Church in Byzantium* (Oxford, 1986)

Lock, P., *The Franks in the Aegean, 1204–1500* (London, 1995)

Morris, R, ed., *Church ad People in Byzantium* (Birmingham, 1986)

Morris, R., *Monks and Laymen in Byzantium, 843–1118* (Cambridge, 1995)

Nicol, D.M., *Church and Society in the Last Centuries of Byzantium* (Cambridge, 1979)

Obolensky, D., *The Byzantine Commonwealth. Eastern Europe 500–1453* (London, 1971)

Runciman, S., *The Eastern Schism* (Oxford, 1955)

Runciman, S., *The Byzantine Theocracy* (Cambridge, 1977)

Runciman, S., *Mistra. Byzantine Capital of the Peloponnese* (London, 1980)

Vlasto, A.P., *The Entry of the Slavs into Christendom* (Cambridge, 1970)

GENERAL WORKS ON CHRISTIAN RELATIONS WITH ISLAM

Goddard, H., *A History of Christian-Muslim Relations* (Edinburgh, 2000)

Gorvers, M. and Bikhazi, R.J., eds, *Conversion and Continuity. Indigenous Christian Communities in Islamic Lands, 8th to 18th centuries* (Toronto, 1990)

THE CHURCHES IN THE LEVANT AND THE CAUCASUS

Frend, W.H.C., *The Rise of the Monophysite Movement. Chapters in the History of the Church in the Fifth and Sixth Centuries* (Cambridge, 1979)

Hamilton, B., *The Crusades* (Stroud, 1998)

Jotischky, A., *The Perfection of Solitude. Hermits and Monks in the Crusader States* (University Park, PA, 1995)

Lang, D.M., *Armenia, cradle of civilization*, 3rd edn (London, 1980)

Mepisashvili, R. And Tsintsadze, V., *The Arts of Ancient Georgia*, trans. A. Jaffa (London, 1979)

Moosa, M., *The Maronites in History* (Syracuse, NY, 1986)

Narkiss, B., *et al., Armenian Art Treasures in Jerusalem* (London, 1980)

Ormanian, M., *The Church of Armenia. Her History, Doctine, Rule, Discipline, Liturgy, Literature and Existing Condition* 2nd edn, trans. G.M. Gergory (London, 1954)

Riley-Smith, J.S.C., *The Crusades. A Short History* (London, 1987)

Skrobucha, H., *Sinai* (London, 1966)

Toumanoff, C., *Studies in Christian Caucasian History* (Washington, D.C., 1963)

THE CHURCHES OF AFRICA

Adams, W.Y., *Nubia, corridor to Africa* (London, 1977)

Bourguet, p. du, *Coptic Art*, trans. C. Hay-Shaw (London, 1971)

Boxer, C.R., *The Portuguese Seaborne Empire* (London, 1969)

Doresse, J., *Ethiopia*, trans. E. Coult (London, 1959)

Gerster, G., ed., *Churches in Rock. Early Christian Art in Ethiopia*, trans. R. Hosking (London, 1970)

Meinardus, O., *Two Thousand Years of Coptic Christianity* (Cairo, 1999)

Meinardus, O., *Monks and Monasteries of the Egyptian Deserts* (Cairo, 1961)

Phillipson, D.W., *Ancient Ethiopia* (London, 1998)

Scholefield, A., *The Dark Kingdoms* (London, 1975)

Tamrat, T., *Church and State in Ethiopia, 1270–1527* (Oxford, 1972)

Trimingham, J.S., *Islam in Ethiopia* (Oxford, 1952)

Ullendorff, E., *The Ethiopians. An Introduction to Country and People*, 3rd edn (Oxford, 1973)

Vantini, G., *Christianity in the Sudan* (Bologna, 1981)

Watterson, B., *Coptic Egypt* (Edinburgh, 1988)

THE CHURCHES OF ASIA

Beckingham, C.F. and Hamilton, B., eds, *Prester John, the Mongols and the Ten Lost Tribes* (Aldershot, 1996)

Brown, L.W., *The Indian Christians of St Thomas. An Account of the Ancient Syrian Church of Malabar*, 2nd edn (Cambridge, 1982)

Gillman, I. and Klimkeit, H-J., *Christians in Asia before 1500* (Richmond, Surrey, 1999)

Manz, B., *The Rise and Rule of Tamerlane* (Cambridge, 1989)

Morgan, D., *The Mongols* (Oxford, 1986)

Morgan, D., *Medieval Persia 1040–1797* (London, 1988)

Moule, A.C., *Christians in China before the Year 1550* (London, 1930)

Murray, R., *Symbols of Church and Kingdom. A Study in Early Syriac Tradition* (Cambridge, 1977)

Neill, S., *A History of Christianity in India. The beginnings to A.D. 1707* (Cambridge, 1984)

Palmer, A., *Monk and Mason on the Tigris Frontier. The Early History of Tur Abdin* (Cambridge, 1990)

Rachewiltz, I., de, *Papal Envoys to the Great Khans* (London, 1971)

Rossabi, M., *Voyager from Xanadu. Rabban Sauma and the first journey from China to the West* (Tokyo, New York, London, 1992)

Tisserant, E., *Eastern Christianity in India. A History of the Syro-Malabar Church from the earliest times to the present day*, authorized adaptation from the French by E.R. Hanbye (Bombay, 1957)

Trimingham, J.S., *Christianity among the Arabs in pre-Islamic times* (London, 1979)

Vine, A., *The Nestorian Churches* (London, 1937)

THE CITY OF JERUSALEM

Biddle, M., *The Tomb of Christ* (Stroud, 1999)

Coüasnon, C., *The Church of the Holy Sepulchre, Jerusalem* (London, 1974)

Prawer, J. and Ben-Shammai, H., eds, *The History of Jerusalem. The Early Muslim period, 638–1099* (New York, 1996)

Walker, P., *Holy City. Holy Places? Christian attitudes to Jerusalem and the Holy Land in the Fourth Century* (Oxford, 1990)

ALTERNATIVE TRADITIONS

Barber, M., *The Cathars* (London, 2000)

Lambert, M., *Medieval Heresy. Popular Movements from the Gregorian Reform to the Reformation*, 3rd edn (Oxford, 2002)

Lieu, S.N.C., *Manichaeism in the Later Roman Empire and Medieval China. A Historical Survey* (Manchester, 1985)

Moore, R.I., *The Origins of European Dissent*, 2nd edn (Oxford, 1985)

Rudolph, K., *Gnosis. The Nature and History of Gnosticism*, trans. R. McL. Wilson (Edinburgh, 1984)

Stoyanov, Y., *The Other God. Dualist Religion from Antiquity to the Cathar Heresy* (London, 2000)

RITUAL MAGIC

Kieckhefer, R., *Magic in the Middle Ages* (Cambridge, 1989)

Maguire, H., ed., *Byzantine Magic* (Washington D.C., 1995)

Meyer, M. and Smith, R., *Ancient Christian Magic. Coptic Texts of Ritual Power* (San Francisco, 1994)

INDEX